# HINDU WIDOWS: A STUDY IN DEPRIVATION

# HINDU WIDOWS:
## A STUDY IN DEPRIVATION

GODAVARI D. PATIL

GYAN PUBLISHING HOUSE
New Delhi-110002

**HINDU WIDOWS: A STUDY IN DEPRIVATION**
[*Women's Studies, Sociology*]

ISBN: 81-212-0647-2



Published in 2000 in India by
Gyan Publishing House
5, Ansari Road
New Delhi 110 002

Laser Typeset at Alphabet, Delhi
Printed at Chawla Offset Press, New Delhi.

***Dedicated to***

*My Loving Father*

***Shri Devendrappa M. Patil***

*and*

*My Loving Sister*

***Kum. Chinnu***

# Contents

# Acknowledgements

With a deep sense of gratitude and everlasting indebtedness, I wish to express my deepest appreciation to my esteemed teacher and guide Dr. Anil. G. Mudbidri, under whose guidance the present study is undertaken. This study could not have been completed without his excellent advice and sincere criticism at every stage of my research work.

I gratefully acknowledge the co-operation of all my respondents who are the main source of the field data for this study. They responded well and co-operated throughout my field work.

I am grateful to the Karnatak University for providing me with the financial assistance. I also wish to thank the ICSSR Western Regional Centre for the sanction of study grants.

My sincere thanks are due to Prof. H. V. Nagesh and Katti. A. P. for their unreserved help in framing the questionnaire.

I am especially thankful to Dr. Vignesh N. Bhat, Chairman, Department of Sociology, Kuvempu University, Shimoga, Dr. Prabha Mahale, Dept. of Anthropology, Karnatak University, Dharwad and Smt. Nandita. A. Mudbidri for their constructive criticisms on the first draft of this thesis and for their suggestions and encouragement.

I am thankful to Mr. Harihar, Computer Section, Karnatak University, Dharwad and Mr. Surendra, Statistician, Agriculture University, Dharwad, who were extremely helpful in data analysis.

I am extremely thankful to the Librarian Mr. R. C. Patil and his staff, Karnatak University for their excellent co-operation.

My sincere thanks are due to Mr. K. Shashidhar Kini for his meticulous typing work.

Finally, I wish to acknowledge an everlasting debt of gratitude to my loving parents, brothers and sister for their interest and constant encouragement in all my academic endeavours.

**Godavari D. Patil**

# Preface

Four years back, while undergoing a law course, I happened to note the unique position of Hindu widows in jurisprudence and law relating to their rights. The unequal legislation for the two sexes, religious tradition and customs made the institution of widowhood more tragic and represented lowest position for Hindu widow.

When I got exposed to the vast literature in the field of women's studies, I learnt that much is written on the status and role of Indian women in general, but very little about Hindu widows. There are very few Indian studies which have taken into account the problems faced by Hindu widows, though the problem has attracted the attention of reformers and social workers.

The plight of widows in this country is highly deplorable. A woman cannot lead an independent life in a male dominated society. She has always been looked down upon with a certain amount of suspicion by others. For a Hindu woman, widowhood is considered a punishment for the crime committed by her in her previous life. Hence, she is looked down upon as a sinner. The death of a woman during the lifetime of her husband is often praised. A widowed woman has no right to participate in any socio-religious functions as her presence is considered inauspicious.

Widows were encouraged to become sati. In the past sati was presented as an ideal for womanhood. Unfortunately this has been revived and a few cases were recently reported in Rajasthan. But today, though the practice of sati is prohibited, the brides are burnt alive not for the same reason but only to inherit her wealth.

Even today, remarriage of widows is not encouraged by the people. We find that widow remarriage is considered a matter of great dishonour and infidelity in Hindu society. Religion prohibits remarriage though it has been legalized.

The problems of the widows are numerous, it is the problem of a woman and a widow, it is the problem of attitudinal change, it is a problem of realistic measures to be taken for their welfare.

Various scientific studies on western widows, encouragement by many people and moreover a sustained interest in this special field have inspired me to take up the present research task. It is my ardent hope that the present study will be a contribution in this field.

The present study was taken up in the district of Dharwad with an aim to evaluate the problems faced by the widows. The study also made an attempt to assess the extent of deprivation faced by them. The study is exploratory in nature, and also makes an attempt to test the significance of relationships between independent, infrastructural and independent variables with dependent variables like deprivation in economic, social, psychological and cultural fields.

The present study points out the need for an indepth analysis on a larger scale in respect of widowhood as a social role, and of sexual involvement of widows. The study is successful to the extent of pinpointing certain requirements like tackling the problem of widows with determination and jointly by women; development of widows' profile; need for follow up and vocational training for illiterate and poor widows, and coordinating the efforts of government with the heads of religious institutions and voluntary organization in changing the attitudes of the people according to the changing times and needs of society.

**Godavari D. Patil**

# List of Tables

ONE

# State of Widowhood and Trends in India

## PART - I

The present study is designed to understand the impact of Deprivation of Hindu Widows and the problem of adjustment of the widows. Hence, keeping in view the objectives of the study the relevant review of literature has been done on the following lines.

1. Death and bereavement
2. State of Widowhood
3. State of Deprivation
4. Consequences of widowhood
5. Economic Deprivation
6. Social Deprivation
7. Psychological Deprivation
8. Cultural Deprivation
9. Widow Remarriage
10. Welfare Measures
11. Hindu Widows - Historical Information.

### 1. Death and bereavement

The post-marital family consisting of the widow or widower is a widely known feature of every society. Facing loss of one of the marital partners is a sad event. Death is an extreme shock. It may come suddenly and without previous warning[1]. It can be a crisis for the family and for the individual[2]. The very term death is enough to create panic among most people. It robs a loved one and thereby destroys the strong ties and close relationships that binds a family. It changes the habits of eating, sleeping, dressing and conversing, habits of sex, and ego support that makes the surviving partner numb and bewildered. Re-organization is often very painful for it involves adjustment and readjustment to a new situation which often comes suddenly[3]. Hence, death can be viewed as social, not biological. The unique qualities of each relationship make the universal experience of death peculiarly painful. No one can truly replace the person who has died[4].

The death of one's spouse is a traumatic event. Loss of the Husband is felt more than any other loss and disorganizes a woman's life deeply[5]. The death of the husband is a devastating blow. For the widow, life may not seem worth living and she may look forward to her own early death[6].

Somerville mentions that death is a significant and universal family experience. However, many people and many families treat bereavement, Crisis, death and widowhood with extreme brevity[7]. Even then, bereavement has not been well studied. Much of this lack can be attributed to the inertia taboos and inherent methodological difficulties that surround studies of this nature. Society in general is against investigating this most universal crisis[8].

Eliot asserts that bereavement is usually unexpected, often a shock seldom planned for, either personally or by the family, though it is the natural form of family dissolution. He rightly quotes that, "as the Renaissance, Dance of Death warned Memento Mori: *hodie mihi, cras tibi* (Remember today for me, tomorrow for you)".

He further says that physically one must recognize bereavement as "a major shock, often requiring physical or medical care like any other illness or accident with time for recovery".

Psychologically, bereavement is a major type in the general class of traumatic frustration-situation. Arrested impulse or thwarted habit is the root of all sorrow.

Sociologically bereavement is the dismemberment of an affectional group by death. It is thus a problem in intrapersonal conflict, accommodation and/or assimilation-disorganization-and in interpersonal accommodation and group reorganization-disintegration[9].

Bereavement and grief represent a crisis and critical transition for the family of the deceased. This is particularly so for the widow who has to face the crisis of not only loosing the spouse but also stepping into the status of the head of the family. She has to bear the onus of being the breadwinner[10]. Waller while studying the social aspects of bereavement points out that bereavement may be the loss of a mate, partner, child, sibling or other close relative or associate and that its effect necessarily varies, with the age of the bereaved, his emotional involvement with the deceased, the manner of death, the other relationships of the bereaved and the degree of emancipation of the bereaved person[11].

Eliot while making a deep and significant analysis of bereavement, classifies some of the ways in which families and their members respond to the crisis of bereavement.

He classifies, the effects of bereavement into immediate and later or primary and secondary, and among them he noted several as typical:

1. Abandon
2. Refusal or rejection of the facts (including dissociation of emotion or sense of unreality).
3. Preternatural or detached calm.
4. Shock, in the neurological sense.
5. Exaltation
6. Self-injury
7. Repression
8. Blame of self or others, revenge.
9. The intense longing of grief.

He opines that the first eight occur in various sequences and in combination with the last, because without grief, the others would not arise.

*The Secondary Reactions*

He says that the following types of responses noted correspond to certain well-known 'mechanisms' of the psychoanalysts:

(1) Escape or attempted escape from the conflict e.g., use oi drugs, moving of residence, suicide, social distractions, or illusions.

(2) Defence and repression e.g., removing all reminders, deliberate forgetting, postural self-control, or certain "mental diseases".

(3) Compensation (in the narrower sense) e.g., rationalization, belief and cults, rituals of guilt or contribution, perpetuation of memory of deceased or of wish or supposed will of deceased, revenge, penance or "overdetermined" grief.

(4) Masochism and exhibition e.g., voluptuaries of grief, recluses, ascetics and the like.

(5) Identification (introjective) e.g., stepping into the role of the deceased or "carrying the spirit" of the deceased.

(6) Transference and substitution (involving projection) e.g., reattachment of affections to new mother, child or spouse; espousal of charities or cause. Most of these behaviour patterns are secondary and socially conditioned. They take time and social interaction for their development. Some mores of bereavement correspond to and also offer channels for these mechanisms.

Many of the above reactions may prove successful or unsuccessful, depending upon the inner resources and current social situation.

*Individual Effects of Bereavement*

A. Total failure to readjust
1. Suicide
2. Early death
3. Insanity
4. Moral disintegration
5. Obsession

B. Partial failure
1. Eccentricities
2. Physical illness or prostration
3. Aboulia, purposelessness
4. Isolation
5. Embitterment, misanthropy, cynicism
6. Reversion to or recurrence of griefs
7. Self-blame or personal hates

8. Fears
9. Loneliness

C. Partial Success

1. Resignation, "God's will", etc
2. Stoicism
3. Stereotyped formula of immortality, misery escaped, etc.
4. Sentimental memorials
5. Effective repression of memories
6. Intensification of affections
7. Extension of affections
8. Deliberate absorption in distractions or duties
9. New or fantasised love objects

D. Conspicuous Success

1. New love object
2. Thoroughgoing religious rationalization
3. Spontaneous forgetting, relaxation of tensions
4. Devotion to life work
5. Identification with role of deceased
6. Creation of constructive memorials
7. Transmutation of the experience into productive reintegration of the personality.

He says that the pattern of family behaviour during bereavement, and after bereavement, is influenced by these types of individual compensatory behaviour. These behaviour patterns are contagious but they are more consciously, imitated or resisted than the immediate impulsive responses.

The most frequent results are infinite combinations of B and C-partial success and partial failure.

*Effect of Bereavement on Family*

The bereavement makes the family change some of its ways, which are as follows:

1. The role of a family member exists in relation to the configuration and functioning of the family as a unit. Death tends to disturb this unity. The shifting of the roles of the various members under bereavement represents a reshaping of the configuration.

2. The consensus of the family in respect to these roles, i.e., in respect to its own pattern, may result; or, family conflict may develop as a sequence to incompatible conceptions of the role of certain members under the new conditions.
3. Such conflicts or jealousies, or the lack of a common personal or domestic object or symbol of affectional attachment (conditioning stimuli) may result in decreased family solidarity.
4. Acceptance of new, interpersonal responsibilities may increase family solidarity.
5. Removal of authority, of habit stimuli, of home, or of support may lead to revision of family folkways.
6. Maturity of children who lose their parents may lead to individualism or turning to their own families.
7. The will of personality, of the deceased, acting psychologically as a dynamic complex in each member's memory, and re-enforced by consensus, may activate the behaviour of the entire family[12]. Men behave differently in bereavement from women, because of differences in cultural expectations and, in part, because they not only have occupational activities demanding their attention, but they are more likely to spend more time away from the objects which remind them of the deceased[13].

As Parkes Murray observes, in his study on bereaved people in London, one-third of them had no contact with a clergy man apart from the funeral service, whereas three-quarters consulted a general practitioner during the six months following the bereavement. He noticed a sharp increase in consultations after bereavement, the reason for seeking advice being different at different ages. Young widows suffer from psychological difficulties whereas old widows suffer from physical symptoms. He further describes the phases, characteristics of grief and mourning, during which the widow was initially shocked or numbed and then suffered from pangs of intense pining. In the final stage there was revival and gradual return to normal life[14].

Thus, bereavement is a compound crisis. It is a painful emotional shock, a sharp change in social status, often an economic catastrophe and usually a philosopical challenge. It calls from reorganizing the habits and routines and ways of a life time of married living[15].

Therefore, Martinson rightly says that knowing about a critical event and preparing for it in advance mitigates the hardship and improves chances of recovery[16].

**State of Widowhood**

Widowhood is unique and its most basic features are as follows.

(a) One must have been married.

(b) Widowhood is not welcomed because most people wish marriage to continue.

(c) The loss is irreplaceable and widowhood cannot be avoided[17].

Widowhood is a crisis in a woman's life, involving new social adjustments for the family as well as for herself[18].

It is an event that constitutes the greatest and saddest change in the life of a woman. It also leads to the loss of status resulting in a state of helplessness and hopelessness[19].

Rosow says that widowhood hits women, particularly, harder than men. A widower, being economically independent, does not feel the stigma, and the loss of the spouse, as much as a woman. Widowhood is, primarily, a female phenomenon. Hence, recent researches have focused on widows more than widowers[20].

It is rightly said that widowhood, at all ages, changes the basic self-identity of many women. This is especially true of traditionally-oriented women for whom the role of wife is central to their lives[21].

Hyman observes that widowhood is one of the sad facts of existence. Millions of women experience this misfortune and generally bear its burden for many years[22].

According to Greg, widowhood is an event that brings about the greatest change in the status of a widow, for it is often accompanied by deleterious consequences. This is not only because of the loss of the husband, but also because of the lack of clear-cut cultural expectations regarding the proper role of the widow[23].

The plight of widows is indeed miserable for, almost inevitably, it carries with it, problems of ill-health, insufficiency of money, unemployment and strained social relations with one's children and one's friends for both men and women[24].

Christianity has accepted widowhood and re-marriage as natural. Widowhood is therefore not considered a very serious problem, since, both men and women enjoy equality, Christian women and widows are treated with respect[25].

In Islam, widowhood, like divorce, is a non-issue. Its acceptability in society should be free from inhibitions and taboos[26]. Even in Jainism widowhood is not a serious problem. Though widow re-marriage is not allowed, they enjoy freedom in the religious, social and political fields. A widow become a direct heir to the property of the deceased husband regardless whether or not she has a son[27].

In India, widowhood represents the last and lowest stage in life for Hindu women.

Caton and Merielli conceptualize Hindu widowhood as a life of agony, pain, suffering and austerity. It is a life which has been inflicted by social customs[28].

Cormack in her study on "The Hindu Women" asserts that there is probably no aspect of womanhood that has received more sympathy than that of widowhood in India. For the majority, widowhood is certainly an unhappy and miserable state[29].

It is observed that throughout India, Hindu women regard widowhood as a punishment for some horrible crime or crimes committed by them in their previous birth, such as disobedience or disloyalty to the husband or having even killed him. Widowhood, and its accompanying miserable existence, is considered as an atonement for some sin committed in a previous birth[30].

In India, widow remarriage is not encouraged, though it is legalized. In the light of such conditions, Mahatma Gandhi rightly remarked, "Enforced widowhood upon little girls is a brutal crime for which we Hindus are daily praying. Widowhood imposed by religion or custom is an unbearable yoke and defiles the home by secret vice and degrades religion, whereas voluntary widowhood consciously adopted by a woman who has felt affection of a partner adds grace and dignity of life, sanctifies the house and uplifts religion itself[31]."

An exploration into the folklores of the different regions of

India widens our awareness about the condition of widows. In the folklore of West Bengal, women considered widowhood as a great curse[32]. Tamil folklore mentions that the condition of the widows in all castes is miserable. Her presence was considered inauspicious and hence, a widow was discouraged from appearing at any social and cultural function. She lived an unseen existence[33]. In the folklore of Orissa, widowhood is considered much more sorrowful than even the death of a loved daughter, for the misery over the loss of a daughter can be overcome, but widowhood dogs a woman till her own death[34].

Moreover, widowhood is a life-event that removes not only persons, closest, support persons but also reduces the size of informal support network at the same time[35].

Brubaker opines that widowhood is a family event and the loss reverberates throughout the later family network. The spouse has lost a mate; children a parent; siblings a brother or sister.

Further, he points out that widowhood represents cut-off of former roles and relationships and commencing of a new set of relationships and expectations[36].

Leslie remarks that widowhood is a long-term proposition. On an average, the period of widowhood lasts from eight to sixteen years as based on his study. Widowhood and accompanying deep sense of loss and frustration comes to an end only with remarriage or with death[37].

In all cultures, widowhood is a crisis in a woman's life. But cultures differ significantly among themselves in their ways of overcoming crises. Some cultures allow their widows to remarry, some allow it only in exceptional cases; some do not allow it under any circumstances. The last course has been adopted by orthodox Brahmanic Hindu culture. A culture that allows widow remarriage does not necessarily become inferior to the one which disapproves of it. But what may bring about the real difference between one culture and another is their reordering of marital values[38].

**State of Deprivation**

In our country the problem of deprivation is a complex phenomenon. The intensity of deprivation is much due to social taboos and cultural prejudices in a traditional society. Deprivation in the nature of discrimination leads to several social problems.

Deprivation is a necessary product of class character of the society. Widows are deprived of the privileges and even the necessities, which every widow has a right to enjoy. Deprivation results in a systematic exploitation and dehumanization of widows.

In the present study the term 'deprivation' has been used to denote, "a social setting in which widows are physically, socially, economically and psychologically handicapped to fulfil their bio-social needs". It has been shown that deprivations and disadvantages create many problems which widows are expected to face all their lives.

The death of a child may be seen as a personal calamity but the death of a husband is seen as altering the social identity of a woman[39]. Widowhood is almost always accompanied by a deep sense of shock due to the sudden, and often unexpected, death of the husband. A woman is stupefied and immobilised with extreme grief. The loss of the husband creates a deep void in her life and she immediately, becomes dependent on her children or relatives, often such a wound is healed only by time[40].

Rane, in her study on "Rehabilitation of Widows: Problems and prospects", argued that widowhood brings sudden and unhappy changes in the life of a woman. Death of a husband causes not only a loss of financial and emotional support[41], but also severe physical and emotional suffering. Often the woman is left feeling helpless and in some cases a deep sense of depression may lead to either a mental disorder or suicide.

Widowhood marks a transition from a marital to a widowed status which is not smooth, for it means not only a loss of status but also a loss of pride, privileges, prestige and independence within the family. For a man, the loss of spouse is only a personal grief but for a woman it means additionally a difficult adjustment to be made. Many women are unable to cope with such a transition. Thus the consequences of widowhood to a woman is more hazardous than to a man[42].

Many a time, a widow faces difficulty in adjusting to her new status because the social norms and taboos put her in most disadvantaged position, and restrict her social interactions. She is confronted with a new set of expectations after widowhood[43].

In a study of the social and economic conditions of widows

in Dharwad, Katti and Nagesh it was reported that, in most communities after the death of the husband, a woman loses some of her privileges and rights in family and in society and in most social and cultural rituals (functions)[44]. In Hindu society a widow is expected to lead a life of an ascetic. She has to wear simple clothes, eat simple (*satvika*) food and keep herself away from all auspicious functions. Remarriage is prohibited for her. In spite of the protection accorded to widows by the regulations and important Acts, their position has not improved much. Thus widows are put in the most disadvantaged position[45].

Often a widow's life is made miserable by her in-laws. She becomes practically a slave, a chattel forced to do all kinds of manual and physical labour. She is meted out harsh treatment and often held responsible for her husband's death[46].

Considering the above cited studies it could be surmised that the death of a husband brings about a stigma, in Hindu society and along with it, severe deprivation of status. Every phase of widowhood is critical, hard, challenging and deranging and brings about severe social, economic, emotional and cultural deprivation.

*Indian Scene*

In India, girls are normally married before the onset of puberty. Men usually marry girls much younger to them in age. Hence, Indian girls become widows earlier, due to the age difference between the two and are destined to widowhood for much of their adult life. Females do not marry again as much as do the males. Moreover, widow remarriage is socially disapproved among the high caste Hindus in India. Early marriage of girls and social disapproval of widow remarriage are found among other communities also. Touba cities the example of Iran where similar conditions are prevalent[47].

Kitchlu in his study on the 'socio-economic conditions of widow in the Union Territory of Delhi', reports that there is a direct correlation between the age of marriage and age at widowhood. In India, girls marry at an early age. The wide age difference between husband and wife is often the reason for the high incidence of widowhood[48]. In India it has been observed that a boy generally gives preference for education. Thus, a man often marries late and not until he is educated and finds employment, while a girl is often married in a hurry before she completes her education. This results in a wide disparity in the age at marriage, of men and women in India. This is one of the causes of high incidence of widowhood. As it is confirmed that according to 1971 and 1981 census the girls who had married at the age of 10-14 years were 11.53 per cent and 6.59 per cent respectively, while in Karnataka the females who married at the age of 10-14 years in 1971 and 1981 were 6.58 per cent and 3.80 per cent respectively.

Thus, it can be said that the institution of widowhood with all its hardships and disadvantages, is a result of discrimination between the sexes, which characterizes all archaic system[49].

In India, the majority of reformers, men and women, have worked tirelessly for the amelioration of the widow's lot. In spite of these efforts, even today widows are treated as second class citizens in our country in addition to being considered as second class members within the family.

**Consequences of Widowhood**

Widowhood can be viewed as a social category consisting of individuals whose life partner is dead. Most couples do not think or refuse to accept that this change of status will befall them, for people are reluctant to face death and its consequences. Few in fact understand what it means to be widowed[50]. It represents a role of status change. When an individual loses a spouse, that individual acquires a new status, widow or widower, instead of wife or husband[51]. Eshleman points out that society makes adjustment to widowed status difficult by placing a taboo on the discussion of death between husband and wife, or parent and children. As a result, the surviving partner and others are often unprepared for the decisions that have to be made[52].

Widowhood is both a crisis, and a problem. When it occurs, its suddenness and intensity make it a crisis and as the individual finds ways of coping, it becomes a problem[53]. Kelphart argues, "widowhood is a problem of many dimensions; numerical-financial-emotional"[54].

Berardo asserted, "Widowhood status presents more serious

problems for both individual and families. It must be viewed as a social, emotional crisis situation and it is a neglected aspect of the family life cycle"[55].

Widowhood also brings about a variety of social problems at the local level being related to adult and child dependency, poverty, unemployment, illness and family disorganization and women's insecure status[56]. Morgan viewed widowhood as a complex transition, with multiple possible consequences[57].

Radhadevi observes that widowhood brings about both subjective and objective consequences. Whereas, subjective consequences can be almost the same for widows and widowers, objective consequences differ due to the distinctively different roles between men and women. The major role of man is that of provider, and of woman as home-maker. When death strikes the spouse, a man loses a home-maker, but a woman loses a provider. Hence the widow faces a much more serious situation than the widower[58]. Apart from these two basic roles, the marital partners play at least eight roles. The spousal loss causes a traumatic role change. The social consequences brought about by widowhood have a damaging effect on the self-concept of a widow.

In every age group women experience more widowhood than men and, in the middle-age group, nearly three times more than men[59]. For the aged, widowhood is a critical situation which involves both social and personal disorganization[60].

The widow faces negative, longterm and severe problems. They seem to be derived from social, economic, cultural and emotional deprivations than from widowhood itself. The problems are not only manifold and severe but they are interrelated and affect each other. And the degree of their seriousness varies with the widow's age, economic conditions, education, caste, family structure, religion, norms and others.

**Economic Deprivation**

One of the most immediate problems following widowhood is economic deprivation. The widows face deprivation due to the economic disadvantages rather than widowhood itself.

The burden of widowhood is not the same for both the sexes. The widow is at a great disadvantage insofar as supporting of the family is concerned[61]. The poverty that follows the loss of the bread winner can send a widow into a demoralizing economic tail-spin. It often forces her to move into a poorer neighbourhood with a restricted budget and out of touch with her former friends[62]. Nimkoff wrote "In Chicago in 1920 about three-fourth widows started working due to sheer financial needs. And many widows who were either unable, or unprepared, to work for a living, became more dependent upon the economic aid of the children, than widowers. The plight of the family bereaved of father is much greater, when the children are young to make financial contribution. In some cases, the family collapses and ceases to exist as a unit and in other cases, the family takes the crisis as a challenge to pull itself together and to reorganize its life on a new basis"[63].

Landis points out that in most homes the husband has almost complete charge of business affairs, aside from those of buying consumer goods for the family. The widow, who knows little about real estate titles, mortgages, contracts, stocks and bonds, and who knows nothing of handling financial affairs, may easily be exploited by others. Almost all widows face two big problems, both closely related (i) money and (ii) finding a job[64], because of their inexperience in dealing with financial matters, and their lack of occupational skills. This makes their economic condition worse, because as Gorden says, "Most of today widows came to maturity in much more traditional times[65].

Morgan in his study on 'Economic Change at Mid-life Widowhood: A Longitudinal Analysis' has found out that the cross-sectional result showed a consistent difference between the income levels and adequacy of married and widowed respondents as a consequence of widowhood. But the longitudinal comparisons showed that many women were poor prior to being widowed. Hence, widowhood is not the major cause of poverty in this group[66].

In India, even today, a woman is a dependent on her husband for support, decision and protection. She has no independent identity, whether she works in the house or in the farm or in a factory, because here the man is the head of the family, owner of the property, and he is in-charge of the family exchequer. Under such circumstances, when a husband dies the wife, who is unprepared for such a situation, faces several problems connected with finance, property and other matters. She has to depend upon herself except for the help received from parents, kinsmen, and others which may not be either adequate or a constant source to depend upon. Her plight is heightened when she is uneducated, poor and ignorant[67]. A widow, whose husband leaves property, may be cheated by others who pretend to help her, if she is not careful and intelligent in self-management. Her plight, in a nuclear family, where the husband alone is the earner and manager, is far worse than in a joint family[68].

Kitchlu, in his study, reported that about 78.48 per cent widows started working after widowhood, due to economic necessity. Among rural widows 30.43 per cent faced problems in getting jobs in comparison to 14.29 per cent of urban widows because the educational attainment of the latter is better than that of the former.

He further reported that Muslim widows had to face problems in getting jobs in comparison to Hindus and Christians, due to their illiteracy. Also, the earnings of Christian widows are higher than their Hindu and Muslim counterparts. The economic condition of the majority of self-employed widows is worse than that of widows in Government employment[69].

Singh et al., in their study on "Problems of Widowhood" write that about 85 per cent of widows faced variety of financial problems. They were unable to purchase items of luxury, maintain "give and take" with friends, previous standard of living, fulfil their husband's liabilities or meet personal and wedding expenses of children[70].

Baidyanath in his report on Kashivasi widows has found that more than half of the widows receive no economic support from their parental or husband's family. About 99 per cent of them follow begging as the primary source of livelihood, but among those whose secondary source of livelihood is begging, the Brahmins outnumber the other three Varnas[71].

Bansal, in her study on "Widows-Marauna", reported that about 58 per cent of the widows were unhappy with their present condition due to their bad economic condition[72].

Finding employment is often a major problem for widows.

Though occasionally, employers may favour widows as a gesture of social responsibility, yet they are not employed easily or paid as much as men, because they have neither proper education nor training. A majority of working widows are employed in low skilled part-time occupations only. Unemployment among widowed mothers is three times higher than other women. Many widows who seek employment were unsuccessful in obtaining jobs. Many widows leave their children uncared for while they work[73]. Middle-class widows have more job-skills and income and more friends, and are more widely engaged in social activities than the working class widows. According to Philiprice the latter experience less grief than the middle-class widows, because they do not have close emotional attachment[74]. It has also been noticed that the home-bound widow feels more oppressed by the stresses of widowhood, than the working widow, because the work may alleviate the distress of behaviour[75].

According to 1981 census, there are 8,574,088 family units in age group 15-49 who have dependent children. A widow who has dependent children faces more economic problems along with other responsibilities, which could be seen in about one-third of all new cases. She is forced to play the new roles of a bread-winner and a caretaker. She undergoes a period of strains and stresses in bringing up her children[76]. The problems of widows are comparatively major because their financial resources usually are considerably less than those of widowers[77]. The widows with dependent children expect some help from the savings or insurance of their husband and also some financial help under Social Security Act. About four-fifths of families are insured with an average of $6,000 insurance per family[78].

Kaur in her study on "Social Adjustment of War Widows" observed that among widows who had a total monthly income of Rs. 300, a majority were found maladjusted. Because of their insufficient financial status they had perceived the fear of worsening economic position[79]. The reduced income, affected their consumption patterns and living arrangements in various ways. They spent more money on food and housing than the average family and this meant there was less money available for other needs[80]. Many a time most of them had to economize on various items of expenditure like milk, vegetables, recreation, clothes, etc[81]. In such situations the children are forced to discontinue their education. They start taking up petty jobs or get self employed to make a contribution to their family income[82]. The unemployed widow becomes dependent upon grown-up children, parents, inlaws or other relatives. She is reduced to a drudge, and, sometimes, she has to face taunts from the family which supports or gives shelter to her[83]. Thus, most widows faced financial difficulties in meeting the basic needs of minor children such as providing good food, clothing and school fees.

When widows start playing dual roles, they cannot adequately supervise or control their children, and thereby they face various negative consequences such as delinquency, mental illness, etc[84].

Berardo in his study on widowhood status in the United States has observed, "widowhood among aged is a critical situation. The aged widows are unemployed and are partly or wholly dependent on the assistance of children, relatives, public or private funds. But often confine to their sisters or such other related kin whether they need advise on solving their personal problems. Therefore, close kinship ties only can mitigate socioeconomic problems of the widows"[85].

Harvey and Bahr in a cross-cultural review of researches on the elderly suggest that the negative characteristics typically found with widowhood are probably attributable to economic disadvantages rather than widowhood *per se*[86].

In the United States a majority of the widowed are aged, their economic condition is usually far below average, particularly in the case of surviving wives and their families[87]. Hutchison, in a study on the life-satisfaction among the low-income elderly, has found that the lower-income widows have more worries about economic problems than do either male counterparts, or the poverty level female counterparts. He also says that the lower-income widows, compared to lower income married, experienced more unhappiness[88]. Hence, Greg in a study has revealed that aged widows who try to maintain some sort of autonomy, need to be respected in terms of their basic rights and freedom[89].

**Familial and Social Deprivation**

Since woman has derived most of her social position from her husband. He is, in most cases, the "Significant other". It is said, a home is everything to a woman, whereas it is a part of a man's life. When such a significant other dies, the role and functions of his widow are completely changed. She often misses the familial roles played by her husband such as sex-partner, caretaker and companion[90]. For most of the traditionally-oriented women the basic self-identity is the role of a mother. Atchleys findings state that a woman with an egalitarian marriage may face lesser identity problems than the woman with traditional marriage[91].

Lopata writes that in American social life the status of the widows tends to be peripheral. Her status, in general is not as high as that of wife. Her single status excludes her from the leisure time activity in a couple companionate environment[92].

Since the couple-based society attaches some kind of stigma to the role of the single person in the transition phase, when the widow is trying to establish a social identity, her "Spoiled identity" from the point of view of her former friends may have negative consequences for her[93]. Anderson says that intimacy support is necessary for the widow during transition phase to build up a new sense of self and social identity in relation to the other world. He further says that both widowed and married women had primary association with their children. Widows, however, are more close to sisters and brothers, than married women. In situations like worry, illness and depression widows relied more on children and siblings than the married women. The close relationships with children based on obligations are not much affected by widowhood[94].

While Morgan, in a study on "Changes in Family Interaction Following Widowhood" reports, "average frequency of interaction with available kin increases for both married and widowed persons, but the number of interactions decreases due to family attrition. Widows are seeing their remaining kin more frequently on the average than the widowers. These changes do not result from the difference in age, race, health or income[95]. Vinick finds that widows are more involved with children, relatives and friends than the widowers, since, several men stated that they had no friends because at this age all of them have passed away[96].

Lopata in her study on "Contributions of Extended Families to the Support System of Metropolitan Area Widows: Limitations of the Modified Kin Network" reports that in the case of Chicago area widows, the extended kin made less contributions to the economic service, social and emotional support systems since, they are not viable resources for the widows to build their support system. In case of younger widows, children and parents are frequent contributors to this support system. Most of the widows did not mention siblings, cousins, nephews or nieces and grand children, who, very infrequently and selectively, contribute to those support systems[97].

In making a transition from married status to widowhood, the surviving partner faces various difficulties not only due to lack of cultural expectation, but also due to lack of supportive relationships. Intimacy support is necessary to build a sense of self and social identity. Research studies have showed that relationships with the kins, neighbours and friends tend to strain and dissolve loneliness. As Lopata says, "The death of the husband breaks up the pattern of engagement, in the life of the wife, in varying degrees and ways. Urbanization and industrialization, and societal complexity, result in a constant shift of people and roles. This fact leaves a rather sizeable number of widows who are relatively isolated or living on a minimal level of contact with a few nearby children, siblings and friends, because they have not been socialized to analyse their environment to choose desired social roles[98].

Lopata, in her study on "Social relations of Black and White Widowed Women in Northern Metropolis" has observed that two-thirds of both white and black widows report little or no contact with siblings. Often, a sibling lived temporarily with the respondent during crisis situations[99]. Lopata, in another study on widows in America, reports that only one-fourth of the widows saw the deceased relatives with any frequency[100]. Kitchlu also observed reduction in the contacts with the relatives and friends of the late husbands[101].

Lopata, in a study on "The Meaning of Friendship in Widowhood" writes; that over half of the widows report that they had no personal friends before and after death of their husbands. In order to know whether the absence of friends lead to loneliness, it was required to measure the level of loneliness in comparison to others. Since, loneliness is often a matter of relative deprivation, the person experiencing it compared his or her level of social interaction to a higher level experienced by others and reported that they did not expect social interaction with people identified as friends. They face problems in maintaining such friendships in widowhood, because, they often feel that being the "fifth-wheel" on social occasions, there is an unwillingness on the part of married friends to include them. They are often left out of such interaction. Among the least educated and disadvantaged widows, friendships are least frequent and least deeply involved. White-collar and middle-class widows wish for friendships and have more personal sources to develop them than the blue-collar widows[102].

For a woman, the spousal loss means a plunge in social status. This curtails her activities and transforms her into an awkward "Fifth-Wheel" at two-by-two social function[103] The Indian woman, soon after widowhood, is excluded from caste rituals and ceremonies. Her social, cultural and economic activities are controlled. Her mode of dressing, eating habits and social contacts all change. She is subjected to total segregation. The reason behind this segregation, putting restriction and disfiguring her is to prevent any kind of intimacy with men[104]. As Gurmeet et al., have observed, a great majority of the widows found it difficult to entertain male visitors in the house and felt the lack of a male escort for functions. They also stated that they missed the companionship[105].

Sometimes, widows are invited by close kinsmen for ceremonies, parties and congregations. But their, deep-felt conviction that the presence of a widow is inauspicious prevents them from participation in these functions. Most of the widows felt a sense of insecurity and loneliness. Their visits to relatives, friends and neighbours also decrease. Widowhood compels them to be away from the social milieu[106]. Thus they are forced into a life of colourlessness, hopelessness and loneliness.

American widows are accultured to live in the homes of male providers. Hence, most of them prefer to live alone rather than be unwanted guests in their children's homes and suffer the loneliness and inconveniences involved[107], whereas in India, a woman/widow cannot have a separate establishment, for she is not culturally trained to lead an independent life. If a widow is young or middle aged with minor children, she has to live with her near relatives. She often needs help to manage the property of the husband, but frequently these very relatives may plot against her and exploit her helpless situation. If the widow is aged, she has to live with her sons, over whom she has no authority. A widow's life in her family and with close relatives becomes miserable, if she does not have any property. Often, due to conflicts between mother-in-law and daughter-in-law, she is made to cook separately.

Her emotions remain bottled-up. And sometimes she is driven out of the family[108].

Baidyanath Saraswati reports in his study, that about 60.22 per cent widows living in the joint family system left their homes under compelling and painful circumstances. A majority of the relatives do not visit the widows in Kashi. These painful experiences within the family seems to be a contributing factor to most widows not maintaining contact with family members. In Kashi, begging is the primary source of livelihood for many widows[109]. Hence, in India, a widow's life is full of loneliness and exploitation except in some sympathetic families.

A younger widow learns to adjust to a life without a spouse in whom she confided and trusted for many years. She establishes, more easily new friendship and discovers ways to integrate herself in the wider community, than her elderly counterpart[110], for whom widowhood is a critical situation which involves both social and personal disorganization[111]. Younger widows face problems of child rearing, returning to work and re-establishment of themselves in the marriage market. Older widows, on the other hand, hold full or part-time jobs or join voluntary organizations, because they do not like to live with their married children. According to Lopata, 49 per cent of widows aged 50 and over in Chicago are solitary dwellers[112]. Besides their body weakness, they face multiple problems such as social, emotional and financial insecurities[113].

Greg, in his study on "The Elderly Widow, Her Family, Neighbours and Friends", has found, widows, whose children are living very closeby have no higher morale than those who do not have children at all or have none living very closeby. The frequency of contact with the children has no significant association with morale, since, the members of family actually do little to elevate widow's morale. In contrast, the frequency of contact with neighbours and friends elevates morale. Family involvement is viewed less meaningful because of the differences in the lifestyles and interests between the elderly widow and her adult children, and also the reversal of roles or interaction between them. If a widow is healthy and financially secure, then she can structure the interactions on her own. Whereas, if the widow is ill or poor, she must rely upon her children to initiate interaction. Dependency changes the nature of interpersonal interaction, then family involvement should be negatively related to morale. As dependency increases, the widow's relations with the family members become more problematic[114]. Due to lack of supportive relationships the aged widows and widowers often find themselves in an isolated situation.

Widows have lower morale and are less affiliated than their married counterparts because they are poorer than the latter[115]. It has recently been discovered that the likelihood of poverty is greater among the female headed households than the male headed households.

Glad writes that elderly widows who are members of other ethnic and racial minority groups, have had less contacts with American society. This foreignness also cuts them off from their own ethnic community, which is Americanizing itself faster, and thereby their loneliness is intensified[116]. Their adjustment is retarded because of lack of education, harmony and strong affection in the home, foreign background, un-Americanization, etc[117].

Duval notes that two-thirds of widows report that their single life is unsatisfactory in loneliness of living. Middle-class widows have more friends than the working class. The widow, thus, may find herself socially marooned in a community[118]. According to Lopata, both white and black older widows lead lonely lives[119]. The social isolation and withdrawal of her relationship with kin network, friends and neighbours lead to higher incidence of mental disorder and a higher suicide rate than their married counterparts. Hence, the condition of the aged widows is deplorable and insecure[120].

It is clear from the above cited studies that the widow is socially incapacitated and her position is deplorable. Widowhood reduces her social roles and makes her socially isolated, thereby social relationships tend to deteriorate.

**Emotional Deprivation**

Among all types of deprivations, that of emotion is harmful to personal development, but, deprivation of love is especially damaging and results in emotional starvation and self-pity at any age[121]. A widow, quite often finds it difficult, and takes a long time to overcome the grief.

The death of a loved one is like an amputation and is an extremely traumatic experience. There is conflict between hopes, which refuse to give up the object, and reality which demands that it shall be given up[122]. Hence, the widow faces problems of overcoming this difficulty.

Usually, there are three stages of grief. The first is a short period of shock during which, the surviving spouse is stunned and immobilized with grief and disbelief. The second is the intense suffering during which the individual shows both physical and emotional symptoms of great disturbance. The third stage is a gradual reawakening of an interest in life[123]. The grief-stricken, bewildered, widow finds no safe corner consoling her. The following are the signs of grief: (1) Physical symptoms (2) Loss of ability to believe the loss/reality. (3) Thinking always about him and expecting him as if he is still alive[124]. The widow becomes physically weak and mentally distressed. Sometimes a widow becomes so highly disturbed that she even doubts her husband's death. In this connection Marris has narrated, in his study, the agony and deep-rooted grief of the widow. He gives and example of a widow with a young daughter and son who is not ready to accept the fact of death of her husband[125]. She remembers her deceased husband time and again. She harbours illusions of hearing his voice and has obsessive memories of the dead husband[126]. Emotional reactions may include anger, guilt, depression, anxiety or preoccupation with the thought of the deceased.

In Peterson and Briley's study on "Widows and Widowhood", the role losses and psychological deprivations caused by the spousal loss are recorded. They also quoted the finding of Schoenbery and others who studied typical and important aspects of grief. They have reported, "About 99 per cent of the consultants predicted that death of a mate causes depression, loss of weight, sleeplessness and despair, 90 per cent predicted that the bereaved would have dreams about the deceased. About 74 per cent and 70 per cent expected the widows to have illusions about the presence of the dead persons and angry thoughts directed toward the deceased respectively. The author felt that widows develop guilt reactions, loneliness, fear, regrets and feeling of abandonment"[127].

According to Barret, the leading problem of widows is loneliness; grief and family difficulties come second while finance and legal affairs are the further problems. They face difficulties in adjusting to the loss and to their new role in the family relationships. Barret further says "Widows suffer from grief as well as stress that male oriented, youth oriented and couple oriented society subjects them to, long after the husband's death"[128].

Mathieu, in his study, has reported that two-thirds of widows had never considered the possibility of widowhood which, inevitably, leaves the survivor ill prepared to cope with the practical or psychological problems like the shock of loss, depression and despair that follow death. Both urban and rural people share a cultural tradition in which the possibility of death is denied[129].

The widow faces problems of adjustment due to individual hindrances like nervousness, moods of depression and morbidity, tendency to worry and general emotional instability[130].

Marris says, "The widow has to adjust to her new state while she is preoccupied with a painful struggle to master her grief. For months, even years after his death, her energies may be so absorbed in this struggle and her feelings so deeply disturbed, as to affect all her needs and her response to those who try to meet them."[131] Widows face a number of emotional problems because often the wife has not been prepared for the death. Widow also faces difficulties in making new living arrangements and new social life. Either she has to live with her adult children or alone. Each choice represents a number of unavoidable problems[132].

Toth and Toth conducted a group work with widows and have reported, "The group members experienced many somatic problems only after widowhood like sleeplessness regularly, headaches, backaches and a general feeling of malaise. They also experienced other symptoms of depression in varying degrees, including a sense of aimlessness, difficulty in making decisions and an inability to get going in the mornings. The widows felt guilt for the sorrow of not doing more to prevent her husband's death"[133]. Lopata's study has revealed that depression, weight loss, insomnia and irritability appears for a few months after the death of the spouse. She also reports of one in five widows never having recovered from grief[134]. Jambagi notes that a majority of widows suffered from psychosomatic diseases. And the health problems lead to the origin of some other problems. If she is not healthy, she becomes a burden to the family and may be neglected or segregated[135].

A widow faces physio-psycho problems because she loses interest in her daily life and neglects her health. Along with these, lack of social contacts, sense of insecurity, isolation and other factors affect her health adversely. She becomes restless, irritated and frustrated due to her distress of mind, pathetic and over-whelmed with the sense of emptiness of life. Widows, particularly young childless and old widows, show withdrawal from friends and relatives and suffer from personal loneliness in life[136].

Loneliness may reflect social isolation, psychological isolation, or a combination of both. The aged widow feels, as if the most central, important aspect of herself has gone and what is left is meaningless and irrelevant. She faces difficulties in establishing new friendships as the former ones are either strained, broken or not easily available[137].

This is because of inability and lack of her skills needed to build new relationships. Thereby loneliness in widowhood is compounded. Many widows experience disengagement from a prior lifestyle and sets of relations and express loneliness as an alienation due to status drop[138]. There is a significant difference in the frequency of loneliness experienced by older women in each marital status. The formerly married women feel lonely more frequently than the married and the never married women. The never married, who see their close friends less often feel lonelier and the formerly married are lonely often if they do not see their close family members[139].

Durkheim writes that there is a connection between widowhood and suicide. "The suicides occur at the crisis of widowhood are really due to domestic anomie resulting from the death of husband or wife. A family catastrophe occurs which affects the survivor. He is not adapted to the new situation in which he finds himself and accordingly offers less resistance to suicide."[140]

Berardo has found that widows, typically, present higher death rates, a greater incidence of mental disorder and a higher suicide rate than their married counterparts because of greater isolation and feelings of insecurity and non-usefulness[141]. Suicides are more common among the widowed than the single, and the rate is lowest among the married[142]. The seriousness of difficulties faced by widows can be seen in the higher rate of suicides than that of married women within the same age group. Harvey and Bahir observe: Widows have more negative outlook than the married. The widows readily express negative feelings, loneliness and depression or unhappiness than the married and they have lower morale than the married[143].

They further write that the damage to the self often accompanies widowhood, some of the widowed commit suicide, others are in mental hospitals and others express anomie feeling, unhappiness, low morale and personal isolation. If the spouse is a "Significant other" damage to the self is likely to follow widowhood. Urban widows have developed a greater sense of insecurity, after losing their husbands, than their rural counterparts[144]. The deprivation of love, security, and sex makes the widows feel insecure, lonely and helpless[145].

Bankoff, in a study on 'Social support and Adaptation to Widowhood', has noted that the death of a husband not only primarily disrupts a woman's social environment but also removes a key relationship in her emotional life. And the data on the effects of social support on psychological well-being of widows indicate that the role of such social supports is important but complex[146].

He further reports that of all types of social supports, intimacy support appears to be the most important for widows in the transition phase, but emotional support is modestly associated with the well-being of widows in crisis-loss phase. Parents and widowed, or single, friends are the two important sources of support in crisis-loss phase. But in the transition phase, widowed or single friends are important sources of support. However, support from their neighbours, parents, children is also positively related to the widow's sense of well-being.[147].

Veroff, Douvan and Kulka's study indicates that widowed women are positive about their marriage and more unhappy about their present and future. Yet, widows are more positive about themselves than either women or men, because they have maintained and built the social network which is helpful to them. Widows who are positive about themselves tend to visit more and to be more satisfied with their friends, than those who are neutral or negative about themselves[147].

During intense grief, a widow should be allowed to talk about her loss with relatives or friends. This helps her to adjust to her new status more easily. Borstein opines that those who had experienced previous losses were less likely to be depressed than those who had not lived through such an experience[148].

**Cultural Deprivation**

In fact, widowhood pervades all the spheres of a widow's life and there is a drastic change in her lifestyle after widowhood. Widows have to start altogether a different life in food habits, dress etc[149]. The norms of widowhood are essentially the norms of asceticism in Hindu Society. The basic emphasis is on simple, Sativic-food, i.e., pure food which does not produce passions, whereas Muslims and Christians are not forced to lead a life of abstinence and are at liberty to enjoy life. There are no restrictions on food habits, dress and remarriage[150].

In general, a Hindu widow is deprived of wearing the Tali, flowers, glass-bangles, nose ring and applying *kumkum*. A widow cannot wear the above insignia of *saubhaghya* under any circumstances. However, the life of an orthodox Brahmin widow is most pitiable. According to strict, orthodox rites, a Brahmin widow had to face, much against her will, the horrible and inhuman rite of tonsure. She is also culturally isolated and is made to spend her time in constant devotion to God, a total separation from wordly affairs and pleasures.

In Maharashtra, the widow had to wear a deep red coloured sari and red bangles to parade her separate identity. In South India, she could not wear blouses and had to wear an almond colour sari. In Bengal eating fish and combing the hair was forbidden. In North India she had to wear a white sari. Most of these customs, it may be noted, are continuing today in some regions[151]. The south Indian widows are more particular in observing these taboos than their North Indian counterparts.

Kitchlu says, that due to widowhood there are drastic changes in the lifestyles of widows although there are group variations. About 62.60 per cent of the widows had undergone change in dress and were not allowed to use *Kumkum* or *Sindhur*, 28.20 per cent widows had to change to simple diet after widowhood. A majority of Urban Christian widows (32.35) were least affected by their change in status in comparison to Hindus (15.57%) and Muslims (11.11%) widows[152].

Even today, widows are discouraged from taking part in any auspicious ceremonies and ritually sacred activities. Nagesh and Katti have observed that the participation of widows in religious activities had decreased after widowhood in rural areas from 97 per cent to 40 per cent and in urban areas from 64 per cent to 58 per cent. Kitchlu has also drawn similar conclusions and feels that widows are still considered as bad women.

Widow remarriage is socially banned in India. However, some cultures allow their widows to remarry, some allow it in exceptional cases and some orthodox Brahmins and Rajputs do not allow it under any circumstances. A widow is made to wear coarse, plain clothes, she is prohibited from wearing jewellery, eating good, and has to lead a hard life of penances. All these are designed to make a widow look unattractive enough for any man to want to marry her.

**Re-marriage of Widows**

In general, the status of widows has been difficult in most societies. In traditional Indian and Chinese societies a widow is not allowed to remarry, or is socially discouraged. While in modern societies a widow is allowed to remarry, the right is subjected to certain restrictions.

In Chinese society, and, to a lesser extent in Japan, widow remarriage is not encouraged. If a son marries a widow, no matter how intelligent, interesting and beautiful she is, he is thought to bring disgrace to the family[153].

And quite often remarriage may be prevented by members of the husband's family. But a large number of widows remarry if the husband's family is poor or if the widow has no son[154]. When a widow does marry she must ride in a black-covered chair instead of real bridal chair, from her residence to that of her intended husband[155]. She is not allowed to take any of her property into a second marriage[156].

In America, remarriage has always been an accepted institution. It is thought to be an easy solution to overcome the problems of widowhood, although it is encouraged between widowed people. But the widowed person is expected to complete a set period of bereavement. Following this he/she can remarry readily. In many communities, if a widow reamaries soon, she is considered to be lacking in respect for her dead husband[157]. This means, a widow is usually required to exhibit her status as widow longer than a man is officially required to.

In Rome, though widow remarriage is allowed, she is required to observe a certain period of mourning before remarriage, the reason is to avoid the *turbatio sanguinis*, "Confusion of the blood". A widow can however, remarry, immediately after giving birth[158].

In India widow remarriage is allowed among some of the lower castes and encouraged especially in rural areas[159] but is in disfavour in all the castes[160].

Census report of 1911 (Mysore) states that, "The marriage of widows is prohibited only among Brahmins and in a very few other castes. Among the rest such marriages are allowed. In few castes like Besta and Uppar a fine has to be paid for the benefit of the caste people if a man marries a widow."[161]

Nair asserts that widow marriage is universal among the tribal people of India and the proper groom is her younger brother-in-law. A person who wishes to marry a widow has to return the bride-price to the deceased husband's family in case widow marries an outsider. The Dhanuks and Chamars of Bihar prefer widows and pay a higher bride price for them[162].

Contrary to popular and widespread belief, Singh's findings in Madhya Pradesh villages confirm that some Brahmins marry widows and separated women. Those who don't do so are known as Byahate and those who do as Karike. Karike is a peripheral group of the caste, the economically well-off, who seek to retain their status, however gain acceptance as near-equals with the Byahate in three or four generations and as equals with them in some more generations[163].

In North India the system of levirate is in practice. Under levirate marriage, a widow has to marry her husband's younger brother, or in the absence of a younger brother, to a cousin. Marriage with the elder brother of the deceased husband is generally not favoured. Jats, Gujars, and Ahirs (all warrior Kshatriya castes) follow this system. Bhangis and Chamars do not have restrictions on marriage of their widows.

Such marriage is not called marriage but 'Kareva'. It is a marriage of convenience whereby society provides protection to a widow or her children and in which there is no formal marriage ceremony. The Kareva normally takes place after 12 months of the death of the husband or in fact, on the day of the first death anniversary. At a small community gathering, the person places bangles on the head of the widow or wraps a piece of cloth around her. After this ceremony, the widow enjoys all the rights and privileges of a married woman[164].

The Punjab Gazetteer of 1904 accurately comments on the "widow inheritance" practised by the Jats and Taneers, "The first husband's brother takes the widow to wife, very often they have already been on very intimate terms. It means the legitimization of previous sexual relationships through the ceremony called 'Kareva' or 'Chadur Puana'[165].

Dube, in his study on widow remarriage in Madhya Pradesh, points out that the prevalence of widow marriage was high due to early marriage of girls: but many of the widows were encouraged to remarry, particularly if a widow had no son[166]. A similar conclusion is drawn by Bose who found that widow remarriage is not only prevalent in rural areas but it is even encouraged, especially among lower castes, but prohibited among Rajput, Brahmin, Purohit and Mahajan castes of North India[167]. Among

Rajputs, Punwar Rajputs allow widow remarriage and sometimes pay a bride price up to Rs 1000 for widows[168].

Mann writes: "In the past, if a Brahmin or a Bania widow married, she was usually excommunicated. But recently the Bania and Brahmins started following widow marriage. They have termed the practice of junior levirate as "Churi Pahrana". The ceremony is observed on the 13th day after the death of the first husband and the deceased husband's brother accepts the widow as his wife"[169].

Baron et al., say that in Kerala, a negative levirate marriage, is in practice. Under this practice a widow is allowed to marry other than the brother-in-law[170].

Almost all the tribes of Chota Nagpur allow their widows the right to marry. They perform such marriages through the *sagai* or *sanga* form. In such second marriages, the rituals of marriage are simple and less elaborate[171].

In South India, the Thanda Pulayan castes in Tamil Nadu permit widow remarriage but not to the deceased husband's brothers. This is also the case among the Halepaike caste. Baron and Ehrenfels however suggest that widow marriage is more prevalent among such of these castes which are Matrilineal or matrilocal[172].

In Karnataka, though widow marriage is in practice among certain lower castes, there are certain restrictions on the choice of the group. The Bedas, Okkaliggas, Holeyas, Madigas, Vaddas, Vayindas, Mandas, Dasari, Bilimagga, Uppar and many other castes do not permit the marriage of a widow with the brother-in-law. The Bedas, Madigas, Bilimagga, Sanyasi and Uppars allow the widow to marry within the close circle of husband's *kula*. The Bilimagga, Sanyasi and Vodda limit her choice of the bridegroom to a still narrower field, prohibiting the members of the widow's father's *kula*. Widow remarriage is allowed among some sections of Lingayats and the practice is called 'Udaki'.

A widow marriage takes place in Krishna Paksha or the dark fortnight of the month. It is never held in the morning but only after sundown. It is performed in a temple or unoccupied house. The Uppars perform the ceremony in a village different from the one in which the first husband and the widow's father live.

Generally remarried women and widows attend such marriage ceremony[173].

In American society, no system of levirate or widow inheritance is in operation, although sometimes a deceased husband's brother may marry the widow. Most widows do not continue a close relation with that group, once the continuing link is gone. It is the duty of the children to retain their late father's family name, but sometimes small children may take the last name of the mother's new husband[174].

Though widow marriage is allowed, the widows receive less encouragement than widowers to remarry. The majority of women are widowed at a more advanced age, and thus it is much more difficult for her, than for a widower, to change her status through remarriage[175]. Hence, proportionately, more widowers than widows remarry. In a recent year 38.4 per cent widowers remarried in comparison to 10.2 per cent widows in all age groups; for widows over 65 years it was only 2.0 per cent[176].

Leslie in a study on "Marriage in a Changing World", has noticed that widowers usually remarry more quickly than widows, and most of them get married within one or two years after the death of their first wives. In comparison, widows often wait for several years, since they have to complete the rearing of all their children before remarrying. He further says that over half of the couples had known each other before they were widowed, as neighbours or members of some church or were associated socially and related by marriage. Men usually marry sisters of their first wives and women favoured brothers of their first husband[177].

Smart and Smart have opined that marriage itself is a complex subject, and the marriage of previously married is more complex. Divorced persons marry more often than single and widowed persons. Widowed persons are happier in their remarriages than their divorced counterparts[178]. Regarding the reactions of the children and peer-groups towards remarriage, Vinick writes: "Majority of them told their children about their plan to remarry and over half had received positive reactions, but their peer-group showed negative reaction initially, later they approved"[179].

Though remarriage is the most satisfactory adjustment to

widowhood, this practice among widows depends upon several conditions like:

(1) Duration of widowhood: Recently widowed have greater chances than those bereaved much previously. The second year of widowhood is considered better for remarriage.

(2) Number of children: There is a correlation between the chances of remarriage and the number of children. More the number of children lesser the chances of remarriage.

(3) Widow's pensions: The widow who receives the pension that terminates upon remarriage may be unwilling to forefeit this benefit, or examines such offers with care[180].

Apart from the above mentioned conditions for widow remarriage, there are important restraints like love and respect for the late husband, concern for the children and apprehension of disrespect by society. Middle-aged widows mention these restraints more than younger and older widows. Employed widows mentioned these restraints more frequently than the unemployed widows[181].

The negative attitude towards remarriage of widows is so strong that even today, people believe that this practice does not have either social or religious sanction. Katti and Nagesh, in another study in Hubli city and some neighbouring rural areas, point out that 97 per cent of the rural respondents and 92 per cent urban, are not willing to marry again[182].

In order to avoid prejudice against widow remarriage and to introduce it among all the castes, an attempt was made during the 18th century by Raja Rajballabha of Deccan, and by the Chief of Kotab of Rajasthan, to get Shastric sanction in support of widow marriage by Pandits. In the first half of the 19th century, the social reformers of Bengal made continuous efforts in that direction and succeeded in abolishing Sati system and legalizing widow remarriage[183].

Ishwar Chandra Vidyasagar conducted the first Hindu Brahmin Widow remarriage in Bengal after the passing of the Widow Remarriage Act on July 26, 1856, in spite of bitter opposition from the orthodox. He emancipated widows, lived for them and even died for them[184]. Babu Sasipada Banurji who had been an advocate of the widow remarriage movement, solemnized the marriage of his widowed niece and rescued her from the hands of her orthodox relatives[185].

Veersalingam, a social reformer from Andhra Pradesh, along with a band of devoted workers, succeeded in performing the first widow remarriage on Dec. 11:1881 at Markandeya, Andhra Pradesh in the teeth of opposition from the orthodox[186].

Bhate, the Secretary of Widow Remarriage Association, Poona, in his book, *Permitting Widow Marriage*, has strongly argued that widow marriage had the sanction of the Hindu laws and texts. He strengthens his argument by quoting the reasons for permitting widow marriage in Hindu society[187].

Pathare Prabhus Association solemnized a marriage of a Brahmin widow openly and publicly on June 1869, an act which received great favour by a very large number of liberal and unprejudiced men belonging to the highest classes of Hindu society[188].

Madhowadas Ragnathdas has explained his personal experiences of marrying a widow in 1872 among Shetti's caste. In the eyes of Hindu orthodoxy, marrying a widow was a crime which was inexplicable. He was accordingly subjected to excommunication by his caste people[189].

In the 1860's the widow marriage and rehabilitation movement made maximum progress in Bengal, followed by Bombay, thanks to the efforts of a number of Indian humanitarians[190].

Agarawal's study on "Widow Marriage in some Rural Areas of Northern India" reveals that the percentage of widow remarriage is high among Muslims (between 35.37 per cent) because they do not put restrictions on widow marriage. And among lower caste Hindus it is 30 per cent whereas among high caste Hindus, it is only around 7 per cent, because of the prohibition of widow marriage among them[191].

In America, during 1905-56 half of those widowed and one-fourth of the divorced women remarried. The remarriage rate is higher among blacks than among whites, due to higher death/divorce rates. The rate is high among lower classes. The remarriage rate among widowed is lower than among the divorced.

Remarriages of widowed persons seems to be successful because they remarry cautiously and slowly[192].

Sudhir Chandra, in an article entitled, "Widow Marriage and Later Nineteenth Century Indian Literature", illustrates the difficulties faced in the operation of an unresolved problem of widow remarriage within the structure of belief itself. He says, "The historiography of social reform in modern India is familiar with the dichotomy between belief and action that, almost invariably, cast a shadow between the profession and practice of social reformers. To this, is attributed the failure of the middle class Hindu social reform movement, and the dichotomy itself is ascribed to the hypocrisy of social reformers"[193].

One more reason for the negative attitude towards widow remarriage, as M.N. Srinivas observes is that due to Sanskritic civilization, the Non-Brahmins wish to rise in the social scale by imitating intolerably-stupid Brahmin customs and ceremonies. The simple tribes like the Soligas, the Korachas and the Dombas present the desire to climb the higher rungs.

He further says that among the Devangas and the Nayindas, widow marriage prevailed originally, but now they prohibit it in imitation of the Brahmins. Among some castes, widow marriage is generally allowed, but is not popular among some groups. For example, among Sajjans, widow marriage is generally allowed but is not allowed among Sajjan Kumbaras. While allowing a widow to remarry the other Non-Brahamin castes except lowest and primitive tribes look down upon the widow. They feel that widow marriage is not socially approved but it is inevitable as it is better to marry than to burn the widow[194].

The above cited review reveals that prohibition of widow marriage is a peculiar phenomenon of Hindu culture. Although marriage of widow is allowed among a few lower castes of Hindus. The married widow is looked down upon with disfavour and the practice is not encouraged. Hence, cases of widow marriages are few. In India, remarriage for divorced and widowed women carries with it a certain stigma, while, in American society, remarriage is thought to be an easy solution to overcome the problems of widowhood. There is a significant difference among the cultures in overcoming the crisis. This is because of their reordering of marital values.

**Welfare of Widows**

There are various legislations passed both before and after independence and important resolutions passed by Indian National Social Conference in order to improve the condition of widows or at least to try to reduce the discriminations against them.

*Before Independence*

(1) Bengal Sati Regulation XVII of 1829 declaring Sati or self immolation of widows illegal.

(2) The Hindu Widow's Re-Marriage Act 1856 legalising the marriage of Hindu widows.

(3) When a Hindu, governed by the Dayabhaga school of Hindu law, dies intestate, leaving any property, and when a Hindu, governed by any other school of Hindu law, or by customary law, dies intestate, leaving separate property, his widow, or if there is more than one widow, all his widows together shall be subject to the provisions of sub section (3) be entitled to the property in respect of which he dies intestate to the same share as a son. Provided that the widow of a predeceased son shall inherit in like manner, as a son, if there is no son surviving of such predeceased son and shall inherit in like manner as a son's son if there is surviving a son or son's son of such predeceased son.

Provided further, the same provision shall apply *mutatis mutandis* to the widow of a predeceased son of a predeceased son.

(4) An interest developing on a Hindu widow, under the provision of this section, shall be the limited interest known as a Hindu Woman's estate provided however that she shall have that same right of claiming partition as a male owner.

(5) Indian Succession Act 1925 there is no distinction between those related through the father and those related through the mother. The husband surviving his wife has the same rights in her property as she would have in his property if she survives him.

(6) The Child Marriage Restraint Act 1929 fixing the minimum age of marriage at 18 years for boys and 15 years for girls.

(7) The Hindu Women's Rights to Property Act as amended in 1938.

(8) Notwithstanding any rule of Hindu Law or custom to the contrary the provision of Section 3 shall apply where a Hindu dies intestate.

*After Independence*

(1) Hindu Marriage Act 1955. It fixes:

1. Minimum age for marriage as 15 years for girls and 18 years for boys. Now it is 18 years for the girls and 21 for the boys.
2. Makes monogany universal.

(2) Hindu Succession Act. 1956.

It confers the right of absolute ownership over property and the woman can make a will leaving her share of property to the heirs. Section 10 provides that the property of an intestate shall be divided among the heirs in accordance with the following rules.

Rule 1 The intestate widow, or if there are more widows than one, all the widows shall take one share.

Rule 2 The surviving sons and daughters and the mothers of the intestate shall each take one share.

Rule 3 The heirs in the branch of each deceased son or each predeceased daughter of the intestate are also entitled to get one share in the property.

(3) Hindu Adoption and Maintenance Act 1956 Section 8, any female Hindu (a) who is of sound mind (b) who is not a minor and (c) who is not married, whose husband is dead or has completely and finally renounced the world or has ceased to be Hindu or has been declared by a court of competent jurisdiction to be of unsound mind, has the capacity to take a son or daughter in adoption. According to Section 9, the consent of father and mother is necessary for giving the child in adoption unless (i) they or one of them is dead or (ii) The father or mother has completely and finally renounced the world or (iii) has ceased to be Hindu or (iv) has been declared by a court of competent jurisdiction to be of unsound mind[195].

The following resolutions were passed in different sessions by the Indian National Social Conference (INSC). They are:

1. Resolution No. 7, Sixth conference Allahabad 1892 INSC. That, the disfigurement of child widows before they attain the age of 18 and even after that age, without the consent of the widows recorded in writing before a Panch and a magistrate be discouraged and caste organizations be formed to arrange for social penalties to be inflicted on those who aid in disfiguring child widows without their consent (Repeated in 12th conference, 1899, 16th conference 1902, 17th conference, 1903, 18th conference 1904 and 22nd conference 1908).

2. Resolution X Tenth conference, Calcutta 1896 INSC. That, in the opinion of the conference, it is desirable not to discourage the remarriage of child widow, when their parents or guardians wish to give them in marriage according to the Hindu Shastras (Repeated at every conference from 12th conference 1899 to 30th conference 1916).

3. Resolution VII, Eleventh conference, Amaravati 1897 INSC. That, the experience of the last 40 years working of the Widow Marriage Act of 1856 has, in the opinion of conference, established the fact that the Act fails to secure to the remarrying widow the full enjoyment of her rights in the following respect-first, that such widow is made to forfeit her life-interest in her husband's immoveable property for doing a lawful act when such forfeiture would not have resulted if she had misconducted herself, secondly, that even in respect of Stridhan property, over which her power of disposal is absolute, there is a general impression that she loses proprietary rights over moveables in favour of her husband's relations who otherwise could not have interfered with her free disposal of the same. Thirdly, in many cases she and her second husband are not only excommunicated but the right of worship in public temples has been denied to them and no relief has been given to them in civil courts. Fourthly in some parts of the country she is subjected to disfigurement before she has arrived at the age of majority with any freedom being given to her to exercise her choice. In all these respects, the law of 1856 has proved inoperative to protect her and the conference is of the opinion that steps should be taken by the Social Reform Associations who favour such reform to adopt remedies to relax the stringency of caste usages and to secure a reconsideration of the principles of the Act with a view to remedy its defects.

4. Resolution XVI, Eleventh conference,- Amaravati 1897, INSC. That, as the law at present stands, there is apparently no protection to a widow or an unmarried girl above twelve or below sixteen, who is a consenting party to an act of personal dishonour at the hands of strangers. In the opinion of the conference, the consent of such a girl between twelve and sixteen should, as in the case of kidnapping be held to be inoperative to protect the man who violates her honour[196].

The Government of Karnataka has undertaken a major policy decision which benefits all destitute widows all over the state. This was the introduction of the widow pension scheme under the social security pension scheme since, 1984. Under this scheme every destitute widow who is a resident of Karnataka and who has no son is entitled to get pension of Rs. 50 per month. It is sent to her by money order through Postal Service[197]. The scheme now covers 54,00,000 lakh widows and entails an expenditure of Rs. 27,00,00,000 crore from the state exchequer for 1989-90, while in Dharwad District 28370 widows are the beneficiaries of this welfare scheme[198].

As in many other countries, we in India have also relied on legislation to bring about social change. Women have been and still are, discriminated against, in family, life, education and training, employment and in several other social and political fields.

Among Hindus, women are assigned inferior status while widows are conferred still inferior status. Despite the protection accorded to widows by legislations and reforms effected by social reformers and social workers there has been no change in the basic position of the widows. Hence it is felt that there is need for conducting such studies.

**Hindu Widows: Historical Information**

To study the status of the Hindu widow in India it is necessary to have a glimpse of her changing status through a historical lens. We will start with the conditions prevailing in the Vedic age because the Hindu civilization goes beyond this period and data is not available on the prehistoric phase as it is unexplored. The portrait of a widow as coming out of the study of Vedic literature is the picture as drawn by several authorities on the Vedic period.

Before we turn to depict the changing status of Hindu widows, we feel that it is essential to know the origin and definition of the term 'vidhava' or 'widow'.

The term 'vidhava' or 'widow' is very old and can be traced beyond the vedic language to Indo-European origin. In most Indo-European languages one finds similar words*. The widow or *vidhava* can be defined as a woman whose husband is dead and who has not married again[199].

According to Sanskrit grammarians the word 'vidhava' is derived from the word *'dhava'* meaning a man or a husband. Although, the word 'vidhava' was in general use, the basic word 'dhava' was not mentioned in the vedic literature. In the 'Nirukta' for the first time the word was used to mean a man or a husband. In the 'Atharvaveda' *'dhava'* is the name of a tree. In the Vedic times the word 'avidhava' -a double negative word in the sense of a woman not widowed was used, instead of a positive word like *sadhava*. Even in the European languages the work *dhava* is not found[200].

The word Vidhava is said to be wrongly split up by the Indian grammarians. The word 'Vi' in the word *'Vidhava'* is not a prefix but part of the main root word. It must be derived from a root like Teutonic 'Wid' to lack, Latin 'Videre' to separate and Sanskrit 'Vidh' to be bereft. Yaska says that when the true derivative meaning was lost in India the word 'dhava' in the sense of a husband came into existence in the Sanskrit language by wrongly spliting up the word *vidhava*[201]. Vidhava or widow therefore is a woman whose husband is dead and who has not married again. Silverman writes, the very word 'widow' has very native connotations. Many widows feel as if it implies they are damaged, a second class citizen. The same associations are not true for the word widower[202].

For the Hindu woman widowhood is more tragic and disastrous because of the superstition and the oppressive, loathsome rituals attached to it. As Abbe Du Bois quotes, "The happiest death for a women is that which overtakes her while she

---

* In Latin-Vidua; Italian-Vedava; Spanish-Viuda; French-Veuv; Old slavonic-vidava; Russian-vidova; Old German-Wituwa; Gothic-Widuowo; old English-Widewe and Wideuwe and Persian-beva.

is still in a married state. Such a death is looked upon as a reward of goodness extending back for many generations; on the other hand, the greatest misfortune that can befall a wife is to survive her husband"[203]. Hindus have a belief in the "Theory of Karma" and therefore every widow thinks that her sorrow or plight is the result of her "Karmas"[204]. It is due to her bad deeds done in previous births that she has to suffer widowhood. The one who has auspicious signs could not be a widow. However, it is important to note that she is not considered among the sinners.

In Hindu society the husband is elevated to such a superior position as to almost enjoy the status of God *vis-a-vis* his wife. A widowed woman is considered as a luckless and unfortunate woman and an object to pity. Quite often she has been compared to a Veena without strings and to a cart without wheels. Thereby the motivation or urge for life is lost to her[205].

Nevertheless, it may be stated that the state of widowhood is a great calamity in all societies, but it is more so in a partriarchal and traditional society like India. The reason for it is that here woman is known as 'Abala' or the one without power and therefore she has to depend upon her protectors. Manu, the Hindu law-giver, infact, states that a woman can never be a free maiden, is to be cared for by her father, brother or husband. A woman considers her husband as her greatest protector and hence his death is a great calamity to her.

### *Vedic Period*

The Hindus of the Vedic period had a patriarchal society. As in the other patriarchal societies, the woman's social, religious or economic status had never been higher than that of men. But, in some respects, the Vedic woman and widow enjoyed certain privileges of which they were deprived of in a later age.

Widows then, were permitted to remarry. This practice seems to have been accepted as normal from the Vedic period onwards[206]. Enough references are found in the Vedas to show that widow remarriage was common though the re-married widow could not aspire to the status of (wife), where she could become the mistress of the house. The use of the word "Parapurva", a woman who has had a second husband, proves that widows remarried. The word

"Didhishu", used in the Rig Veda, means the second husband of a woman. This shows that marriage of widows was not opposed. The custom of a widow marrying the brother of her deceased husband seemed to be common. Hence, the word "Devara" literally means a woman's brother-in-law[207].

The economic condition of widows was not unsatisfactory. A widow was given her husband's share in the property. A brotherless maiden was an heir to her father's property. A man was reluctant to marry such a maiden, apprehensive that her father may make her a *putrika*, or an appointed daughter. As it is believed that the woman's *parinahya* was not her absolute property. But a childless widow inherited her husband's property by right[208]. A widow who had a son by Niyoga (levirate) received her dead husband's property as the guardian of the property during her son's minority. If a widow remarried, her financial difficulties and problems were solved, since her second husband looked after her.

*Niyoga (Levirate)*

The institution of Niyoga was in practice during the time of Dharmasutras since, in the Rig Veda we find the widow married to her brother-in-law[209]. But there is no reference to the necessity of his producing an heir for his dead brother and even in, Grhaya Sutras there is no ritual connected with Niyoga. There are differences of opinion among different Dharmasutras about its practice, as it can be assumed that the institution of Niyoga came into Aryan society from some non-Aryan source. For a long period the sacred law was inclined to adopt the growing custom, although with misgiving[210].

The term Niyoga is of later origin, but its implications were freely practised in the Rig vedic times. Frequent allusions are made in the Rig Veda to the practice of levirate. We have several references to the wives of weaklings procuring children from agencies other than their legally married husband[211].

Under the system of Niyoga a widow, or a woman whose husband was not virile, was allowed to have conjugal relations with her brother-in-law, who was regarded as the most eligible person for this duty, or some other near relation, till she gave birth to an offspring. It is also significant to note that there is no reference in the whole of the Rig Veda to a woman marrying the elder brother of her deceased husband. Even today, a widow's marriage with her husband's elder brother is taboo.

A widow was allowed to have two sons through Niyoga. Such a son had the right to perform the funeral oblations. Like Vedic Indian, in early societies also, a son by levirate was always preferred to a son by adoption. Hence, adoption of a son by a widow was in vogue but it was looked down upon with disfavour.

*Widow Burning*

We do not have any reference to burning of widows in the whole range of the Rig Veda[212]. The vedic hymns refer to the remarriage of widows rather than their self-immolation. Widow-burning was, evidently, a defunct custom at this time. It was represented only by the symbolic ritual of the widow lying besides her husband on the funeral pyre, until upon which she was asked to rise up. Both the Rig Veda and Atharva Veda expected the widow to get up from the pyre and marry the husband's younger brother[213].

Immolation can be expected to have existed among the early Indo-Aryans in some form or the other. This Indo-European custom of widow burning came to an end when Aryans entered India and had become only a symbolic ceremony. But Prof Sarkar observes:

> The Vedic literature shows very few traces of such a custom; partly, no doubt because these texts are priestly in character, and widow burning is known to have prevailed elsewhere, mainly among non-priestly warrior families, and partly because, even amongst the ruling classes, cases of widow burning were rare and prevented throughout the Vedic period as shown by authentic Kshatryia dynastic traditions; while in the "Brahman" society Sex-relations seem to have been too lax to admit of the prevalence of such a practice[214].

The status of a woman began to decline gradually in the partriarchal vedic society where importance is attached to the birth of a male child which, in turn, become responsible for the gradual rise in the status of man. The widow was given inferior position as she was unfortunate enough to lose an all-powerful protecting male partner.

### *Epic Period, Sutra Period, Buddhistic Literature*

The position of the widow in the epic period, the Sutra period and as found in the Buddhistic literature, gives a full picture as these are the connecting links between the Vedic and the Smruti period.

The deterioration in the status of widows commenced from the epic period. From Shantiparva of the Mahabharat, we can generalize about the miserable position of widows through the words of a she-pigeon, who says, "Widows, even if mothers of many children, are still miserable. Bereft of husband, a woman becomes helpless and an object of pity with her friends. Limited are the gifts from the son to a woman. The gifts that her husband alone makes to her are unlimited. A woman has no protector, no happiness without her lord"[215]. Hence his death is a great calamity to her. Her hopes and happiness are shattered for even if she has several sons[216], a widow feels uprooted and her honour is destroyed[217]. Even a woman of aristrocracy is feared this calamity of widowhood. It is therefore but natural that widows are full of selfpity. They referred to themselves as 'Anatha' and the state of widowhood as 'Paschimavastha'[218] which means the later state". This implies, that just as the sun going to the west loses its splendour and light so does the widow.

### *Niyoga*

During the Vedic period the custom of widow marriage was in practice, whereas during the Epic period Niyoga came into existence. As Jayal says, no account of a woman's life in the Epics would be complete without the mention of the practice of Niyoga. The reason behind this practice, again, might be the husband's desire for securing spiritual and family interests. Such sons were, known as 'Kshetraja' i.e. born of Kshetra, or field i.e. wife. He was always preferred to a son by adoption and had a legal status in the family[219]. Most of the heroes of the Mahabharta were born of levirate (Niyoga). In epics, Niyoga was practised for spiritual or dynastic interests.

In ancient times, in several civilizations, the custom of levirate was quite common. A parallel custom is found among Jews where a widow becomes her husband's brother's wife without any ceremony. If he refused to marry her, she could spit on his face[220].

Gray and Gulliver point out that Lobeder, Gussi and Shambala of Africa practise the levirate, a custom by which a man could marry his brother's widow. The levirate husband acts as a substitute for the dead man. They further say that "levirate" can be distinguished form "widow-inheritance". This process, maintains the discrete unity of the bereaved family group, thus the members retain exclusive rights to their own estate.

In the first case the arrangements for the widow could be termed as "husband-succession". The 'Sonjo' practice husband succession[221].

*Widow remarriage*

Remarriage was another course for a widow. Among the Aryan widows examples of remarriage are not to be found in the Epics. There are instances of non-Aryan widows marrying Aryans. Mahabharat says, "a child widow can remarry and her sons by the second marriage can offer oblations to the manes"[222]. Hence, Mahabharat sanctions widow remarriage in positive terms and gives a social as well as religious, status to the children by second marriage of a widow. Child widows therefore remarried without fear of social Ostracism. During this period Niyoga was preferred to widow remarriage. Though widow marriage was mentioned in some form in great Epic it was slowly dying.

*The Custom of Sati*

The custom of widow burning was known, but not prevalent, when the Epics were composed. In the later parts of the Epics we do find a few references to Sati. This custom came into existence by about 400 A.D.[223].

During this period we do have scores of instances of widows surviving their husbands and offering them funerals oblations. They also accompanied funeral processions. In cases of calamity when all the male members of a family were wiped out, the burning of the pyre[224] and the watering rite[225] after the corpse was burnt, were performed by widows. Unlike modern standards, the behaviour of these widows was comparatively free of restrictions. On the whole, the position of widows during Epic period was not so honourable as in the past.

### *Sutra Period*

It was clear from version that widowhood was both undesirable as well as inauspicious in the Sutra period. Hence, prayers were constantly chanted both before and after marriage for the longevity of the husband. No such prayers are said by the husband for the longevity of the wife. Polygamy was prevalent, hence he did not dread being a widower. From the time of Sutras the position of widows became more pitiable than before because the Sutras ordered a widow to avoid, for the duration of a year, the use of honey, meat, spirituous liquor and salt, and to sleep on the ground. At the expiry of six-months, she could with the permission of her Guru, bear a son, by her brother-in-law, in case she had no son. Although widow was permitted remarriage, her social status was inferior. Hence, widowhood was much dreaded by women.

#### *Widow Burning*

The custom of widow burning was not prevalent in the Sutra period. Although widowhood was dreaded, the widow was not expected to immolate herself on her husbands funeral pyre. Apastambiya Gruhya Sutra states that the widow was brought back from the funeral pyre either by the dead husband's brother or an old trusted servant[226].

### *Buddhistic Period*

During this period a widow did not suffer any social and moral degradation due to widowhood. No stigma was attached to her by the society. There were no restrictions on her dress or food habits and she did not have to shave her head. She used to participate in socio-religious functions[227] as in the later periods. Widow enjoyed high social status and maintained the social status of pre-widowed days.

#### *Widow Remarriage*

Widow remarriage was permitted as freely as the marriage of a widower. As Honer opines, "there were no religious or social obstacles to be overcome in being remarried; but as if it were a step that could quite easily be taken without raising any scandal[228].

In practice, a widow faced difficulties in remarrying as much as any other widow anywhere else in the world owing to her greater age, look, poverty and number of children.

According to Buddhist literature also, a widow's position has never been elevated. Her condition, in our society, has been the same through the track of centuries. Vasantara Jataka describes the condition of widowhood: "Terrible is widowhood, she eats the leaving of all, a man may do her any hurt, speak unkindly, a widow may have ten brothers yet is a nacked thing, oh terrible is widowhood"[229].

*Widow Burning*

The custom of widow burning was not practised during this period[230]. In Gautama's preachings there is no reference to this custom of sati. Hence the custom did not exist.

*Widow Inheritance and Succession Rights*

During this period, husbands left their property to their widows rather to sons and daughter in preference. There were no rules laid down against widow inheriting her husband's property, "If the husband left any property to the widow; often she managed it all by herself"[231].

***Smruti Period***

During this period, the Buddhism declined and Brahmanism which was detriment to the status of woman and the widow was re-established.

The Hindu law-givers of this period imposed certain duties on widows, who did not ascend the funeral pyre but chose to survive the husband All the sages, prescribed a life of severe discipline and penance on such widows for their whole life.

*Niyoga*

The custom of 'Niyoga' was condemned by Smriti writers when chastity (celibacy) had become the main qualification of marriage. Manu disapproved this custom of Niyoga as fit for cattle. The custom of Niyoga appears very strange and unacceptable to the modern mind. However, 'niyoga' is still practised in some communities in India.

*Widow Remarriage*

During the Smriti period, widow marriage was prohibited, and thus, widows were not allowed to marry even the husband's brothers. As Manu expressed "in the sacred texts no where the appointment of widows is mentioned nor is the remarriage of widows prescribed in the rules concerning marriage"[232]. In most of the smritis there is no passage which permits the marriage of widows. However, Manu permitted the marriage of only virgin widows. But Narada and Parashara permit widow-remarriage.

*Practice of sati*

The practice of sati is not sanctioned by the older Smritis of Manu and Yajnavalkya. It is however alluded to, and recommended by, many of the later authorities such as Arti, Harita, Usanas and Parashara. The practice prevailed as early Alexander's invasions, about 325 B.C. Travellers like Strabo, Megasthenes and Diodarus who accompanied Alexander, allude to this practice. The custom of sati had been well established by the end of 6th century A.D. The law givers from Smriti period, forced the widows to lead a life of austerities, fasting and abstinence from pleasure.

Manu, the Hindu lawgiver says:

1. "Until her death, let her be patient of hardships, self-controlled, and chaste and strive to fulfil that most excellent duty which is prescribed for wives who have one husband only.

2. At her pleasure, let her emaciate her body by living on pure flowers, roots and fruits but she must never mention the name of another man after husband has died.

3. A virtuous wife, Manu says again is one, "who after death of her husband constantly remains chaste, reaches heaven though she has no son, just like those chaste men[233].

There are numerous texts prescribing the number of meals a day that a widow may take, the nature of bed she is to sleep upon and other particulars relating to her conduct. In short, she is ordered to lead a pious life for the spiritual benefit of herself as well as of her dead husband.

But Vishnu, the later Smriti writer, prescribes an alternative to widows either to survive their husband or to burn themselves[234].

The manms/codes of Hindu law which are commended for

a widow to lead a chaste life are not only moral precepts. Unchastity of the widow affects not only her social status but also her proprietary position. But the injunctions, to emaciate her body and to live on frugal and abstemious diet, were in the nature of religious or moral injunction.

The age of later Smritis commentators and digest writers (C. 500 AD to C 1800 AD).

The unjust, foolish social customs like child marriage, sati, polygamy reduced the status of women to the level of mere goods and chattel. They were regarded as Nari-Sudras. The status of widows was still more inferior.

*Widow Remarriage*

During this period, widow remarriage in general was prohibited. Altekar says that the prohibition of widow marriage began to be imposed from about 1000 A.D. even on the child widows. It was totally prohibited in Hindu society from about 1100 AD. In Hindu society, upper caste widows were prohibited from remarrying, whereas lower caste widows were allowed to do so[235]. During the last century due to sanskritization and the desire to increase their respectability, the lower caste began to impose upon themselves the prohibition of widow remarriage.

Alberuni the famous Muslim traveller who came to India, in 11th century A.D. states, "If a wife of a Hindu loses her husband by death she cannot marry another man. She has only to choose between two things, either to remain a widow as long as she lives or to burn herself"[236]. And the latter eventually is considered preferable because as widow she is ill-treated as long as she lives.

Among the high castes of Rajputs, the second marriage of women were never permitted, though, in some lower castes, such as Kadoa Kunbi a widow was eligible for Natra or second marriage.

*Tonsure*

The practice of tonsuring widows was prevalent among many high castes until recently. The origin of tonsure is not definitely known. None of the Vedas or Grahya Sutras or Epics refer to the practice. Widows retained their hair but did not part it.

Widows were obtained to lead a strict, ascetic life. And an

ascetic is expected to remove the hair on the head. Hence, the custom of disfiguring the Indian widow appears to have originated from this source.

Tonsure is believed to have come into vogue in about the 8th Century A.D. Once widow marriage was prohibited, society desired to make the widow as unattractive as possible so that no man would ever want to marry her. With this idea in mind, the widow was tonsured and made to wear white clothes only, sleep on the bare floor, and partake of a frugual meal only once a day. This deprived her of all her good health and good looks so that even if she wanted to marry, no man came forward to do so.

Veda Vyasa in 10th Century A.D., says "If a widow does not become a sati, she should shave her head"[237]. This is the first Smriti to mention the custom. Some Puranas and the Skanda Purana Kashikhanda advocating tonsure, seem to be clearly a later interpolation.

From 12 Century AD, tonsure was prevalent all over India. It prevailed more in the south than in the North of the country Foreign travellers who visited India in the 16th Century AD mention having seen tonsured widows.

Horner asserts that this system is believed to have been followed by the Brahmins due to the influence of Buddhism where the Buddhist nuns underwent tonsure in imitation of the Monks[238]. However, Kane seems to suggest that a widow was tonsured, just as the son of a deceased man underwent tonsure, as a matter of purification and as a symbol of bereavement[239]. Though the cruel practice of tonsuring is dying out, it is still practised by some orthodox sects of Brahmins in Southern India, but in Northern India it is generally not practised[240].

*Widows Dress*

From ancient times widows wear white. *Manusmriti* asks the widow who is appointed for *niyoga* to wear white[241]. The idea might probably have been borrowed from the Buddhist or Jain nuns who wore white clothes, when they renounce the world, since the widow too, was supposed to have renounced the world. Later, black became the colour of mourning, since this depicts darkness and unhappiness. She was forbidden to wear any jewels.

*Practice of Sati*

Widows had to follow strict rules and restrictions. So they frequently preferred Sati to the tiresome life prescribed for them. Most widows voluntarily ascended the funeral pyres of their husbands. Sometimes the heartless relatives of widows burnt them forcibly, because they were either afraid that they might misbehave and bring disgrace to the family, or wanted to misappropriate her share in the family property. This cruel procedure of Sati was widely practised during this period.

The institution of 'Sati' which was peculiar to Hindu widows came into existence from about the 700 A.D. 'Sutee' was not originally a religious practice but the supposed consequence of a widow's grief at the death of her husband. A widow was expected to prepare herself for a frightful death by burning herself on her husband's corpse. Sir Henry Maine opines that the superstitious belief, coupled with the Brahmanical dislike of the enjoyment of property by women, had led to the practice of sati, and was intended to fight the ancient rule of civil law, which made her tenant for life in respect of her husband's property[242]. The rewards dangled before a sati were, as Sankha and Angiras say, that she who follows her husband in death, dwells in heaven for 3.5 crores of years[243].

Sati became more frequent among royal families in northern India and quite common in Kashmir during the period of 1500 to 1800 A.D. The custom of sati had however, obtained the status of a well recognized, but optional practice in Hinduism[244]. The practice of sati was also prevalent among the Rajputs and Marathas of Central India.

Several Muslim emperors discouraged sati and adopted measures to prevent it as far as possible. Traverneir, the French traveller who came to India during Aurangzeb's time observed, "there is no woman that can burn herself along with her husband's body till she has the leave of the governor of the place where she inhabits, who being a Mohamedan and abhorring that execrable crime of self murder, is very shy to permit her"[245].

During the Muslim period, women faced a number of hardships and cruelty due to backward practices like — child marriage, purdah system, sati, enforced widowhood, prostitution and devadasi system. This era led not only to the degeneration of women's physical, mental and social life, but her rights in the educational, social, religious and economic fields were also lowered gradually.

From time to time, protestant movements like Buddhism, Jainism, Vaishnavism, Veerashaivism, Sikhism and the Bhakṭi movements made sincere efforts to improve the status of women. They regarded women as mothers and wives but inferior to men. Orthodox forces in society, however, erased the salutary effects brought about by these revolutions.

### *British Period*

The British were the first rulers who unified the country as a whole and were liberal in thinking. They believed that rational thinking had to be the basis for all customs and institutions and all customs and institutions not so based had to be done away with.

Liberalism and the rational thinking of the British, set the educated Indians to thinking about Indian problems like child marriage, female infanticide, the practice of sati, prohibition of widow-remarriage among high caste Hindus and the need for emancipation of women.

The social reform movement in the British period gave rise to various schools of thought. (1) The Liberal school of thought wanted to free women and bring them on par with men, because to them, this was true democracy (2) The Revivalist school of thought which wanted to bring the ancient period into the modern era, but were confused as to which ancient period. But the orthodox section opposed both these movements. Raja Ram Mohun Roy and Ishwar Chandra Vidyasagar belonged to the liberal school of thought.

#### *The Practice of Sati*

In spite of the cruelty of this practise, its incidence was on the increase throughout the 17th and 18th centuries, because at this, time religion had become corrupted and people were governed by the priests. The Hindus, at this time, were unenlightned and strict followers of customs and conventions. People firmly believed that a man's sins were completely washed out, if his widow was burnt alive with his dead body. However, in 1829, the custom of sati was abolished during the tenure of Lord William Bentinck by Regulation XVII, mainly through the active exertion and moral influence of that "Friend of humanity" Raja Ram Mohun Roy, in spite of many orthodox petitions against its prevention. This Act of 1829 declared the observance of sati penal within British India; it continues to linger to Rajasthan even today[246]. Several cases pointing to resurgence of sati were reported recently.

*Widow Remarriage*

The controversy over the sanction, by the Shastras, of the marriage of Hindu widows was put to an end by a distinguished Sanskrit scholar, Pandit Ishwar Chandra Vidyasagar. He proved, with quotations that widow remarriage was not prohibited either by Vedas or by the Sutras or even by the Shastras, in his book *Widow Remarriage*, which created a terrific uproar in the society of 19th Century. He based his argument on the famous text of Parasara and maintained that the institutes of Parasara must be held specially binding in the present age[247].

The sage Parasara permits a widow to remarry. The passage runs as follows:

The institutes of Parasara are considered as the law for Kaliyug that is, widow marriage is meant exclusively for the present age[248].

Hindu widow's marriage was legalised by the Act XV of 1856 known as an, "Act to remove all legal obstacles to the marriage of Hindu Widows" and enacted that the issues of such marriage would be legitimate, any customs and any interpretation of Hindu law to the contrary not withstanding (Section, I)[249]. The prejudice against widow remarriage was so deeprooted that the said Act did not receive any effective response for more than a century.

**Widow in Hindu Law**

It is not possible to define the legal status of Hindu widows by any general statement.

*Right of Inheritance*

For a long time the widow was not recognized as an heir because Niyoga was a common practice. Hence she could get her husband's share in the family property if not as a direct heir but as a guardian of her minor sons. By 1200 AD when Niyoga disappeared and childless, widows came on the scene, then Hindu Society realized the necessity of recognizing the widow as an heir to her husband's property. The widow, no doubt, was regarded as a limited heir. This limited heirship was given to her with reluctance by society, since one of the functions to be discharged by the person who inherited a man's property was the performance of his Shradhas. Since women were not permitted to perform any religious ceremonies, it seemed to follow that women could not hold any property. Even Medhatithi (Kulluka on Many IX 187) generally a liberal writer, holds that the widow is prohibited from inheriting her husbands wealth[250].

Brahaspati gives the widow the right to inherit her husband's property, as well as offer funeral oblations to the deceased husband in the absence of a male issue[251].

Vigneshwar, who wrote *Mitakshar*, II, 135, 136 says, "The chaste and regularly married wife of a sonless man who dies separated and not reunited inherits his estate"[252]. Yajnavalkya, II 131 lays down that when members of a family reunited, after separation, the surviving coparcerners will succeed to the deceased husband's property and not the widow.

According to Dayabhaga law, which is prevalent in Bengal, a widow of a man without a son, even in a joint family, succeeds to his share in the family property and there is no difference between joint family property and his separate property and moveable and immoveable property. The Mitakshar school requires the husband to be separated from the joint family and she has absolute power over the moveable property. A widow has no power to bequeath moveable property inherited by her from her husband. Under Mitakshar, a widow is not competent to make gift of the moveables inherited[253]. A widow, who has not been faithful to her husband at the time of his death, is not entitled to inherit his property. But, once the husband's estates have been vested in her (which could only be so if she was faithful at the time of his death). She cannot be divested of it by her subsequent infidelity[254].

*The Hindu Women's Right to Property Act of 1937*

Today, under this Act, the widow gets a share in the joint family property, as well as in the separate property of her husband. But prior to this Act, the birth of a son, or adoption, deprived her from inheriting the property, even if the son was born posthumously.

The widow is a limited heir to her husband's property means (1) that she cannot alienate the property; she cannot sell, mortgage or gift away the property (ii) She is only entitled to the income out of it. (2) after her death the property reverts to her husband's heirs.

One of the important conditions for inheritance is that the widow has to be faithful at the time of her husband's death. Her subsequent infidelity does not matter.

Today, a widow who changes her religion or who remarries forfeits her husband's property.

Though she is a limited heir to the moveable and immoveable property of her husband in practice she is the absolute owner of the former if it is in her hands. Although a widow cannot sell, mortgage or gift away her inherited property, she can alienate her life interest in the property[255].

*Maintenance*

A widow does not succeed to her husbands property is entitled to maintenance out of her husband's separate or joint property. Her right to maintenance however is dependent on the possession or her husband's property by the husband's heir whether by survivorship or by inheritance.

Even during her life time, if she was living away from the husband, she does not lose her right to maintenance. This right is conditional upon her chastity. Unfortunately the proof of her chastity is taken into account. And other private income and property are all deducted when allotting maintenance to her.

According to all the schools of Hindu law the obligation to maintain the widow is not absolute. It is conditioned by the fact that the man who inherits the dead man's property such as the son, or brother of the dead man, becomes responsible in maintaining the widow. However if the dead man does not leave behind property then the widow could not claim maintenance[256].

Mr. Justice Mahmood in his judgement, in the context of granting maintenance said "The amount of maintenance should not be determined with reference to the principle that the life of a Hindu widow should be a peculiarly ascetic character and that she should have only a starving allowance". The austerities enjoined on Hindu widows are matters not of legal obligation but only of moral injunction and cannot be enforced by courts of Justice.

"The courts should bear in mind that Hindu widows are by ancient custom, debarred from remarriage and should fix the maintenance at a sum sufficient to the degree of the widow being driven to immorality"[257].

A widow cannot be deprived of her right to maintenance by will or by making a gift of whole property by her husband. But if the husband's property is sold for his debts or for joint family debts or even without any cause, she cannot ask the purchaser for value, unless she has acquired a previous charge on the estate for her maintenance. The husband's debts take precedence over the maintenance of the widow and the infant child[258].

The only person who is under legal obligation to maintain, out of his own property, the widow of a deceased Hindu, is her own son. The others will only maintain out of the husband's property.

*Adoption*

With regard to the question as to the power of a widow to adopt or give away a son in adoption, all the schools based their conclusions on the text of Vashistha which says, "Never let a woman give or accept a son unless with the assent or her lord". But different schools interpreted the text differently and expressed divergent opinions with regard to the power of a widow to adopt and its limitations.

The Bombay school views that the widow of a separated coparcerner, who inherits her husband's estate, can adopt without the consent of her husband, in the absence of an expression of or implied prohibition by him. The basic theory on which it is based is as Nilakantha says, "Even a woman has like the Sudra, authority to adopt, because women and Sudra are governed by the same rule" thus a widow's right to adopt to her separated husband is inherent and nor mererly delegated.

Before the Hindu womens right to property Act of 1937, the birth of a son or adoption deprived the widow of her inherited property. The adopted son received the whole of his father's property to the exclusion of the widow. Her estate was diverted and thereafter she could not alienate any portion of the husband's estate for any purpose. Adoption would deprive her of her husband's property, but after adoption she received only a maintenance.

After the 1937 Act, the widow is a co-heir along with the adopted son[259].

*The Widow Remarriage Act of 1856*

This Act has been a revolutionary step in the social and legal reforms pertaining to the widow. After 1856 Act, a widow's second marriage is legal and her children by her second marriage are considered legitimate and are heirs to their fathers property. Even in those castes which permit widow remarriage, the widow, upon her second marriage loses all her rights to her first husband's property.

This Act gives rise to a curious anomaly. If the widow leads an immoral life after she inherits her husband's property, she can remain an heir to the property, but if she is chaste and remarries, the property passes on to her husbands next-of-kin. A widow by her second marriage loses her preferential right to the guardianship of her children by the first husband, except where such marriage was allowed by custom. She does not lose her future right of succession.

For the purpose of remarriage of a widow who is a minor and whose first marriage has not been consummated, she must get consent from her father, mother, brothers or that of a close male relative. If her first marriage is consummated, her own consent is sufficient as well as necessary. The mother-in-law can give her consent for the second marriage but not after consummation. A minor widow is one who is under 16 years of age[260].

## HINDU CODE BILL

The Hindu Code Bill applies to all Hindus and in all provinces of India.

*Adoption*

Any Hindu widow over 18, can adopt a son provided her husband had not expressly forbidden her to do so, or her power to adopt has not terminated. A Hindu widow's right to adopt shall not revive after it has once been terminated.

The Maharashtrian widow is entitled to make an adoption on the presumed authority from him, and this she may do whether he had died a joint or a separate member of the family.

The Hindu code, like the Hindu Law, does not permit the adoption of a daughter.

If the widow is not 18, but if her husband had named a certain boy for adoption, she can adopt him. A widows right terminates when she remarries, or if her son dies leaving a son, or a widow or son's widow or if the widow ceases to be a Hindu[261].

*Widow's Interest in Coparcenery*

When a coparcener dies, his widow and daughter shall, amongst themselves, have interest in the property, in case of an unmarried daughter, an interest equal to half of that of the son, and in the case of a married daughter, one quarter of that of the son. The share of the widow of the predeceased son, will be equal to that of the son of the predeceased son.

*Women and Property*

Any property acquired by a woman after the commencement of the Hindu Code Bill would be her absolute property. The Code eliminates what has been known to Hindu law as woman's estate. Both moveable and immoveable property, even when acquired during widowhood, shall be the woman's and widow's exclusive and absolute property.

A Hindu woman's estate shall devolve upon the heirs of the last full owner if obtained by inheritance or if obtained by partition.

Dowry would be the bride's absolute property.

*Intestate Succession*

Intestate woman's property would devolve first upon the husband and children or if the husband is dead to all children equally. If a woman dies without mentioning her heirs, her property goes to her mother or father or husband's heirs, etc.

If a man dies leaving only a widow or daughter, the widow or daughter takes his whole property.

For intestate succession no distinction will be made between an undivided and a divided son or divided and reunited son or between a married daughter or an unmarried daughter or a childless daughter or a daughter with children.

An unchaste wife (unless a court of law has found) and any remarried widow cannot succeed to the husband's property.

In Bombay, women who receive property of the family of their birth, own it as absolute owners. The same privilege will now be conceded to females who acquire property belonging to their families by marriage in Bombay and it will be extended to all families in the rest of India after the code is passed.

*Maintenance*

A father-in-law will have to support his widowed daughter-in-law only in so far as he has the means to do so and if she cannot support herself in any other way. No maintenance will be given to her when she remarries or she becomes unchaste.

A widow, a widowed daughter-in-law, a father, a mother, an unmarried but needy daughter, the widowed daughter of a deceased person should be maintained from the husband's or the son's or the father-in-law's or the father's estate.

A widow is entitled to maintenance out of her husband's share in the joint family property, from those coparcerners who hold that by survivorship.

The widow does not forfeit her right to property or maintenance merely on account of her going and residing with her family. Accordingly the claim for arrears of maintenance cannot be resisted on the ground that the widow went away to live with her brother.

Share of deceased coparcener at the time of partition determines quantum of widows maintenance.

The right of a widow for maintenance and partition of joint family legally arises because of the fact that her husband left an interest in the joint family at the time of his death. There is nothing in this Act to suggest that the position of the son's widow has improved in this respect under the Act.

The Hindu Code has brought about some important changes, one of them is it abolishes the woman's estate and makes the woman's property absolute[262].

## THE HINDU SUCCESSION ACT 1956

This Act has introduced revolutionary changes as far as widows are concerned. This act applies to Hindus, Jains, Sikhs, Buddhists and others who are Hindus. The clauses are as follows: The property of an intestate shall be divided as follows.

Rule 1: The intestate's widow or all widows together shall take one share.

Rule 2: The surviving sons and daughter and the mother shall each take one share.

Rule 3: The heirs in the branch of each predeceased son, or each predeceased daughter of the intestate shall take between them one share.

1. Among the heirs in the branch of the predeceased son share shall be so made that his widow (or widows together) and the surviving sons and daughters get equal portions; and the branch of his predeceased sons get the same portion.
2. Among the heirs in the branch of the pre-deceased daughter share shall be so made that the surviving sons and daughters get equal portions[263].

*Property of a Female Hindu to be her Absolute Property*

Any property possessed by a female Hindu whether acquired before or after the commencement of this Act, shall be held by her as full owner thereof and not as a limited owner.

"Property" includes both moveable and immoveable property acquired by a female Hindu by inheritance or devise or at a partition or in lieu of maintenance or arrears of maintenance or by gift from any person, whether a relative or not; before, at or after her marriage or by her own skill or exertion, or by purchase or by prescription or any other manner whatsoever and also any such property held by her as Stridhan immediately before the commencement of this Act.

Nothing contained in sub-section above can apply to any property acquired by way of the gift or under a will or any other instrument or under a decree or order of a civil court or under an award where the terms of the gift, will or other instrument or the decree, order or award prescribe a restricted estate in such property[264].

*General Rules of Succession in the case of Female Hindus*

1. The property of a female Hindu dying intestate shall devolve.

Firstly, upon the son and daughters (including the children of any pre-deceased son or daughter) and the husband. Secondly, upon the heirs of the husband. Thirdly, upon the mother and father. Fourthly, upon the heirs of the father. Lastly upon the heirs of the mother[265]. The biggest change brought about by this act is that it has done away with what is called. "The limited estate of a woman". Any woman acquiring any property by any of the ways mentioned above, is considered her absolute owner of the property except where it is specifically stated otherwise. This makes the widow an absolute heir to the property inherited by her from her husband. This Act solves many problems of the widows. Even as a daughter, a woman receives the same share as a son. A woman's property (intestate) devolved upon her sons and daughters.

This Act is a blessing to the widows. Dwarkinath opines that there is no system of jurisprudence, where the status of the widow has passed through such varying stages of legal development as in Hindu law[266].

It is clear from the above cited studies that no authority either in Vedas or Upanishads prescribed stern austere measures for widows. According to Altekar it is a sheer misinterpretation of Vedas. During the medieval period, several cruel, restrictive practices came to be introduced into Hindu society much to the detriment of widows. And it is surprising to note that till today the Hindu widows are governed by age old oppressive and abominable customs. Hence their lot in Hindu society is miserable and unenviable.

*Trends and Differentials in the Incidence of Widowhood in India*

In the socio-demographic literature, marital status occupies an important place. Marital status like age and sex is an important demographic characteristic of any population. Usually the population by age and sex is categorized into two groups viz, the never married (single) and the ever-married. Among ever-married, currently married set up the largest proportion. In a number of demographic studies, marital union or marriage level, trends, differentials and determinants of age at marriage have been given more attention as they have implication on fertility rate. However, enough attention has not been given, to the study of problems of widowed, divorced or separated firstly because they constitute an insignificant proportion of the total population. Secondly due to the increase in the age at marriage, the proportion of widowed has been gradually declining. Thirdly, it may also be due to the difficulty in collecting information from widow[267]. In most of the societies, the size of the family and family building process are determined by the patterns of marital dissolution and remarriage and also by the patterns of age at first marriage. The dissolution of marriage which includes widowhood and divorce, brings about demographic and socioeconomic implications like marital union but the effect is reversed. Both widowhood and divorce represent withdrawal from the married population and tend to have effects on fertility[268]. Davis and Blake (1956) highlighted the importance of widowhood as an important intermediate variable affecting fertility. The age at widowhood and the extent of remarriage determine the fertility differentials. In traditional societies, the influence of widowhood on fertility would be higher than in modern societies because of the higher age difference between the spouse and prohibition of widow marriage in certain communities. Whereas, in modern societies, the age difference between the spouses is less, widow remarriage is permitted and the age at widowhood is relatively at a later age[269].

The extent of spouse-loss in either sex in a population will depend on several factors such as the rate of mortality in the opposite sex, the age distributions, the shape of the mortality curve, the age at marriage, the distribution of the differences, the ages of husband and wife, the rate of population growth and the rate and age pattern of remarriage[270].

In India, the widowed form a major group while in developed countries, divorced or separated form a major group. For instance, in India during 1980 the divorced or separated formed only 0.3 per cent; in U.S. this percentage was 6.7. However in India during 1981 the percentage of widowed to the total population was 5.2 and in U.S. this was 5.7 per cent[271].

The recent trends and differentials in the incidence of widowhood in India in general and Karnataka in particular are discussed as below.

In India the prevalence of widowhood is higher than widowerhood. Table 1.1 includes the data of post independence period only, since the data of the pre-independence period seemed to be unreliable, as they show great fluctuations.

**TABLE - 1.1**
**PREVALENCE OF WIDOWHOOD IN INDIA AND KARNATAKA**

| | *India* | | *Karnataka* | |
|---|---|---|---|---|
| *Years* | *Males* | *Females* | *Males* | *Females* |
| 1951 | 5.00 | 12.80 | 4.31 | 15.36 |
| 1961 | 3.69 | 10.82 | 3.16 | 12.36 |
| 1971 | 4.14 | 12.67 | 2.27 | 10.35 |
| 1981 | 2.43 | 8.06 | 1.82 | 9.59 |

*Source:* Census of India, 1951, 1961, 1971 & 1981.

In India from 1951 to 1961 the percentage of widowhood remains more or less stable around 12 per cent. However, in 1981 this figure has come down by four points. On the other hand there is a steady decline in the percentage of widowerhood which was 5 per cent in 1951 and has come down to 2.4 per cent in 1981. In Karnataka also the percentage of widowhood which was 15.4 per cent in 1951 has come down to 9.6 per cent in 1981, while the percentage of widowerhood in 1951 was 4.3 has come down to 1.8 per cent in 1981.

The prevalence of widowhood is determined by the decline in mortality, sex differentials in mortality in adult and old ages and the incidence of marriage of widowed persons.

Widows have been outnumbering widowers as can be seen in Table 1.2 because females live longer than males. Also men usually marry women quite younger in age and lesser widows remarry. The sex differential immortality in late adulthood and old age are universally favourable to women. These factors cause increase in the incidence of widowhood.

**TABLE - 1.2**
**AGE AND SEX SPECIFIC PREVALENCE OF WIDOWHOOD IN INDIA - 1961, 1971 AND 1981**

| | *Prevalence of Widowhood* | | | | | |
|---|---|---|---|---|---|---|
| *Age Group* | *Male* | | | *Female* | | |
| | *1961* | *1971* | *1981* | *1961* | *1971* | *1981* |
| 10-14 | 0.07 | 0.04 | 0.02 | 0.13 | 0.05 | 0.03 |
| 15-19 | 0.29 | 0.02 | 0.09 | 0.52 | 0.34 | 0.21 |
| 20-24 | 0.90 | 0.58 | 0.38 | 1.29 | 0.88 | 0.69 |
| 25-29 | 1.67 | 1.25 | 0.78 | 2.89 | 1.94 | 1.50 |
| 32.34 | 2.61 | 1.99 | 1.34 | 6.42 | 4.09 | 3.12 |
| 35-39 | 3.67 | 2.66 | 1.94 | 11.14 | 7.04 | 5.42 |
| 42-44 | 5.98 | 4.43 | 3.31 | 20.66 | 14.38 | 10.86 |
| 45-49 | 8.24 | 5.90 | 4.46 | 28.84 | 20.66 | 15.96 |
| 50-54 | 12.37 | 9.64 | 7.34 | 45.47 | 36.60 | 29.71 |
| 55-59 | 15.53 | 12.07 | 8.97 | 50.24 | 41.22 | 31.79 |
| 60-64 | 21.83 | 17.15 | 14.11 | 69.62 | 62.41 | 56.05 |
| 65-69 | 25.87 | 20.41 | 17.21 | 71.84 | 64.59 | 58.55 |
| 71+ | 36.10 | 30.45 | 27.04 | 84.38 | 80.36 | 77.55 |
| Age not stated | 2.92 | - | 1.53 | 5.64 | - | 5.58 |

*Source:* 1. Social and Cultural tables, 1961, Census of India.
2. Country monograph series - 10: Population of India (UN)
3. Family Welfare Year book, 1982-83.

There has been a steady decline in the levels of mortality in all the age groups for both the sexes, as could be seen in Table 1.3. The female death rates are not only lesser than that of males from early adulthood onwards but also steadily widens in margin between the sexes as age progresses.

**TABLE - 1.3**
**AGE SPECIFIC DEATH RATES BY SEX IN INDIA 1970 AND 1980**

| *Age Group* | *Age Specific Death Rates* | | | |
|---|---|---|---|---|
| | *Males* | | *Females* | |
| | *1970* | *1980* | *1970* | *1980* |
| 0-4 | 51.7 | 40.1 | 55.1 | 43.5 |
| 5-9 | 4.6 | 3.3 | 5.0 | 4.0 |
| 10-14 | 2.0 | 1.7 | 2.4 | 1.7 |
| 15-19 | 2.5 | 2.0 | 3.7 | 2.9 |
| 20-24 | 2.9 | 2.3 | 4.6 | 3.8 |
| 25-29 | 3.3 | 2.2 | 4.9 | 4.0 |
| 30-34 | 4.0 | 8.4 | 5.2 | 3.6 |
| 35-39 | 4.7 | 4.7 | 5.7 | 4.6 |
| 40-44 | 8.0 | 7.2 | 5.9 | 5.5 |
| 45-49 | 11.0 | 9.6 | 8.0 | 7.3 |
| 50-54 | 17.9 | 14.6 | 12.9 | 10.4 |
| 55-59 | 25.5 | 21.5 | 16.5 | 16.7 |
| 60-64 | 42.7 | 35.0 | 31.4 | 27.3 |
| 70+ | 117.1 | 98.5 | 104.0 | 85.3 |
| All ages | 15.8 | 12.4 | 15.6 | 12.4 |

*Source*: SRS Bulletin

The percentage of widowed population in each age-group by sex and residence has been given in Table 1.4, and the percentage distribution of widows and widowers of India has been presented in Table 1.5 at three points of time, by residential status of the population. Table 1.4 and 1.5 shows the rural and urban differentials in the prevalence of widowhood in India. In urban areas both widowhood and widowerhood appear to be at lower rate upto 45 years age-group. In the later age-groups the rate of widowhood increases sharply. For instance in rural areas the size of widowhood is more than five times higher than widowerhood, in the 60-64 years age group. It is also noticed that in the later age-groups widowhood appears slightly more in urban areas. This may be due to the unfavourable mortality pattern for males in urban areas.

In Table 1.5 it is noticed that there is a progressive decline both in widowhood and widowerhood over time, in both rural and urban areas and male, female distribution of population. In 1961, the percentage of widowed was 10.8 which has declined to 8.1 by 1981.

**TABLE - 1.4**
**PERCENTAGE OF WIDOWED POPULATION IN EACH AGE-GROUP BY SEX 1981 INDIA**

| *Age* | *Male/Female* | *Total* | *Rural* | *Urban* |
|---|---|---|---|---|
| All ages | Male | 2.43 | 2.71 | 1.56 |
| | Female | 8.06 | 8.23 | 7.46 |
| 10-14 | Male | 0.02 | 0.02 | 0.01 |
| | Female | 0.03 | 0.04 | 0.01 |
| 15-19 | Male | 0.09 | 0.11 | 0.03 |
| | Female | 0.21 | 0.23 | 0.13 |
| 20-24 | Male | 0.38 | 0.46 | 0.17 |
| | Female | 0.69 | 0.75 | 0.53 |
| 25-29 | Male | 0.78 | 0.95 | 0.37 |
| | Female | 0.50 | 0.59 | 0.24 |
| 30-34 | Male | 1.34 | 1.60 | 0.67 |
| | Female | 3.12 | 3.22 | 2.81 |
| 35-39 | Male | 1.94 | 2.28 | 1.00 |
| | Female | 5.42 | 5.50 | 5.14 |
| 40-44 | Male | 3.31 | 3.38 | 1.89 |
| | Female | 10.86 | 10.83 | 10.98 |
| 45-49 | Male | 4.46 | 5.01 | 2.75 |
| | Female | 15.96 | 15.68 | 16.97 |
| 50-54 | Male | 7.34 | 8.05 | 4.92 |
| | Female | 29.71 | 29.41 | 30.87 |
| 55-59 | Male | 8.97 | 9.73 | 6.41 |
| | Female | 31.97 | 30.74 | 35.99 |
| 60-64 | Male | 14.11 | 14.88 | 10.94 |
| | Female | 56.06 | 55.60 | 57.92 |
| 65-69 | Male | 17.21 | 17.85 | 14.61 |
| | Female | 58.55 | 57.72 | 61.94 |
| 70+ | Male | 27.04 | 27.74 | 24.06 |
| | Female | 77.55 | 77.24 | 78.78 |
| Ages Not | Male | 1.53 | 2.04 | 0.76 |
| stated | Female | 5.58 | 7.00 | 3.70 |

*Source*: Census of India, 1981 Series 1. Paper 2 of 1983 Key Population Statistics based on 5 per cent Sample Data, Registrar General, India.

Table 1.6 provides the percentages of widows and ever married women in 1981 for Hindus, Muslims, Christians, Sikhs and Buddhists. Among Hindus 84.49 per cent were widows, and 83.89 per cent were ever married women, among Muslims respective percentages were 10.17 per cent and 10.57 per cent, among Christians they were 2.32 and 2.19., among Sikhs they were 1.21 and 1.78 per cent and among Buddhists the percentages were 0.80 and 0.71 per cent. It is observed among all the religions that Sikhs had minimum proportion of widows and Buddhists had maximum proportion of widows. It is also noticed that the differences in the proportion of widows by age were negligible among all the religions except Sikhs.

**TABLE - 1.5**

**PERCENTAGE OF WIDOWED AND WIDOWERED BY RURAL/ URBAN STATUS FOR INDIA AT 1961, 1971 AND 1981**

| *Widowed/Widowered* | *1961* | *1971* | *1981* |
|---|---|---|---|
| Widowed | | | |
| 1. Total | 10.82 | 8.86 | 8.06 |
| 2. Rural | 11.01 | 9.03 | 8.23 |
| 3. Urban | 9.90 | 8.15 | 7.46 |
| Widowered | | | |
| 1. Total | 3.69 | 2.94 | 2.43 |
| 2. Rural | 3.90 | 3.19 | 2.71 |
| 3. Urban | 2.76 | 1.97 | 1.56 |

*Source*: Census of India, 1961, Part-II-C (i), Social and Cultural Tables, Census of India 1971, Series 1 India, Part II-C(ii), Social and Cultural Tables, Reports and Tables based on 5 per cent sample data, series 1, India Part II-Special Census of India 1981.

**TABLE - 1.6**

**PATTERN OF WIDOWHOOD BY RELIGION IN INDIA: 1981**

| *Age Group* | *Hindus* A | B | *Muslims* A | B | *Christians* A | B | *Sikhs* A | B | *Buddhists* A | B |
|---|---|---|---|---|---|---|---|---|---|---|
| 10-14 | 0.87 | 0.04 | 0.45 | 0.12 | 2.25 | 0.03 | 2.54 | 0.07 | 3.41 | 0.15 |
| 15-19 | 1.31 | 0.43 | 2.02 | 1.13 | 2.51 | 0.41 | 0.57 | 0.13 | 3.07 | 1.17 |
| 20-24 | 1.66 | 1.31 | 2.46 | 2.47 | 2.00 | 1.39 | 0.59 | 0.71 | 3.25 | 2.59 |
| 25-29 | 2.42 | 2.09 | 2.86 | 2.78 | 2.59 | 2.42 | 0.84 | 1.16 | 3.28 | 2.62 |
| 30-34 | 4.04 | 3.02 | 4.34 | 3.49 | 4.28 | 3.24 | 1.75 | 2.13 | 4.74 | 3.07 |
| 35-39 | 6.27 | 4.45 | 6.30 | 4.59 | 6.48 | 4.67 | 3.03 | 3.04 | 8.73 | 4.42 |
| 40-44 | 11.79 | 7.13 | 12.80 | 7.29 | 12.41 | 6.63 | 5.34 | 4.76 | 12.10 | 6.67 |
| 45-49 | 16.81 | 9.18 | 17.36 | 8.60 | 15.84 | 8.92 | 7.77 | 6.43 | 20.18 | 9.74 |
| 50+ | 49.36 | 72.34 | 48.92 | 69.55 | 44.37 | 72.29 | 31.50 | 81.57 | 51.20 | 69.57 |
| All | 15.73 | 100.0 | 15.02 | 100.0 | 16.52 | 100.0 | 10.61 | 100.0 | 17.49 | 100.0 |
| Mean age at widowhood: | 35.08*22998343 | | 34.29*2767996 | | 34.43*631645 | | 33.89*329211 | | 32.67*217716 | |
| | (84.49) | | (10.17) | | (2.32) | | (1.21) | | (0.80) | |

*Source*: Census of India, 1981 Series 1 India, Part II -Special Report and Tables based on 5 per cent sample data.

* Refers to mean age to widowhood.

Figures in the brackets refers to the percentages of total widows.

It is noticed in Table 1.7 that 24.5 million that is 90 per cent of total widows were reported to be illiterates, whereas the corresponding number among ever-married was 79. The percentage of widows among illiterate, ever-married women was 17.73 per cent. The corresponding percentage among literate, middle class has come down to 9.75 per cent. A sharp decline in the percentage is noticed i.e. 3.34 among matriculate and above 2.17 among graduates and above. The reasons for proportion of widows may be due to existing differentials in adult male mortality and age at marriage at each category of educational level. In each category of educational level, a reduction in widows rate in all the age groups is noticed. In the younger age group, the percentage of widows ranged from 1.94 per cent among illiterates to 0.31 per cent among graduates and above and in the age group of 50 and above it ranged from 49.93 among illiterate to 20.75 among graduates and above, this percentage showed a consistant sharp decline in each category of the educational level.

**TABLE - 1.7**

**PERCENTAGE OF WIDOWS AND EVER MARRIED WOMEN BY AGE AND EDUCATIONAL LEVEL 1981 INDIA**

| *Age Group* | *Illiterate* | | *Literate but Below Middle* | | *Educational Level above Middle* | | *Matriculate but Below Graduate* | | *Graduate and Above* | |
|---|---|---|---|---|---|---|---|---|---|---|
| | *A* | *B* | *A* | *B* | *A* | *B* | *A* | *B* | *A* | *B* |
| 10-14 | 0.91 | 0.09 | 0.78 | 0.10 | 0.82 | 0.10 | 0.59 | 0.01 | 0.00 | 0.00 |
| 15-19 | 1.52 | 0.64 | 1.27 | 1.18 | 0.73 | 1.51 | 0.58 | 1.03 | 0.31 | 0.09 |
| 20-24 | 1.94 | 1.33 | 1.77 | 3.39 | 1.05 | 5.15 | 0.72 | 5.45 | 0.31 | 2.67 |
| 25-29 | 2.67 | 1.83 | 2.58 | 4.60 | 1.83 | 7.99 | 1.12 | 8.76 | 0.49 | 7.50 |
| 30-34 | 4.29 | 2.71 | 4.02 | 5.39 | 3.05 | 8.40 | 2.04 | 10.34 | 1.42 | 14.10 |
| 35-39 | 6.55 | 3.98 | 5.86 | 6.88 | 4.33 | 8.39 | 3.15 | 9.94 | 2.20 | 11.72 |
| 40-44 | 12.30 | 6.72 | 9.75 | 8.16 | 7.78 | 9.57 | 6.31 | 11.93 | 4.58 | 14.08 |
| 45-49 | 17.17 | 8.19 | 15.29 | 10.68 | 12.38 | 11.22 | 10.17 | 12.05 | 7.60 | 12.51 |
| 50 & above | 49.93 | 74.51 | 41.06 | 59.62 | 33.16 | 47.67 | 27.10 | 40.49 | 20.75 | 37.34 |
| All ages | 17.73 | 100.00 | 9.75 | 100.00 | 5.06 | 100.00 | 3.34 | 100.00 | 2.17 | 100.00 |
| Mean age at Widowhood | 37.74*24498993 (90.00) | | 34.60*214316 (7.88) | | 35.29*352693 (1.30) | | 36.19*192511 (0.70) | | 37.36*32565 (0.12) | |

*Source*: As mentioned in Table 1.6

* Refers to mean age at widowhood

Figures in the brackets refers to the percentages of total widows.

It is also observed that the percentage of widows, in the age-group of 50 and above declined rapidly from 74.51 among illiterates to 37.74 among graduates and above. This shows that female education plays an important role in reducing the proportion of widowhood not only now but also in the past. It is also surprising to note that 18.25 million widows, that is 67 per cent of the total, were not only illiterate but also aged 50 and above.

Table 1.8 provides the mean age of widowed and widowered by age 45, 50, 60 and 70 years. These estimates give an idea about the average length of married life before the death of either of the spouse. As mentioned earlier, early widowhood is one of the factors which tends to reduce the length of fertile union. The mean age at widowhood for those getting widowed by age 45 is 36.5 years and for widowered 32.2 years. And for those getting widowed and widowered by age 70, the mean age is 56.1 years and 58.5 years respectively. It is observed that mean age at widowhood is always higher than their male counterparts until the terminal age, where it is reversed.

**TABLE - 1.8**

**MEAN AGE AT WIDOWHOOD AND WIDOWERHOOD BY RESIDENTIAL STATUS FOR INDIA 1981**

| *Widowhood/ Widowerhood* | *Mean Age at Widowhood* | | | *Mean Age at Widowerhood* | | |
|---|---|---|---|---|---|---|
| | *Rural* | *Urban* | *Total* | *Rural* | *Urban* | *Total* |
| 45 years | 36.33 | 37.12 | 36.52 | 32.21 | 31.96 | 32.19 |
| 50 years | 41.42 | 41.84 | 41.52 | 37.51 | 38.49 | 37.76 |
| 60 years | 48.54 | 48.70 | 48.52 | 46.13 | 48.36 | 46.67 |
| 70 years | 56.24 | 55.64 | 56.12 | 57.94 | 60.51 | 58.52 |

*Source*: Computed from Reports and Tables based on 5% Sample Data, Series 1 India Part - II - Special Census of India. 1981.

Table 1.9 provides the intercensal estimates of mean age at widowhood for those getting widowed at age 45 for India and Karnataka. During the past three decades the increase in the mean age at widowhood is because of improvement in the mortality. It was 33.2 years in 1941-51, 34 years in 1951-61 and 35 years in 1961-71 decade. Agarwala has noticed that, "In India the mean age at widowhood was more than 30 years except for the 1911-21 and 1931-41 decade. The low mean age at widowhood for the 1911-21 decade was presumably because of the influenza epidemic which followed World War I and in the 1931-41 decade, due to a large number of child marriages which took place before the enforcement of the Child Marriage Act. The spouses of these girls experienced high mortality hence the mean age at widowhood declined"[272]. In the 1911-21 decade, the mean age at widowhood was low in Karnataka presumably because of the influenza epidemic. It is observed that this age has been rising in Karnataka also. In 8 years of time there has been an increase of 6 years in the mean age at widowhood in both India and Karnataka.

**TABLE - 1.9**

**MEAN AGE AT WIDOWHOOD OF THOSE GETTING WIDOWED BY AGE, 45 INDIA AND KARNATAKA, 1901-11 TO 1971-81**

| Decades | *Mean age at widowhood in different decades* India | Karnataka |
|---|---|---|
| 1901-1911 | 31.2 | 29.5 |
| 1911-1921 | 29.8 | 25.5 |
| 1921-1931 | 34.1 | 33.0 |
| 1931-1941 | 28.8 | 32.2 |
| 1941-1951 | 32.2 | 33.1 |
| 1951-1961 | 34.0 | 36.5 |
| 1961-1971 | 35.1 | 34.7 |
| 1971-1981 | 36.2 | 35.9 |

Source: Agarwala S.N. *India's Population Problems*. Tata, McGraw Hill Publications, 1977, Delhi.

* Figures upto 1951 include divorced, also Figures upto 1951 refer to old Mysore.

Source: Data upto 1951 census of India 1951 Mysore Vol., XIV, 1954 Bangalore.

1961 census of India, 1961 Mysore Vol. XI, Part II-c(i) Social and cultural Tables, 1966, Delhi

1971 census of India, 1971, Series 14, Mysore Part - II-c(ii) Social and Cultural Tables, 1981, Delhi

1981 census of India, 1981, Series 9, Karnataka part - II Special Report and Tables based on 5 per cent sample data 1984 Delhi.

The recent trends and differentials in the incidence of widowhood in Karnataka State, could be seen in Table 1.10. It is observed that this incidence among both the sexes in all the age-groups and in both rural and urban areas has declined. During 1921-81 the prevalence of widowerhood among total male population declined from 6 per cent to 2 per cent and from 16 per cent to 5 per cent among ever married males. While, during the same period, the prevalence of widowhood declined from 20 per cent to 10 per cent among the total female population and from 49 per cent to 18 per cent among the ever married females. Though the gap between the prevalence of widowhood and widowerhood has narrowed over the years, it is as high as 8 per cent among the total female population and 14 per cent among ever married females in 1981.

Table 1.11 provides the percentage distribution of widowed females for the country and Karnataka at three points of time, 1961, 1971 and 1981. Similar distribution by residence has been given in Table 1.12. It is observed from the Table 1.11 that there has been a decline in widows in Karnataka, as observed earlier for the country. In Karnataka during 1961, the percentage of widows was 12.36 which declined to 9.59 per cent by 1981.

The rural/urban situation as depicted in Table 1.12 suggest that the percentage of widowhood is slightly more in rural areas than in urban areas. This incidence among both males and females is relatively higher in rural areas than in urban areas. Though, there is a decline in the incidence in both the areas, the gap between the urban and rural areas still exists, since the health facilities are concentrated in the latter.

It is observed from Table 1.13 that district-wise, incidence of widowhood was not relatively same for males and females in 1961, 1971 and 1981. In some districts like Mandya, Mysore and South Karnataka, the incidence widowhood is relatively high, while the incidence of widowerhood is low. In some other districts like Chitradurga, Hassan and Kolar the incidence is low, the corresponding incidence of widowerhood is high. In Bangalore, Coorg and Dharwad the prevalence of widowhood among males and females is the same. There is no significant change in the relative position of the districts in 1961, 1971 and 1981. The changes observed in different districts may be due to the differences in the practice of remarriage of widowed persons.

## TABLE - 1.10
## TRENDS AND DIFFERENTIALS IN WIDOWHOOD IN KARNATAKA

| Year | | Per cent to Total Population | | | Per cent to Ever-Married Population | | |
|---|---|---|---|---|---|---|---|
| | | Male | Female | Difference F – M | Male | Female | Difference F – M |
| 1 | 2 | 3 | 4 | 5 | 6 | 7 | 8 |
| 1921 | Total | 6.1 | 20.1 | (14.0) | 15.7 | 49.3 | (33.6) |
| 1931 | Total | 5.1 | 17.7 | (12.6) | 13.0 | 42.3 | (29.3) |
| 1941 | Total | 5.1 | 16.3 | (11.2) | 13.1 | 39.2 | (26.1) |
| 1951 | Total | 4.3 | 15.4 | (11.1) | 11.2 | 37.0 | (25.8) |
| 1961 | Total | 3.2 | 12.4 | (9.2) | 7.5 | 22.5 | (15.0) |
| Age | 15+ | 5.4 | 21.6 | (16.2) | 7.5 | 23.1 | (15.6) |
| | 25+ | 7.4 | 30.1 | (22.7) | 8.0 | 30.5 | (22.5) |
| | 35+ | 10.4 | 44.7 | (34.3) | 10.7 | 45.2 | (34.5) |
| | 45+ | 15.3 | 61.3 | (46.0) | 15.6 | 62.0 | (46.4) |
| Rural | | 3.4 | 12.8 | (9.4) | 7.9 | 23.0 | (15.1) |
| Urban | | 2.3 | 10.8 | (8.5) | 5.9 | 20.8 | (14.9) |
| 1971 | Total | 2.3 | 10.4 | (8.1) | 5.6 | 19.9 | (14.3) |
| Age | 15+ | 3.9 | 18.2 | (14.3) | 5.6 | 20.3 | (14.7) |
| | 25+ | 5.5 | 25.6 | (20.1) | 5.9 | 25.9 | (20.0) |
| | 35+ | 7.6 | 37.4 | (29.8) | 7.8 | 37.7 | (29.9) |
| | 45+ | 11.1 | 53.9 | (42.8) | 11.3 | 54.3 | (43.0) |
| Rural | | 2.5 | 10.8 | (8.3) | 6.0 | 20.5 | (14.5) |
| Urban | | 1.7 | 9.0 | (7.3) | 4.4 | 18.2 | (13.8) |
| 1981 | Total | 1.8 | 9.6 | (7.8) | 4.5 | 18.5 | (14.0) |
| Age | 15+ | 3.0 | 16.0 | (13.0) | 45.5 | 18.6 | (14.1) |
| | 25+ | 4.3 | 22.8 | (18.5) | 4.7 | 23.2 | (18.5) |
| | 35+ | 6.1 | 33.3 | (27.2) | 6.2 | 33.5 | (27.3) |
| | 45+ | 9.0 | 47.9 | (38.9) | 9.1 | 48.1 | (39.0) |
| Rural | | 2.1 | 10.0 | (7.9) | 5.0 | 18.9 | (13.9) |
| Urban | | 1.2 | 8.7 | (7.5) | 3.3 | 17.4 | (14.1) |

* Figures up to 1951 include divorced also.

*Source*: Data upto 1951 : Census of India, 1951. Mysore, Vol XIV, 1954, Bangalore.

1961: Census of India, 1961, Mysore Vol IX Part II-c(i) Social and Cultural Tables, 1966, Delhi.

1971: Census of India, 1971, Series 14 Mysore Part II-C(ii) Social and Cultural Tables 1981, Delhi.

1981: Census of India, 1981, Series 9 Karnataka Part II Special Report and Tables based on 5 per cent Sample Data, 1984, Delhi.

**TABLE - 1.11**
**PERCENTAGE OF WIDOWED FEMALES FOR INDIA AND KARNATAKA IN 1961, 1971 AND 1981**

| India/State | Percentage of Widowed Females | | |
|---|---|---|---|
| | 1961 | 1971 | 1981 |
| India | 10.82 | 8.86 | 8.06 |
| Karnataka | 12.36 | 10.5 | 9.59 |

**TABLE - 1.12**
**PERCENTAGE OF WIDOWED FEMALES BY RESIDENTIAL STATUS FOR INDIA AND KARNATAKA IN 1961, 1971 AND 1981**

| India/State | Rural | | | Urban | | |
|---|---|---|---|---|---|---|
| | 1961 | 1971 | 1981 | 1961 | 1971 | 1981 |
| India | 11.01 | 9.03 | 8.23 | 9.19 | 8.15 | 7.46 |
| Karnataka | 12.81 | 10.77 | 9.95 | 10.77 | 9.00 | 8.67 |

Source: Census of India 1961, Part II-c(i) Social and Cultural tables, Census of India 1971 Series 1 India: Part II-c(ii) Social and Cultural Tables, Reports and Tables based on 5 per cent sample data, Series 1 India, Part II-special census of India 1981.

Widows face increased economic problems after the death of the bread winner. They are forced to work in order to earn a living. The work participation rate is higher among widows, particularly among elderly widows than ever married women as shown in the National Sample Survey 1961. At the same time the data also indicates that unemployment and poverty are higher among the widowed.

Table 1.14 shows the dominance of widows in informal sector activities like agriculture, trade, commerce and other services. It is observed from the table that the majority are absorbed in agriculture, where they get work easily, since that category does not require much skill or education. The work participation rates of widows in rural and urban areas are 26 and 21 in 1971 and 27 and 18 in 1981 respectively, whereas for married women the corresponding areas in 1981 are 24 and 13. The same tendency is noticed both in rural and urban areas, in all the age groups. The gross years of active life for widows in rural and urban are 17.0 and 14.6 respectively whereas for evermarried women the corresponding figures are 10.8 and 6.0 years.

**TABLE - 1.13**

**PERCENTAGE OF WIDOWED TOTAL POPULATION AND EVER MARRIED POPULATION IN KARNATAKA BY DISTRICT IN 1961, 1971 AND 1981 CENSUS**

| | *1961* | | | | *1971* | | | | *1981* | | | |
|---|---|---|---|---|---|---|---|---|---|---|---|---|
| | *% to Total Pop.* | | *% to Ever Married Pop.* | | *% to Total Pop.* | | *% to Ever Married Pop.* | | *% to Total Pop.* | | *% to Ever Married Pop.* | |
| | *M* | *F* | *M* | *F* | *M* | *F* | *M* | *F* | *M* | *F* | *M* | *F* |
| *1* | *2* | *3* | *4* | *5* | *6* | *7* | *8* | *9* | *10* | *11* | *12* | *13* |
| Bangalore | 2.4(3) | 10.8(2) | 5.9(4) | 19.3(2) | 1.7(3) | 8.0(2) | 4.2(2) | 16.0(2) | 1.3(1) | 8.5(4) | 3.3(1) | 17.1(6) |
| Belgaum | 2.9(6) | 12.4(11) | 6.7(7) | 21.8(7) | 2.3(8) | 10.8(13) | 5.3(7) | 20.0(12) | 1.7(5) | 10.0(12) | 4.1(5) | 18.4(12) |
| Bellary | 4.0(18) | 13.6(16) | 9.2(18) | 21.4(16) | 2.7(15) | 11.3(14) | 6.5(14) | 20.9(14) | 2.0(8) | 9.8(11) | 4.8(9) | 18.5(13) |
| Bidar | 3.0(7) | 12.0(8) | 6.4(6) | 20.1(3) | 1.5(1) | 8.6(4) | 3.3(1) | 15.4(1) | 1.6(4) | 8.8(7) | 3.7(3) | 16.1(2) |
| Bijapur | 3.2(9) | 13.9(17) | 7.0(8) | 23.7(14) | 2.5(10) | 12.3(17) | 5.6(9) | 21.8(15) | 1.9(7) | 11.2(5) | 4.4(7) | 20.1(15) |
| Chikmagalur | 3.5(11) | 10.9(4) | 8.5(13) | 21.4(5) | 2.5(10) | 8.6(4) | 6.6(15) | 18.3(5) | 1.9(7) | 7.9(1) | 4.9(10) | 16.5(3) |
| Chitradurga | 4.0(18) | 11.9(6) | 9.7(19) | 22.4(9) | 2.9(18) | 9.7(7) | 7.3(19) | 19.1(16) | 2.2(10) | 8.6(5) | 5.4(12) | 17.1(6) |
| Coorg | 2.1(1) | 8.0(1) | 5.2(1) | 16.5(1) | 1.9(5) | 7.6(1) | 5.0(6) | 16.8(3) | 1.7(5) | 8.1(3) | 4.2(6) | 17.0(5) |
| Dharwar | 3.7(19) | 13.1(14) | 8.9(15) | 24.2(17) | 2.6(14) | 11.4(15) | 6.7(17) | 22.2(16) | 1.9(7) | 10.6(13) | 5.1(11) | 20.8(17) |
| Gulbarga | 3.5(11) | 14.4(18) | 7.4(9) | 23.8(15) | 2.5(10) | 11.8(16) | 5.4(8) | 20.6(13) | 1.9(7) | 11.1(14) | 4.4(7) | 19.8(14) |
| Hassan | 3.7(16) | 11.7(5) | 9.1(16) | 22.8(11) | 2.5(10) | 9.4(6) | 6.3(13) | 19.3(8) | 1.9(7) | 8.8(7) | 4.8(9) | 18.0(9) |
| Kolar | 3.9(18) | 12.0(8) | 8.7(14) | 21.4(5) | 2.9(18) | 10.5(11) | 6.8(18) | 19.8(10) | 2.0(8) | 8.7(3) | 4.9(10) | 16.6(4) |
| Mandya | 2.4(3) | 12.8(13) | 5.7(2) | 22.9(12) | 1.8(4) | 10.3(9) | 4.4(3) | 19.5(9) | 1.4(2) | 9.4(8) | 3.4(2) | 18.1(10) |
| Mysore | 2.6(5) | 12.4(11) | 6.1(5) | 22.4(9) | 2.0(6) | 10.5(11) | 4.9(5) | 19.8(10) | 1.6(4) | 9.6(10) | 3.9(4) | 18.4(12) |
| North Kanara | 3.2(9) | 13.5(15) | 7.9(12) | 25.7(18) | 2.3(8) | 12.3(17) | 6.1(11) | 25.2(19) | 1.8(6) | 9.5(9) | 4.8(9) | 22.5(18) |
| Raichur | 3.6(14) | 15.3(19) | 7.8(11) | 25.7(18) | 2.7(15) | 13.1(19) | 6.1(11) | 23.0(18) | 2.1(9) | 11.6(16) | 4.9(10) | 10.4(1) |
| Shimoga | 3.1(8) | 10.3(3) | 7.5(10) | 20.9(4) | 2.2(7) | 8.2(3) | 5.8(10) | 17.7(4) | 1.6(4) | 8.0(2) | 4.4(7) | 17.3(7) |
| South Kanara | 2.1(1) | 11.9(6) | 5.8(3) | 23.5(13) | 1.6(2) | 10.4(10) | 4.7(4) | 22.4(17) | 1.4(2) | 9.4(8) | 3.9(4) | 20.3(16) |
| Tumkur | 3.7(16) | 12.0(8) | 9.1(16) | 22.2(8) | 2.7(15) | 9.9(8) | 6.6(15) | 19.2(7) | 2.3(11) | 9.3(7) | 5.7(13) | 17.5(8) |
| State Total | 3.2 | 12.4 | 7.5 | 22.5 | 2.3 | 10.4 | 5.6 | 19.9 | 1.8(6) | 9.5(9) | 4.5(8) | 18.3(11) |

Figures in parenthesis indicate their ranks. *Source*: as in Table 10.

### TABLE - 1.14
### WORK PARTICIPATION RATES FOR CURRENTLY MARRIED AND WIDOWED WOMEN IN 1971 AND 1981 BY AGE, PLACE OF RESIDENCE AND MAIN ACTIVITY, INDIA

| | | 1971 | | | | | | | 1981 | | | | | | |
|---|---|---|---|---|---|---|---|---|---|---|---|---|---|---|---|
| *Age* | | *Rural* | *Urban* | *I* | *II* | *VII* | *VIII* | *IX* | *Rural* | *Urban* | *I* | *II* | *VII* | *VIII* | *IX* |
| 10-14 | M | 18.5 | 12.8 | 14.3 | 70.1 | 0.3 | 0.7 | 3.3 | 28.0 | 15.3 | 16.0 | 72.0 | 0.06 | 0.2 | 1.0 |
| | W | 32.0 | 46.7 | 2.4 | 74.2 | - | 1.2 | 2.4 | 29.8 | 7.9 | 14.4 | 74.5 | - | 0.9 | - |
| 15-19 | M | 21.5 | 9.3 | 22.2 | 58.3 | 0.8 | 0.9 | 3.7 | 34.0 | 11.7 | 22.5 | 60.7 | 0.5 | 0.2 | 1.6 |
| | W | 33.0 | 20.7 | 18.8 | 58.5 | - | 1.8 | 4.5 | 33.3 | 26.7 | 18.7 | 63.0 | 0.6 | 0.3 | 3.8 |
| 20-24 | M | 22.8 | 10.0 | 22.7 | 52.3 | 1.4 | 1.1 | 5.5 | 34.2 | 11.7 | 24.5 | 52.8 | 1.4 | 0.3 | 3.1 |
| | W | 38.7 | 30.0 | 16.8 | 58.0 | 2.0 | 2.1 | 6.4 | 45.4 | 33.2 | 15.9 | 58.7 | 2.7 | 0.5 | 6.3 |
| 25-29 | M | 24.7 | 13.0 | 22.4 | 50.5 | 1.9 | 1.2 | 7.2 | 36.2 | 15.4 | 24.6 | 50.0 | 2.2 | 0.4 | 5.6 |
| | W | 46.6 | 40.6 | 21.3 | 49.7 | 4.1 | 2.4 | 8.6 | 52.3 | 42.8 | 21.4 | 50.0 | 2.9 | 0.7 | 7.0 |
| 30-39 | M | 26.1 | 15.1 | 23.4 | 50.5 | 2.5 | 1.3 | 7.5 | 38.1 | 19.0 | 30.9 | 59.7 | 3.1 | 3.5 | 5.9 |
| | W | 48.4 | 44.9 | 26.3 | 46.4 | 3.7 | 2.0 | 8.2 | 59.1 | 44.9 | 22.6 | 49.0 | 4.1 | 0.7 | 6.3 |
| 40-49 | M | 25.9 | 15.5 | 26.8 | 49.6 | 2.9 | 1.7 | 6.6 | 36.2 | 17.9 | 29.8 | 49.6 | 2.7 | 0.2 | 5.4 |
| | W | 42.8 | 34.3 | 28.0 | 47.0 | 4.4 | 1.7 | 7.6 | 48.7 | 34.2 | 25.8 | 49.2 | 4.7 | 0.6 | 6.2 |
| 50-59 | M | 21.5 | 12.9 | 28.9 | 48.7 | 3.5 | 1.1 | 6.1 | 28.4 | 12.6 | 33.8 | 46.8 | 3.8 | 0.3 | 4.3 |
| | W | 29.3 | 21.5 | 29.9 | 46.6 | 4.9 | 1.4 | 6.9 | 32.9 | 39.6 | 26.9 | 50.0 | 5.2 | 0.4 | 6.3 |
| 60+ | M | 13.0 | 8.1 | 31.3 | 45.6 | 4.3 | 1.2 | 5.3 | 16.0 | 6.8 | 34.8 | 47.8 | 3.9 | 0.3 | 3.3 |
| | W | 12.0 | 8.7 | 34.3 | 41.5 | 6.3 | 1.2 | 6.5 | 12.6 | 6.7 | 31.2 | 46.2 | 6.9 | 0.3 | 4.5 |
| Total | M | 23.8 | 12.9 | 23.9 | 51.5 | 2.2 | 1.2 | 6.4 | 34.5 | 16.4 | 26.5 | 51.2 | 2.3 | 0.3 | 4.8 |
| | W | 26.0 | 20.6 | 29.0 | 46.0 | 4.7 | 1.6 | 7.3 | 27.2 | 17.9 | 27.1 | 49.2 | 5.1 | 0.5 | 5.7 |

*Note*: I-Cultivators, II-Agricultural Labourers, VII-Trade and Commerce, VIII-Transport, Storage and Communication, IX-Other services

*Sources*: Census of India 1971 and 1981, Series 1, Part-II-B(ii). General Economic Tables, 1977, 1987 Delhi.

Widows work for a longer period than their currently married counterparts. Usually, rural women spend a longer period at work than the urban women, be it widows or currently married.

In Table 1.15, the work participation rates of widowed women in different divisions for 1971 and 1981 show their dominance when compared to their married counterparts. This shows that women enter into informal sector activities, where entrance is easy.

**TABLE - 1.15**

**WORK PARTICIPATION RATES FOR CURRENTLY MARRIED AND WIDOWED WOMEN IN 1971 AND 1981, BY AGE RESIDENCE, KARNATAKA STATE**

| | | *1971* | | *1981* | |
|---|---|---|---|---|---|
| *Age* | | *Rural* | *Urban* | *Rural* | *Urban* |
| 10-14 | M | 18.11 | 12.80 | 28.7 | 15.3 |
| | W | 31.97 | 46.67 | 29.8 | 7.9 |
| 15-29 | M | 21.47 | 9.27 | 34.0 | 11.7 |
| | W | 33.04 | 20.68 | 45.1 | 26.7 |
| 20-24 | M | 22.04 | 9.28 | 34.2 | 11.7 |
| | W | 38.74 | 30.02 | 45.4 | 33.3 |
| 25-29 | M | | 12.98 | 36.2 | 15.3 |
| | W | 46.55 | 40.56 | 52.3 | 42.6 |
| 30-39 | M | | 15.05 | 38.1 | 19.0 |
| | W | 48.40 | 44.87 | 59.1 | 44.8 |
| 40-49 | M | | 15.45 | 36.2 | 19.2 |
| | W | 42.78 | 34.30 | 49.7 | 34.2 |
| 50-59 | M | | 12.90 | 28.4 | 17.9 |
| | W | 19.98 | 21.50 | 38.1 | 19.0 |
| 60+ | M | | 8.11 | 16.0 | 12.7 |
| | W | 11.96 | 8.70 | 11.6 | 6.7 |
| Total | M | 23.83 | 12.88 | 9.8 | 15.4 |
| | W | 26.01 | 20.55 | 27.2 | 17.9 |

Table 1.14 indicates that except rural 60+ age group all the rates are high for widows when compared to that of currently married women. In both rural and urban areas there is more or less the same rate of participation at the central adjacent age groups. For widows the 30-39 age group has the highest rate.

The previous tables further indicate that the distribution of workers by industrial divisions. When India as a whole is considered, the industrial division "trade and commerce" has only shown a definitely higher proportion of widows. The same was true also in rural India for "other services". This gives the impression that "Trade and commerce" and, to a certain extent, "other services" are the industrial divisions that absorb the late entrants to the labour market.

**TABLE - 1.16**

**GROSS YEARS OF ACTIVE LIFE FOR 1971 AND 1981**

| | *1971* | | *1981* | |
|---|---|---|---|---|
| | *Rural* | *Urban* | *Rural* | *Urban* |
| M | 10.80 | 5.95 | 15.95 | 8.42 |
| W | 17.03 | 14.63 | 23.31 | 15.31 |

**TABLE - 1.17**

**PERCENTAGE DISTRIBUTION OF WORKING WIDOWS AND CURRENTLY MARRIED WOMEN BY INDUSTRIAL DIVISIONS, 1971 AND 1981 KARNATAKA STATE**

| | *1971* | | | | | *1981* | | | | |
|---|---|---|---|---|---|---|---|---|---|---|
| | *I* | *II* | *VII* | *VIII* | *IX* | *I* | *II* | *VII* | *VIII* | *IX* |
| M | 23.90 | 51.52 | 2.17 | 1.16 | 6.41 | 26.6 | 51.3 | 2.4 | 0.4 | 4.8 |
| W | 29.04 | 45.99 | 4.72 | 1.59 | 7.28 | 27.1 | 49.2 | 5.1 | 0.5 | 5.5 |

Table 1.16 gives the age and residential wise distribution of widows and currently married by work participation in Karnataka. Work participation rate for widows in rural and urban areas in all the age groups is higher than their counterparts. The work participation rate is lesser for widows only in the age group of 60+. The gross years of active life for widows in rural and urban areas during 1971 and 1981 are 17.03 and 14.63, 23.31 and 15.31 years respectively.

Table 1.17 shows the industrial division, "Trade and Commerce" has a definitely higher proportion of widows, because this is the only industrial division that absorbs the late entrants (widows) to the labour market. But in general, the distributional pattern of the workers among widows and currently married women between different industrial divisions does not carry much. Between urban and rural areas this difference is more in urban areas than in rural areas.

**Future Trend**

It is noticed from the illustrations in the literature, that India, at present, is undergoing a significant demographic transition. The improvement in the health status and decline in mortality rates in late adulthood have proved to be favourable to females. In course of time, due to this the proportion of aged females will increase, among whom a significant proportion will be widows, since widows marry infrequently.

In India by 2000 A.D. the proportion of males and females who fall in the age group of 65 and above will be 3.66 and 3.98 per cent respectively. That means in the proportion of males there would be an increase of 7.3 per cent and 17.4 per cent in the proportion of females. In our country by 2001 A.D. the females aged 50+ would be 83.5 million and widows expected to be 45 million.

## PART - II

### 1.1 Introduction

The present study deals mainly with the various problems faced by widows in traditional Hindu society, as well as the socio-economic and demographic implications of widowhood. From a sociological point of view widowhood may be perceived as a change in the status of women caused by the dissolution of marriage and which necessitates the establishment of new ties within the family, with the kin group and the community[273].

The importance of the study of widowhood lies in the fact that the death of one's spouse precipitates a period of crisis. It is also a traumatic experience for almost everyone within the family unit. It brings about a number of economic and social consequences both for the members of the immediate family and the community[274]. The consequences are apt to be more serious in case of death among middle aged spouses, who leaves a wife and young children as dependents. The most affected persons in our traditional society are young widows[275]. The death of the husband has a serious consequence on the widow. Apart from the severe emotional stress of coping with the loss of a husband, it often means the widow has to undertake the problems of looking after the socioeconomic needs of the family. The problem becomes more acute in the case of young illiterate widows. In such cases a woman who is herself dependent, is suddenly faced with the task of mustering resources to look after her children who now look to her for everything.

Women generally occupy a secondary position in most societies and do not enjoy socio-religious or political life. Even today in spite of changes as those granted to married women, they are deprived of the necessities which every human being has a right to enjoy. Consequently, social norms and taboos consign the unfortunate widows to an even more disadvantaged position. They are considered a bad omen and inauspicious and thereby restricted in their socio-religious functions. Widows who are young, poor and uneducated face even more problems. Thus, when the position of widows is deplorable, the condition of Hindu widows who are governed by the age old oppressive and rigid customs is indeed lamentable. The position of a Hindu widow is miserable and her lot is unenviable. The present study is concerned with Hindu widows, living in the urban and rural areas of Dharwad district.

The main focus of the study deals with the problems faced by widows, the factors responsible for her predicament and the manner in which they attempt to overcome them. The major interest of the present study is to investigate the circumstances under which widows face deprivation. This study also tries to find out the consequences caused by the various kinds of deprivation to the widow herself, her family and to society in general. This study of widowhood provides us not only with the adequate understanding of the magnitude of the problems and its prospects in future, but also deals with the various ramifications and implications of widowhood and the state of deprivation faced by them. So far most of the studies undertaken have examined only the socio-economic aspect of the problem. Hence, this study makes an attempt to understand the sociological implications of widowhood, particularly the deprivation faced by a widow in the economic, social, psychological and cultural spheres.

## 1.2 The Problem

The position of a widow in society is a crucial topic which sociologists have to discuss and elucidate. The treatment which she receives is often an index to the attitudes of society towards women as a class.

What is the general lot of widows? What are the problems faced by them? What are the changes in their lifestyles? Does she marry again if she so desires? Did her husband leave any property so that she could lead an honourable and independent life after his death? These are the main questions which we have to explore in connection with the position of widows. The tragic alienation of a widow today, is casually related to continued loss of her status and dignity in the remote past.

From available literature on widowhood, one finds that several factors are responsible for the deprived position of widows. There is no uniform pattern of widowhood either in terms of conditions leading to such a phenomenon or in terms of the consequences pattern. There is also no uniform lifestyle for widows. The lifestyles vary not only according to the location in the social system be it an upper class area or a middle-class area, or the slum, urban or Rural areas, but by their own combination of characteristics. Patterns emerge when such factors as educational level of the women are compared to their social life and space. So it emerges that the more educated and trained widows are able to enter into and maintain more social roles and social relations. On the other hand, poor, uneducated, ignorant and illiterate widows face difficulties in entering and maintaining social roles and social relations.

The present study is entitled, "Hindu Widows: A Study in Deprivation". Deprivation of certain necessities and privileges, certainly affects physical development, and acute deprivation may affect the development of personality too. The state of deprivation of widows constitute the main focus of the study rather than the variety of problems faced by them. The present study is an attempt to understand the various kinds of deprivation faced by widows, the effects of deprivation on them and how they manage to overcome them. An attempt is also made to understand the Hindu value system which has created the institution of widowhood.

Some of the questions which the researcher has tried to take up for investigation are as follows : Are there any changes in the socio-economic conditions of women, after widowhood? What are the problems faced by them? What are the factors that may be considered as responsible for their low social status? The types of treatment they received before and after widowhood? Are there any differences in the lifestyle of widow of both rural and urban areas? What are their reactions towards death, widowhood and position of widows in Hindu society? The views of widows on various aspects of their life, remarriage of widows, future plans, for themselves and their children. Suggestions for the welfare of the widow were also sought.

The sample widows are drawn from diverse social backgrounds. Hence, the views of widows about their status and roles differ. Socio-economic background, size of the family, value system of every caste, are important factors that decide the nature of the problems, which widows have to face in their life, which also may explain the diverse ways of life of widows. The present investigation considers the differences in the background characteristics of widows of both rural and urban areas as well as the differences in the nature of socio-emotional support and caste value systems, in order to understand how far such differences contribute to the state of deprivation and the problems of adjustment of widows.

### 1.3 Scope and Objectives

The problem of widowhood has elicited considerable interest in the minds of researchers in recent times. Widowhood is a complex transition, with various possible consequences, both subjective and objective. In the Indian context the problem assumes considerable importance, as the age difference between husband and wife is higher, widow remarriage is highly restricted. The influence of widowhood on fertility is higher than in modern societies. An increasing trend towards the small family norm, nuclearization of families and continuous erosion of family, kinship ties even in rural areas of our society, seems to have a bearing on the problems of widowhood. It has been rightly said that widowhood is a combination of the problems of the woman and the widow. Hence, in order to understand the complex phenomenon of widowhood, a systematic study of the various problems faced by widows, the causes, the consequences and the effects on the personality of widows, the difficulties in adopting to widowhood and how they manage to overcome the problems, becomes essential.

There is a growing research literature on widowhood. Most of it is concerned with the explanation of psychological and emotional adaptations to bereavement and the socio-economic conditions of widows.

Hence, the present study, which is an attempt to find out the causes and consequences of economic, social, psychological and cultural deprivation, assumes importance.

The present study work is confined to the study of 300 widows belonging to Dharwad city and surrounding villages in Dharwad Taluk. The field of investigation was restricted to the above mentioned areas, because of the limited resources and time available to an individual researcher.

For the selection of samples among Hindus, a systematic procedure was used to obtain a representative sample, belonging to various castes, which are classified broadly into three groups, viz. Hindu low caste, Hindu intermediate caste and Hindu Upper caste.

**Aims of the study**

The present study takes into account the various problems faced by widows, causes and consequences and efforts made by them to overcome the problems. This study also takes into cognizance the opinion, attitudes of widows towards status of Hindu widows, factors that improve their status and remarriage of widows. Hence, it pertains to the analysis of relationships between background factors and the problems and the differences between the rural and urban area and between the upper, the intermediate and lower castes.

The following are some of the major aims of the present study.

1. To study the changes brought about by widowhood in the socio-economic conditions of widows.

2. To ascertain the socio-economic background of the deceased husbands of the widows.
3. To ascertain the difficulties faced by widows in the upbringing of their children and the reasons responsible for the same.
4. To assess the extent of deprivation faced by them in fields like economic, social, psychological and cultural and the manner in which they manage to overcome them.
5. To elicit, their opinion towards widow remarriage, their future plans regarding themselves and their children and their suggestions for the welfare of widows.

**1.4 Methods and Procedures**

As mentioned earlier the present study is an attempt to explain the state of deprivation faced by widows in the fields like economic, social, psychological and cultural, the problems of adjustment of widows and the factors which have an impact on the life of widows. The requisite data is obtained through the interview method with the help of a structured interview schedule. The interview method is considered as the basic field technique through which the widows were approached and the responses received from them were recorded in the field itself.

**Selection of the Field**

Since the present study is a rural-urban comparative study, Dharwad city and the surrounding villages form the rural part of Dharwad Taluk were selected. For urban sample, ward nos. 4 and 5, that is Malmaddi and ward nos. 16 and 17, i.e., Mrutunjayanagar from Dharwad city, where Hindus are substantial in number were selected for the study. Malmaddi comprises of a predominantly Brahmin population, where a Rayara Math (a Brahmin monastery) is situated. Mritunjayanagar comprises of a predominantly Lingayat population with a fair sprinkling of some of the predominant lower castes and where the Murugha Math (a Lingait monastery) is situated. In the selection of areas, for purposes of geographical stratification, the Dharwad Taluk was subdivided into four zones by drawing a vertical and horizontal line

*Attitudes and Orientations*

Under this head, relevant questions are included to ascertain the respondents orientations and attitudes toward death and widowhood, the status of widow in Hindu society, the remarriage of widows.

The questions also included certain number of brief statements, the responses to which could be either in the affirmative or negative. These items mainly included either favourable or unfavourable attitudes toward marriage, and status of widows.

*Future Plans and Suggestions*

Under this head questions are included to ascertain information from the respondents about their future plans regarding themselves and their children and suggestions for the state and others to work for the welfare of the widows.

**Pilot Study**

A pilot study was conducted before the main interview schedule was finalized in order to ensure the suitability of the questions and the sample. This study included the interview of 50 widows, 25 each from the rural and urban areas who belonged to different castes in Hindu religion like upper castes, lower Hindu castes, intermediate and dominant Hindu castes. This study was carried out in Hubli city and surrounding villages. The sample of widows selected from both the areas varied in caste, age and income.

A draft of interview schedule comprised of structured answers was used for the purpose of the pilot study. The pilot study helped the researcher to add a few more direct questions and responses so as to meet the objectives of the study. The responses were given codes and scores so as to make the analysis easy.

**The Sample**

*Sampling Procedure*

The present study is confined to the study of 300 widows who are the inhabitants of Dharwad and surrounding villages, with 150 from the rural and 150 from the urban area. The 1988 house tax list of the Dharwad-Hubli corporation was used to determine which wards were to be sampled and which streets constituted a given block. Next, a list of households in which widows lived was made by using the snow-ball technique, which served as the source of the sample. Two-way stratified simple random sampling method was used for the selection of widows. Since the name and addresses of widows are not maintained either by the corporation or village panchayats as the case may be, the researcher found it difficult to trace the widows for the purpose of the study. However, with the given objectives of the study namely: the impact of deprivation, it was decided to select a sample in such a way as to ensure adequate representation of various variables like caste, age, income, area and education. The respondents were selected based on the following criteria.

1. Respondent should be a Hindu.
2. Respondent who had been widowed for not less than five years.
3. Five SC/ST/Backward classes respondents in each locality/village.

To identify the widows in the respective localities the help of leaders of different agencies/associations like Mahila Mandals, Mandal Panchayati and other prominent local persons was sought. The purpose of the study was thoroughly explained to them and cooperation from their end was sought. Personal visits were made to every household to collect the basic information, and recorded on a separate paper. Only those families where widows were present, a further detailed information was collected on the pre-coded structured schedules by interview method. The same sampling procedure was used even in the rural areas.

**Sample Characteristics and Distribution**

The sample was designed to have a total of 325 respondents. But due to non-availability of respondents belonging to particular category, only 300 respondents were taken into consideration.

The number of respondents selected for the study from Dharwad city and different villages is given in the Table 1.18.

**Interview Procedure**

Of the 25 respondent households with eligible respondents, 25 (10-Rural, 15-Urban) potential respondents declined to be interviewed. This represented 7.69 per cent of the eligible respondents. Among those who did not wish to be interviewed a majority of the cases refused to participate claiming to have no time or were unwilling to meet the researcher on personal grounds, or were unwilling to narrate their personal problems to an outsider. Some were unwilling to recall the sad events. Eight (2-R, 6-U) of those were unable to participate because of poor health or physical disability or were out of station.

Three hundred widows (92.31%) of the eligible widows were interviewed in their homes between January 1988 and March 1988. The youngest respondent was 18 and the oldest was 102.

**TABLE - 1.18**
**TABLE SHOWING THE WARD-WISE AND VILLAGE WISE DISTRIBUTION OF RESPONDENTS SELECTED FOR THE STUDY**

| *Urban* | *Number of Respondents* |
|---|---|
| 1. Ward No. 4 and 5 | 75 |
| 2. Ward no. 16 and 17 | 75 |
| *Rural (Villages)* | |
| 1. Daddikamalpur | 24 |
| 2. Mandihal | 28 |
| 3. Ghongadikop | 18 |
| 4. Govankop | 18 |
| 5. Lakamapur | 18 |
| 6. Dasankop | 18 |
| 7. Nuggikeri | 18 |
| 8. Yerikop | 18 |

## 1.5 Framework of Analysis

*Variables for the Study*

The major variables used in the present study are as follows:

(a) Independent variables - caste, age, income, education area

(b) Infrastructure variable - Property left by the husband

(c) Dependent variable - Deprivation

1. Caste-depending on the religion, widows are broadly classified as 1) Hindu Lower caste (2) Hindu Intermediate caste (3) Hindu upper caste.
2. Age - based on the age, the widows are classified into three groups such as, young widows: 0-30 years; Middle aged: 30-60 years: Aged widows: 60 above.

3. Locality widows are classified on the basis of locality to which they belonged - (1) rural (2) urban
4. Income - depending on the level of income widows are classified into :
    1. High income group
    2. Middle income group
    3. Low income group
5. Background variable - This includes husband's occupation, his income and property left by him as important factors - Husband's occupation is divided into high, medium and low.
    (i) High occupation - comprises the professionals and managers, who have secured university degrees and training.
    (ii) Medium occupation - includes principally, white collar workers, such as clerks where completion of secondary education is mandatory to secure jobs.
    (iii) Low occupation - comprises mainly manual occupations i.e. semi-skilled and skilled workers, whose educational level is low, including illiterates.
6. Attitudinal Variable - This variable concerns the subjective aspects of a widow's life. The findings regarding the attitudes toward the status of widows in Hindu society and the marriage of widows, etc., are brought under this variable. The attitudes are measured in terms of favourable or unfavourable responses to the questions. The above mentioned variables are considered for analysing and interpreting the data. These variables are taken into consideration because they are expected to influence the deprivation level and adjustment of the widows.

It is presumed that caste, age, income and locality are some of the social characteristics which have influence over the deprivation faced. Besides, background variables like occupation, income and property left by the deceased husbands also affect the deprivation level/ process. It is also considered that attitudes of the respondents are also possible variables affecting deprivation level and adjustment process.

## Methods used for Qualifying the Variables

The following methods are used for qualifying the data regarding the dependent variables.

### *Deprivation Level*

The deprivation level of respondents is measured with reference to the problems faced by the widows in economic, social, emotional and cultural fields. For this purpose a deprivation index was developed as suggested by Anastasi 1961.

$$\text{Deprivation Index} = \frac{\text{Number of correct positive responses}}{\text{Total number of deprivation items}} \times 100$$

There are four types of deprivation. They are (1) Economic Deprivation (2) Social Deprivation (3) Emotional Deprivation and (4) Cultural Deprivation.

And each deprivation item is credited with one and two scores and each wrong/negative answer with zero score. The details regarding the individual items included in the deprivation test and their scoring pattern are furnished later on in this book. The raw deprivation score of each individual is converted into the above deprivation index.

## Hypothesis

The following hypothesis are framed in order to test them in the light of the findings of the present study.

1. The income of the husbands has an influence on the widow's level of economic deprivation.
2. Absence of father influences the children's behaviour.
3. Caste has influence on the level of cultural deprivation, of widows.
4. There is a significant difference in the social deprivation level of rural and urban widows.
5. Husband's age at death has influence on the economic deprivation of widows.
6. There is a significant difference in the emotional deprivation of rural and urban widows.

**Statistical Methods and Tools Used**

The data thus collected is analysed into two stages. Initially a two dimensional contingency table was constructed taking one independent variable and a dependent variable. The findings are analysed with the help of relative frequencies in regard to the variables that are identified. Other relevant statistical techniques used in chi-square value which indicate the degree of association/ difference between variables. Statistical tests are applied wherever the findings are not obvious, when the results of analysis reveal findings that are obvious in nature, percentages calculated are considered for interpretation of data and explaining the difference between one or more variables. The chisquare test of independence and student 't' test are carried out to find out the significant difference between the independent and the dependent variables. The formula used for chisquare.

$$X2 = \frac{E\,(O_i - E_i)^2}{E_i}$$

Where $O_i$ = observed frequency,

$E_i$ = expected frequency

The formula used for 't' tests is

$$t = \frac{\overline{X}_1 - \overline{X}_2}{\sqrt{\frac{S_1^2}{n_1} + \frac{S_2^2}{n_2}}} - t_n + n_2 - 2$$

where $X_1$ = Sample mean of I group

$X_2$ = Sample mean of II group

$$S_1 = \sqrt{\frac{\Sigma X_1^2}{n_1} - \frac{(\Sigma X_1)^2}{n_1}}$$

Standard Deviation of I group.

$$S_2 = \sqrt{\frac{\Sigma X_2^2}{n_2} - \frac{(\Sigma X_2)^2}{n_2}}$$

Standard Deviation of II group.

where $n_1$ = Sample size of I group

$n_2$ = Sample size of II group

### 1.6 Theoretical Support

Etymologically the word deprivation is derived from the verb "to deprive" which means to dispossess or strip (a person or an object) and it implies a "felt loss". The word deprivation literally refers to dispossession or loss of privileges, opportunities, material good and the like. It usually means a taking away of what one owns, or has a right to. As C.D. Lewis explains its meaning by quoting an example as "the feeling that the system under which we live deprives the majority of the chances of a decent life".[276]

The term deprivation is sometimes used by researchers in different ways. Rubin Richard et al., express that there are two distinct meanings for the term: (1) the taking or withholding — usually deliberately, of something from another to which he is used or otherwise entitled, (2) according to behavioural scientists, the technical meaning of the term refers to the absence of a variable from the environment of an organizm. They further say that the popular use generally regards deprivation as negative, worst, not worthy of approval and a means of last resort. The technical use of the term is free of value judgements. It merely describes an existing condition which may or may not be desirable.[277]

Sinha in his study on "Towards and Ecological Framework of Deprivation" says that the term deprivation refers to certain deficiencies in the environment. The deficiencies are not only there but are also experienced by the individual. It in turn causes an impact on the functioning of the individual. When one refers to deprivation the emphasis is on that aspects of environment which are deficient or wanted in some respects. In the conceptualization of deprivation, importance should be given to the environment or the setting in which the individual operates.[278]

Hunt says that the deprivation has been equated with "failures to provide opportunity to have experience".[279] Adams asserts that the deprivation refers to deficiencies in experiences and conditions of learning.[280] Gordon has stated that deprivation in his study concerns with deficiencies in the stimulus conditions of the childhood. The identification of deprivation has been attempted through the living area and membership of specific social groups.[281]

Davis and others in their study on "Social Deprivation and

Cognitive Functioning of Lower Class Children" have devised some independent indices of deprivation but they cover a narrow and partial range of deprivational variables, that is, they have covered only the social variables.[282]

Ojha is of the opinion that the concept of deprivation is used in various ways. High powered international bodies while describing lifestyles in different countries of the world refer to some countries which fall short of their conception of good living as "deprived".[283]

He further says that the discrimination suffered by the disadvantaged among the Scheduled Castes and Tribes is not less severe than what the low among the high castes have suffered at the instance of their own men. Even among the high castes, people belonging to lower category of high caste are socially discriminated by other high castes. The less well-to-do among both the high and low castes remain underprivileged in more than one ways. In the same way, the cogenitally or otherwise deformed ones among the rich feel deprived in comparison to the poor having no such deformities incapacitating them, whichever caste they belonged. The physically or the mentally handicapped are perhaps the real "deprived ones" than the normal ones.[284]

In medical and psychological studies, the term "deprivation" has been used in diverse ways. But a number of recent studies in natural life settings have led to crystallization of various empirical referents in this term.[285] In psychological studies it has often been employed to denote "social disadvantage" or "cultural alienation"[286] Monks describes deprivation as "insufficient satisfaction of basic psychological needs, and deficiencies in individual family settings".[287]

Tripathi and Misra considered deprivation as a prolonged process relative to a defined social setting.[288] They further say that a critical scrutiny of the various ways in which the term deprivation has been used has led to a belief that in spite of its diverse definitions there underlies unity in its implications.

The above are some of the ways in which the term deprivation has been used by some of the social scientists to describe various situations. However, one may narrow down the definition of deprivation as relevant to this research work.[289]

Nurcombe has stated, "deprivation refers strictly to a dispossession or loss of privileges, opportunities, material goods and the like. It may occur with reference to three interrelated sets of basic needs — physical, psychological and sociocultural.[290]

Langmeir has viewed deprivation as a general phenomenon and defined the same as "insufficient satisfaction of basic needs for a longer period." According to him it is a phenomenon which includes sensory, cognitive, emotional and social deprivation. These aspects overlap one another. They can be studied separately in specific conditions or in experimental situation.[291]

Misra and Tripathi have developed the concept of prolonged deprivation with the intention of including all aspects of life in which deprivation has been recognized as a phenomenon. They have defined prolonged deprivation as, "a multidimensional psychological construct embracing a wide range of environmental and organizmic variables and refers to a dispossession or loss of privileges, opportunities, material goods and the like relatively for a longer period".[292]

In the above mentioned definition it can be said that the term deprivation has been used to denote deficient environmental conditions and impoverished experiences along different dimensions of deprivation.

Misra in his study on "Motivational Structure and Prolonged Deprivation" has analysed the motivational structure as related to different degrees of experimental deprivation. The experiential deprivation significantly influences the strength of achievement and approved motives and anxiety. It is also found that the different motives, interpersonal and task-related are positively related to anxiety which disrupts the effort towards goal attainment[293].

Again, Misra and Tripathi in their study on "Prolonged Deprivation and Status Perception" report that the status perception varies as a function of deprivation level. The 'low deprived group' showed a very high level of status striving. The past and present status of 'high deprived group' was very low compared to middle and low deprived groups[294].

Deprivation is a phenomenon which brings about systematic exploitation. Widows are perhaps those who belong to the deprived section of society. They are deprived of the privileges, and necessities. Widows are discriminated in Hindu society.

The plight of Hindu widows is perhaps more glaring given the traditional social structure in India. Deprivation or disadvantages in the nature of discrimination leads to several problems. These problems in turn narrow down a widow's behavioural alternatives or makes her physically, socially, economically and psychologically handicapped to fulfil their biosocial needs or to achieve their self-fulfilment.

**Types of Deprivation**

The "Psychological Abstracts" index lists over two dozen types of deprivations, such as stimulus, cultural, egoistical, economic, social, political, educational, material and environmental. To this one can add various types of need deprivation such as food, water, sexual activity and the like[295]. These are some of the prevailing concepts of the term 'deprivation' observed in current researches. Any of these concepts could be with various degrees of precision used to denote deprivation.

*Economic Deprivation*

Economic deprivation can be understood in terms of the levels of poverty in every country. There are other factors along with economic factors that causes economic deprivation. The nature and composition of these factors vary from one country to another[296].

When a family does not get adequate food even when all the members spend their resources of time, energy and money on earning their livelihood, the family experiences deprivation caused by the non-fulfilment of basic needs due to poverty. For such families, energy levels and time for leisure activities are limited. Almost every member has to contribute to the family income in order to survive. In a majority of such cases, even the children are involved in procuring cash or kind for their wherewithal for survival. Their economic pressures force them to join the labour force early and the children of the poor are even deprived of a childhood[297].

Valentine asserts that the distinctive feature of life of the poor can be determined primarily by the structure of society as a whole and by forces beyond the control of the poor[298].

Pealtie holds that the poor develop such value systems that suit their poverty conditions. They adjust their values and aspirations to suit their social and economic deprived conditions[299].

In this sense, perhaps, one of the most important problems following widowhood is economic deprivation. Most widows face deprivation due to an economic catastrophe brought about by the death of the breadwinner. The life in a deprived economic condition is difficult. Widows face several problems connected with money, property, employment and other related economic matters. The loss of a bread-winner can send them into a demoralizing life of dependency. Due to this, widows develop low self-esteem, a sense of inefficacy and passivity in their social life.

*Social Deprivation*

Being deprived of opportunities for social contacts, like being deprived of affection and love can play havoc with the personality pattern. As Mussen et al., have said, "a child's lack of peer group contacts, because of social isolation, family restrictions, unfavourable social attitudes on the part of the child's condition, may result not only in immediate unhappiness but also subsequent difficulties in interpersonal relationships[300].

Gordon has stated that terms such as 'socio-economic deprivation', 'socially disadvantaged' and 'culturally alienated' reflect deficiencies in social conditions[301].

Whiteman and Deutcsch have considered social deprivation as a relative term referring exclusively to specific types of environmental factors. According to them, any environmental factor may be considered deprivational: (1) if that factor is associated with certain social grouping such as socio-economic status and race and (2) when the environmental variable is associated with impaired performance[302].

Tannenbaum has concluded that social deprivation may be characterized as a condition in which particular external and internal factors merge to narrow a person's behavioural alternatives for achieving self-fulfilment[303].

David, Beres has viewed social deprivation as "experiences wherein an individual is deprived of the opportunity to develop his capacities to work, to provide for his needs and to enjoy the dignities of life"[304].

Recent research studies have shown the importance of social interaction for normal human development. As Hurlock observes, the lack of social contacts brings about socio-psycho problems. This in turn causes social deprivation[305].

She further says that social deprivation leads to social isolation. Social isolation is specially damaging to the personality development. It is so in a culture which places high values or moral codes or restrictions on behaviours or social relations. The damage comes in part from lack of opportunities to participate in social activities and in part from the feelings or inadequacy which the deprived person feels in comparison with others[306].

Social deprivation is most damaging to certain age groups such as the very young and the old. During the period the individual is neither self-sufficient nor occupied with duties and responsibilities.

How damaging social deprivation is to the personality pattern depends on many factors and conditions, the most important of which are the age at which the deprivation occurs, how long it lasts, what causes it, how extensive it also depends on the person's social contacts[307].

Many elderly people suffer as severely from social deprivation as from emotional deprivation because the two go hand in hand. While social isolation leads to poor morale and mental disorganization at any age, it is particularly harmful among the elderly. The problem is all the more acute among elderly widows[308].

The causes of a person's social deprivation may be external or internal. Some causes can be better controlled than others. Geographic isolation is easier to control than isolation due to social rejection. As a general rule, social deprivation among the younger age level is primarily due to obstacles within themselves, and among the older age levels, due to environmental obstacles[309].

Deprivation is far more damaging to persons who desire social contacts than to these who are self-sufficient or who voluntarily withdraw. Thus, an extrovert person feels the impact of deprivation more than an introvert.

Geschwender opines that social deprivation always has an adverse effect on personality. Loneliness, feeling of being rejected and being forced to become socially isolated makes the person frustrated. All these are damaging to the self-concept. The more value the social group puts on social participation, the more damaged the person is psychologically by social deprivation. If deprivation is extensive and prolonged it inevitably leads to unhealthy social attitudes and mental illness[310].

In India, widows have been prohibited from participating in socio-religious functions because they are considered inauspicious or bad omen. Hence, widows often feel left out of social interaction after widowhood. The feeling of being deprived on social occasions or feeling of an unwillingness on the part of married friends to include, makes them socially segregated. For a woman, widowhood means a plunge in social status.

A reduction in the social contacts and supportive relationships of the widows leads to social isolation, insecurity feeling, loneliness. This is more so in case of elderly widows.

Social deprivation is thus damaging to the self-concept. One may conclude that the more opportunities the person has for social activities, the better adjusted and happier the person will be.

*Emotional Deprivation*

Emotional deprivation refers to the denied stimulus objects which arose emotional reactions. In its broadest sense it refers to any kind of emotional reaction. The psychologists and sociologists refer to 'love' reactions[311].

Hurlock further says that just as some children can grow up in an environment which protects them from unpleasant emotions, there are many children who can have plenty of opportunities to experience unpleasant emotions and who are deprived of opportunities to experience the pleasant ones. It is to this second group that the term "emotional deprivation is ordinarily applied"[312].

She further argues that studies of emotional deprivation have increased our understanding of the role emotions play in personality development. A deficiency of emotional experiences, pleasant ones, especially during early years of life, leads to poor personal and social adjustments[313].

Goode opines, "deprivation of any emotion is harmful to the personality, but deprivation of love is especially damaging"[314]. As Jersild says, "there is something emotionally satisfying about being loved and there also is something very practical about it". Thus, he emphasizes the need for care and emotional satisfaction[315]. Hurlow speaks of love as a wondrous state, deep, tender and rewarding[316]. Many adults experience deprivation of love, especially in old age and after the death or divorce of a spouse. Deprivation can be almost as damaging to the self-concept in adulthood as in childhood[317].

Recent studies have shown that lack of opportunities to experience other pleasant emotions result in psychological damage. Here widows of all ages are deprived of opportunities to experience curiosity, happiness, joy or elation. The loss of a spouse brings about the deprivation of love and affection for women especially during young age while for men during old age. Thereby they become apathetic and frustrated[318].

Hurlock observed that deprivation of opportunities to love and be loved delays the normal patterns of physical and mental development. Some of the specific effects of emotional deprivation have been reported to be:

Physical, as seen in listlessness, emaciation, loss of appetite, quietness, general apathy and psychosomatic illness.

Social, as revealed in handicaps in learning, how to get along with people, lack of responsiveness to the advances of others, lack of cooperation and hostility.

Emotional, as shown in lack of emotional responsiveness and interchange (the empathic complex) feelings of insecurity, resentments as expressed in a social behaviour, restlessness, anxiety, temper, tantrums and many other forms of mal-adjustive behaviour[319].

The effects of deprivation of love on the personalities of widows will depend on how much rejected they feel. A feeling of rejection leads to self-pity, anxiety, irritability and negativism at an early age.

The severity and persistence of effects of deprivation of love depends on the extent of deprivation, when it occurs, how long it lasts and whether the satisfaction of love can be substituted from a normal and available source. Deprivation of love is especially damaging to the self and results in emotional starvation and self-destruction at any age.

The death of a loved one can be an alarming experience while that of a husband is especially traumatic, which often causes self-damage and psychosomatic problems like shock of loss, depression, despair, loneliness, fears, feelings of abandonment, loss of weight and sleeplessness, etc. The widows take a long time to overcome the psychological deprivations and grief caused by the spousal loss. Some of the important effects of emotional deprivation are unhappiness, emotional insecurity, anomie, mental disorders or sometimes even suicide.

*Cultural Deprivation*

Chaubey et al., observe that cultural deprivation is, "a state resulting from removal or withdrawal of the given culture". A study of cultural deprivation would therefore mean either taking away the individual from the culture to which he belongs or placing him in an environment devoid of that culture. In operational terms it would mean preventing individual's access to the material life and blocking his access to the living styles social norms, customs, values, ethos, etc., of his groups[320].

Das defines cultural deprivation as, "a complex set of conditions which favour intellectual sub-normality in a child" and that is how the term 'cultural deprivation' is being used in contemporary psychology. The ill-effects of cultural deprivation not only affects intelligence but also verbal ability of children who have normal intelligence[321]. Wight et al., observe that cultural deprivation must account for deficiencies both in experience and in the conditions of learning[322]. Deutcsch says, "a different emphasis in approach to the problem of cultural deprivation is represented in terms such as 'motivational inadequacy', 'cultural maladaptations' and 'learning deficit'[323].

Himes in his study on "Some Work-Related Cultural Deprivations of Lower-class Negro Youths" says, "in the present study, cultural deprivation is understood to refer to residual personality characteristics that issue from socialization under specific institutionalized preconditions"[324].

According to Hunt cultural deprivation is, "failure to provide an opportunity to have the experiences required for adequate development of the semi-autonomous central process demanded for acquiring skill in cognitive process."[325]

Samant finds four objectively measurable factors such as, economic status, caste, parental education and place of residence, together provide a reliable index of the level of socio-cultural deprivation[326].

In short, cultural deprivation is failure to provide the experiences required for adequate development of human personality.

In India, women have to re-start an altogether difficult life after widowhood. In Hindu society the norms of widowhood are the norms of asceticism. There are restrictions on food habits, dress and remarriage of the widows. They are forbidden to attend socio-religious functions. They are also prohibited from wearing saubhagya insignia under any circumstances. They are culturally isolated and are made to spend their life in constant devotion to Gods. They are also separated from worldly affairs and pleasures.

The state of deprivation is often coupled with stigma. Many women see widowhood as a social stigma. They are discriminated as inauspicious. Exclusion of widows from full social acceptance brings about social isolation and reduces life chances. Their wants and needs are considered less valid than the married women. As a result they are treated as less than their married counterparts.

## REFERENCES

1. Landis, P.H.: *Your Marriage and Family Living*, McGraw-Hill, New York, 1954, p. 319
2. Smart, M.S. and Smart L.S.: *Families-Developing Relationship*, Macmillan Publishing Co. New York, 1976, p. 412.
3. Christensen H.T.: *Marriage Analysis-Foundation for Successful Family Life*. Ronald Press Co. New York, 1950, p. 64.
4. Goode, W.J.: *The Family*. Prentice Hall of India New Delhi, 1965, p. 98.
5. Bankoff, E.A. Social Support and Adoptation to widowhood. *Journal of Marriage and the Family*, Vol. 45. No. 4. 1983, p. 827.
6. Bock, E.B. and Webber I.L.: Suicide Among the Elderly; Isolating Widowhood and Mitigating Altractives, *Journal of Marriage and the Family*, Vol. 34. No. 1. 1972, p. 24.
7. Somerville, V.M.: Death Education as part of Family Life Education. *The Family Coordinator*, 1971, p. 209.

8. Womble, D.: *Foundations for Marriage and Family Relations*. Macmillan, New York, 1966, p. 491.
9. Eliot, Thomas. D.: Bereavement : Inevitable but not Insurmountable in Becker, Howard and Hill Rueben. (Eds), *Family Marriage and Parenthood*. D.C. Health and Company Boston. 1948, p. 644.
10. Lindeman, E.: "Symptomology and Management of Acute grief", *American Journal of Psychiatry*. Vol. 101, No. 2, 1944, p. 141.
11. Waller, Willard: *The Family - A dynamic interaction*. The Drydon Press, New York, 1956, p. 471.
12. Eliot, Thomas D: The Bereaved Family. In Landis J.T. and Landis M.G. (Eds) *Readings in Marriage and the Family*, Prentice Hill Inc., New York, 1953, pp. 288-294.
13. Eliot, Thomas D.: "........ of the shadow of Death" *Annals of the American Academy of political and social Sciences*, Vol. 229, No. 1, 1943, pp. 94-95.
14. Murray. P.C.: "Bereavement", *British Medical Journal*, Vol. 3, No. 1-6, 1967, p. 232.
15. Duval, E.M.: *Family Development*, J.B. Lippincott Co., New York, 1971, p. 468.
16. Martinson, F.: *Family in Society*, Dodd Mead, New York, 1970, p. 354.
17. Brubaker, T.H.: *Later Life Families*, Sage Publications, London, 1985, pp. 94-95.
18. Fritz, M.A.: A study of Widowhood in *Sociology and Social Research*, Vol. XIV, No. 1, 1929, p. 553.
19. Singh, Gurmeet *et. al.*,: Problems of widowhood. *The Indian Journal of Social Work*, Vol. XLVII, No. 1, 1986, p. 67.
20. Rosow, I.: *Social Integration of the Aged*. The free Press, New York, 1967, pp.
21. Philiprice, F.: *Marriage and Parenthood*. Allyn and Bacon, Boston, 1979, p. 305.
22. Hyman, H.H. *Of time and Widowhood*. Duke press policy studies, Durham, 1983, p. 3.
23. Greg, A.: The Elderly widow and her Family Neighbours and Friends. *Journal of Marriage and the Family*, Vol. 38, No. 4, 1976, p. 757.
24. Duberman, L.: *Marriage and other Alternative*, Praeger Publishers, New York, 1977, p. 614.
25. Jogula, J.M.: The Christian perspective and practice in Nagesh, *et. al.*, (Eds) *Widowhood in India*, SDMET and J.S.S., Dharwad, 1988, p. 150.
26. Kareem, A.S.: Widowhood in Islam, *Ibid.*, p. 157.
27. Sanghave, V.: Position of widows in Jaina community, *Ibid.*, pp. 162-163.

28. Caton, A.R. and Merielli, E.: Home and Marriage in *The Key Progress: A Survey of the status and conditions of women in India*, Oxford University Press, London, 1930, p. 125.
29. Cormack, M.: *The Hindu Women*, Bureau of Publications, Teachers College Columbia, New York, 1953, p. 173.
30. Pandita, Ramabai: *The High Caste Hindu Women*, D.K. Publishers, Delhi, 1984 (C 1888), p. 95.
31. Gandhi. M.K.: *Women and Social injustice*, Navajivan publishing House, Ahmedabad, 1942, p. 103.
32. Akshaya. Kumar: in Gupta Sankarsen (Ed) *Indian Folklore-A short survey of their Social Status and Position*, Indian Publications, Calcutta, 1969, p. 198.
33. Vanamala: in Gupta Sankarsen, *Ibid.*, p. 198.
34. Das in Gupta Sankarsen, *Ibid.*, p. 233.
35. Ohio State University: Sibling Support and older widow's well-being. *Journal of Marriage and the Family*, Vol. 50, No. 1, 1988, p. 173.
36. Brubaker. T.H.: op. cit., pp. 94-95.
37. Leslie, G.R.: *The Family in Social Context*, Oxford University Press, New York, 1979, p. 614.
38. Saraswati, Baidyanath.: *The Kashivasi Widows*, ICSSR Project Report, New Delhi, 1983, p. 63.
39. Madan, T.N.: The structural implications of Marriage Among Kashmiri Brahmins: *Contribution to Indian Sociology*, NS. Vol. 9, 1975, p. 221.
40. Aradhya, B.M.M.: What it means to be a widow, Social Welfare, Vol. XXXIV, No. 9, 1987, p. 3.
41. Rane, A: Rehabilitation of widows: Problems and prospects a paper presented at the national seminar on widowhood in India organized Jointly by JSS and SDMET Ujire, p. 1.
42. Hanumanth, R. and Umamani. K.S.: Incidence of widowhood in Karnataka a paper presented at the National seminar on widowhood in India sponsored jointly by JSS and SDMET Ujire, p. 2.
43. Thekkamalai, S.S.: Problems and Adjustment of widows. A case study, a paper presented at the above seminar, p. 2.
44. Katti, A.P. and Nagesh H.V.: A Socio-economic study of widows; A report submitted to the Institute of Economic research, Dharwad, 1983, pp 43-44.
45. Gurmeet, *et. al.*, op. cit., p. 67.
46. Kamal Kumar: Deoral Before and After, *Social Welfare*, Vol. XXXIV, No. 9, 1987, p. 7.
47. Touba, J.R.: In Das. Mansing and Bardis, P.D. (Eds): *Family in Asia*, Vikas Publications, New Delhi, 1978, p. 233.

48. Kitchlu, T.N.: A Study of Socio-economic Conditions of Widows in Union Territory of Delhi, Report submitted to Delhi University, 1982, p. 5.
49. Banerjee, G.: *Hindu Law of Marriage and Stridhana*, Mittal Publications, Delhi, 1984, p. 202.
50. Silverman, P.R. : Widowhood and preventive Intervention in Zarit. S.H. (Ed.) Readings in Aging and Death-contemporary Perspectives Harper and Row Pub., New York, 1977, p. 175.
51. Smart, S.M. and Smart, L.S.: op. cit., pp. 412-413.
52. Eshleman, J.R.: *The Family*, Allyn and Bacon, Inc., Boston, 1974, p. 606.
53. Smart, S.M. and Smart, L.S.: op. cit., p. 413.
54. Kelphart, W.M.: *The Family Society and Individual*, Houghton Mifflin Co., Boston, 1981, p. 391.
55. Berardo, F.M.: "Survivorship and Social Isolation-The case of the Aged widower". *The Family Coordinator*, Vol. 19, No. 1, 1970, p. 11.
56. Phelps, H.A.: Contemporary Social Problems, Prentice-Hall Inc., New York, 1983, pp. 516-540.
57. Morgan, L.A. "Economic change at midlife widowhood-A longitudinal Analysis". *Journal of Marriage and the Family*, 1981, Vol. 43, No. 4, p. 899.
58. Radhadevi: Work Participation of widows in India-A census Analysis, a paper presented at the National Seminar on widowhood in India, op. cit., p. 1.
59. Farmer, M.: *The Family*, Longman Group Ltd., London. 1979, p. 919.
60. Berardo, F.M.: Social Adaptation to Widowhood among a Rural-Urban Aged Population Washington. *Agricultural experimentation bulletin*, College of Agriculture Washington State University, p. 4.
61. Nimkoff, M.F.: *The Family*, Houghton Mifflin Co., Boston, 1934, p. 425.
62. Glad, D.: Don't cry infront of your Friends in Zarit S.H. (Ed) *Readings in Aging and Death: Contemporary perspectives*, Harper & Row Pub., New York, 1977, p. 171.
63. Nimkoff, M.F., op. cit., p. 426.
64. Landis, P.H.: op. cit., p. 321.
65. Kelphart, W.M.: op. cit., p. 292.
66. Morgan, L.A.: op. cit., p. 899.
67. Bidarkoppa, G.S.: Position and Problems of Hindu Widow. *Journal of Karnataka University Social Sciences*, Vol. VII, 1971, p. 80.
68. Aradhya, B.M.: op. cit., p. 3.
69. Kitchlu, T.N.: op. cit., p. 7-9.
70. Singh, Gurmeet, *et. al.*, op. cit., pp. 68-69.
71. Baidyanath, S. op. cit., p. 51.

72. Bansal, V.: *Widows-Marauna*, Ph.D. Thesis ICSSR, New Delhi, 1979, p. 320.
73. Philiprice, F.: op. cit., p. 305.
74. *Ibid.*, p. 305.
75. Abrahams, R.B.: Mutual help for the widowed, *Journal of Social Work*, Vol. 17, No. 5, 1972, p. 59.
76. Christenson, H.T.: op. cit., p. 433.
77. Berardo op. cit., p. 14.
78. Truxual, and Merrill: *Marriage and the Family in American Culture*, Prentice-Hall Inc., New York, 1953, p. 502.
79. Kaur, S.: Social Adjustment of war widows. M.A. Dissertation Punjab University, 1974, p. 63.
80. Nye, F.I. and Berado F.M.: *The Family-Its Structure and Interaction*, The Macmillan Co., New York, 1973, pp. 617-619.
81. Kitchlu, T.N. op. cit., p. 5.
82. *Ibid.*, p. 5.
83. Rao, Nagamani: Widowhood. In Jessie. B. and Nayak. T. (Eds) *Indian Womanhood Then and Now*, Satprakashan Sanchar Kendra Indore, 1983, pp. 83-84.
84. Anderson, T.B.: Widowhood as a life Transition: Its impact on Kinship Ties. *Journal of Marriage and the Family*, Vol. 46, No. 1, 1984, p. 105.
85. Berardo, F.M.: Widowhood status in the United States perspective on a neglected aspect of the Family Life-Cycle, *The Family coordinator*, Vol. 17, No. 1, 1968, p. 191.
86. Harvey, C.D. and Bahar, H.M.: Widowhood Morale and Affiliation. Journal of Marriage and the Family, Vol. 36, No. 1, p. 104.
87. Nye, F.I. and Berardo, F.M.: op. cit., p. 617.
88. Hutchison, I.W.: The significance of Marital status for morale and life satisfaction among lower-Income elderly. *Journal of Marriage and the Family*, Vol. 32, No. 2, 1975, p. 190.
89. Greg, A.: op. cit., p. 757.
90. Lopata, H.Z.: Social relations of Black and White Widowed Women in Northern Metropolis is Hubers J (Ed) *Changing Women in changing Society*, The University of Chicago Press, Chicago, 1973, p. 247.
91. Philiprice, F. op. cit., p. 305.
92. Lopata, H.Z.: Widowhood in America in Peter. J. Stein *et. al.*, (Eds) *The family Functions, conflicts and symbols*, Addison Wesley Pub. Co., London, 1977, p. 326.
93. Bankoff, E.A. op. cit., p. 386.
94. Anderson, T.B.: op. cit., pp. 105-109.
95. Morgan, L.A.: Changes in Family Interaction Following widowhood. *Journal of Marriage and the Family*, Vol. 46, No. 2, 1984, p. 330.

96. Vinick, R.: Remarriage in old Age. *The Family Coordinator*. Vol. 27, No. 2, 1978, p. 360.
97. Lopaṭa, H.Z.: Contributions of extended Families to the support system of Metropolitan Area widows: Limitations of the Modified kin net work, *Journal of Marriage and the Family*, Vol. 40, No. 2, 1978, p. 362.
98. Lopata, H.Z.: The social Involvement of American widows. *American Behavioural Scientist*, Vol. 14, No. 1, 1970, pp. 44, 56.
99. Lopata H.Z.: op. cit., 1973, p. 247.
100. Lopata H.Z.: Widowhood, in a American City. Schenckman Publishing Co., Cambridge, 1973, pp. 265-266.
101. Kitchlu, T.N. op. cit., p. 14.
102. Lopata H.Z.: The Meaning of Friendship in widowhood in Troll *et. al.*, (Eds) *Looking Ahead*, Prentice-Hall Inc., New Jersey, 1977, pp. 96-104.
103. Glad, D.: op. cit., p. 171.
104. Aradhya, B.M.M. op. cit., p. 3.
105. Gurmeet, *et al.*, op. cit., pp. 69-70.
106. Kitchlu, T.N.: op. cit., p. 11.
107. Glad, D. op. cit., p. 171.
108. Bidarkoppa, G.S. op. cit., p. 80.
109. Saraswati, B. op. cit., p. 56.
110. Green, E.J. *Marriage and Family - A Basic Self Instruction*. McGraw Hill Book Co., New York, 1977, p. 150.
111. Berardo, F.M.: op. cit., p. 191.
112. Lopata H.Z.: op. cit., 1977, p. 328.
113. Srinivasan, P.: Problems of the Aged in India, Yojana, Vol. XXVI, No. 10, 1982, p. 9.
114. Greg, A.: op. cit., pp. 762-764.
115. Harvey, C.D. and Bahr, H.M. op. cit., p. 97.
116. Glad, D.: op. cit., p. 171.
117. Fritz, M.A.: op. cit., p. 425.
118. Duval, E.M.: op. cit., p. 470.
119. Lopata H.Z.: op. cit., 1973, pp. 241-248.
120. Bock, E.B. and Webber, I.L.: op. cit., p. 24.
121. Hurlock, E.B.: *Personality Development*, Tata McGraw Hill, New Delhi, 1970, p. 211.
122. Waller, W: op. cit., pp. 491-588.
123. Battee, R.N. and Lewis, M.I.: *Aging and Mental Health*, 2nd Edn., St. Louis Mosby, 1977, p. 298.
124. Jambagi, S.: *Life and Activities of Lingayat Widows*. M.A. Dissertation, Karnataka University, 1964, p. 65.
125. Marris, P.: *Widows and Their Families*, Routledge and Kegal Paul, London, 1958, p. 10.

126. Kaur, S.: op. cit., p. 64.
127. Peterson, A.J and Briley, M.L.: *Widows and Widowhood—A Creative approach to being alone*. Follett Publishing Co., Chicago, 1977, pp. 38, 45-48.
128. Barret. in Peterson. *et. al., Ibid.*, pp. 46-47.
129. Mathieu in Peterson *et. al., Ibid.*, p. 48.
130. *Ibid.*, p. 48.
131. Marris, P.: op. cit., p. 10.
132. Kelphart, W.M. op. cit., p. 392.
133. Toth, A. and Toth, S.: Group work with widows, *Social Work*, Vol. 25. No. 1 1980 pp. 64-65.
134. Lopata H.Z.: 1973 op. cit., p. 51.
135. Jambagi, S. op. cit., pp. 67-68.
136. Bidarkoppa, G.S. op. cit., p. 81.
137. Hutchison, op. cit., p. 228.
138. Lopata H.Z.: Loneliness. Forms and Components, *Social Problems*, 1969 pp. 248-253.
139. Essex, and Nam: Marital Status and loneliness among old women: The differential importance of close family & Friend. *Journal of Marriage and the Family*. Vol. 49, No. 1, 1987, pp. 93-106.
140. Durkheim, Emile: *Suicide: A study in sociology*. The Free Press, New York, 1951, p. 259.
141. Berardo F.M.: op. cit., pp. 11-25.
142. Sainsbary, P.: Suicide in London, Mousley Monograph, No. 1, Chapman & Hall, London, 1955, p. 81.
143. Harvey, C.D. and Bahir, H.M. op. cit., p. 98.
144. Nagesh H.V. and Katti, A.P. op. cit., p. 72.
145. Aradhya, B.M.M. op. cit., p. 12.
146. Bankoff, E.A.: op. cit., pp. 832-833.
147. Veroff, Douvan, and Kulka (quoted by Kohan, J.A.) in McGuigan, D.G. (Ed.) *Women's Lives - New Theory, Research and Policy*, Michigan Centre for continuing Education of Women, Michigan. pp. 305.
148. Borstein, P.E. *et. al.,*: The Depression of Widowhood after Thirteen months. *British Journal of Psychiatry*. Vol. 122, No. 4, pp. 561-566.
149. Das, Veena. in Sudhir Karkar (Ed) op. cit., p. 98.
150. Sinha B.B.: *Society in Tribal India*, B.R. Pub. Co., Delhi, 1982, p. 139.
151. Lopamudra, op. cit., p. 13.
152. Kitchlu, T.N. op. cit., p. 11.
153. Wolf, A.P.: Women, Widowhood and Fertility in pre-modern China, in Dupuquire *et. al.*, (Eds) *Marriage and Remarriage in population of the past*, Academic press, New York, 1981, p. 139.
154. Anshe, R.N.: *The Family-its Function and Destiny*, Harper and Brothers publication, New York, 1949, p. 130.

155. Wolf, A.P. op. cit., p. 139.
156. Peterson, and Briley: op. cit., p. 168.
157. Landis, P.H.: *Marking the most of Marriage*, Appelton-century crofts Inc., New York, 1955, pp. 605-606.
158. Gardner, Jane. F.: *Women in Roman Law & Society*, Groom Helm London, 1986, p. 51.
159. Dubey, B.R.: Widow-Remarriage in Madhya Pradesh, *Man in India*, Vol. 45, No. 1, 1965, p. 50.
160. Census of India - Mysore 1931, Vol. I, p. 46.
161. Census of India - Mysore 1911, Vol. I, p. 100.
162. Nair, P.T.: *Marriage and Dowry in India*, Minerva Associates, Calcutta, 1978, pp. 7-8.
163. Singh, T.R.: Widow Remarriage Among Brahimans. A sociological study. *The Eastern Anthropologist*, Vol. 22, No. 1, 1969, pp. 75-87.
164. Agarawal, S.N.: Remarriage Rates in some Delhi villages. *Medical Digest*, Vol. 30, No. 9, 1969, pp. 551-552.
165. Gazetteer of Punjab, 1904.
166. Dubey, B.R. op. cit., p. 50.
167. Bose, A.B.: Some characteristics of widows in Rural society *Man in India*, Vol. 46. Jan-March, 1966, p. 230.
168. Baron, O. *et. al.,: Mother Right in India*. OUP. Hyderabad. 1941. p. 55.
169. Mann, R.S.: *Social Structure, Social Change and Future trends*. Rawat Publications, Jaipur, 1979, pp. 52-79.
170. Baron, O. *et. al.*, op. cit., p. 55.
171. Das, V. op. cit., p. 99.
172. Baron, O. *et. al.*, op. cit., p. 55.
173. Srinivans, M.N., *Marriage and Family among the Kannada Castes of the Mysore State*. M.A. Dissertation. Bombay University, 1938 pp. 153-9.
174. Lopata, H.Z. op. cit., 1977, pp. 327-328.
175. Berardo, F.M.: op. cit., p. 14.
176. Duval, E.M. op. cit., p. 470.
177. Leslie, G.R.: *Marriage in a Changing World*. John Wiley and Sons, New York, 1971, p. 384.
178. Smart, M.S. and Smart, L.S. op. cit., pp. 214-216.
179. Vinick, R. op. cit., p. 360.
180. Truxual, A.G. and Merrill, F.E.: op. cit., p. 502.
181. Singh, G.: Restraints to widow remarriage Social change September, 1988, pp. 59-62.
182. Katti, A.P. and Nagesh, H.V.: *A Socio-Economic study of widows In Hubli City and Neighbouring Villages* (Unpublished) J.S.S. Institute. Vidyagiri, Dharwad, p. 106.
183. Narain, V.A.: *Social History of Modern India*. Meenakshi Prakashan. Meerat, 1972, pp. 72-73.

184. Nair, T.: The First Hindu Widow Remarriage, *Bhavans Journal*, Vol. 17, No. 1, 1970, p. 39.
185. Tattavabhushan, S.: *Social Reform in Bengal* - A side sketch Papygras, Calcutta, 1982, p. 125.
186. Editor: The First Widow Marriage. *Triveni*, October 1970, pp. 48-54.
187. Bhate, G.C.: *Permitting Widow Marriage*, Tatva Vivechaka Press, Bombay, 1907, pp. 1-16.
188. Bhim, R.: *Marriage of Hindu Widows* (2nd Edn) Indu Prakash Press, Bombay, 1869, p. 1.
189. Madhowadas, R.: Story of a widow Re-Marriage S.K. Khambata and Co., Bombay, 1890, p. 1.
190. Vasta, R.S.: The Remarriage and Rehabilitation of the Hindu widows in India 1856-1914. *Journal of Indian History*, Vol. 54, 1976, p. 719.
191. Agarawal, S.N.: Widow Marriage in some Rural Areas of Northern India *Demography*, Vol. 4, No. 1, 1967, p. 127.
192. Duberman, L.: op. cit., pp. 198-209.
193. Sudhir, C.: *Widow remarriage and Late Nineteenth Century Indian Literature*, (For Private circulation only), 1985, p.1.
194. Srinivas, M.N.: op. cit., pp. 152-154.
195. Editor: Legislation on Women. Social Welfare, Vol. XXIX, No. 11-12, 1983, p. 20.
196. Hate, C. A.: Hindu Women and Her Future. New Book Co. Ltd., Bombay.
197. Karnataka Government: Dari Deepa. Information Broadcast Department, 1985, pp. 116-165.
198. Karnataka Government: Dharwad District- Six Year's Progress. 1983-1989. Information Broadcast Dept., Bangalore, 1989, p. 6.
199. Dutt, N. *Origin and Growth of Caste in India*, Vol. I, Firma, Calcutta, 1968, p. 247.
200. *Ibid.*, p. 247.
201. *Ibid.*, p. 248.
202. Silverman, P.R.: *Widowhood* and Preventive Intervention in Zarit. H.S. (Ed) *Readings in Aging and Death-contemporary perspective*, Harper and Row Pub., New York, 1970, p. 175.
203. Abbe, Du. Bois.: *Hindus Manners, Customs and Ceremonies*, Beauchamp C I E Oxf. University Press, London, p. 350.
204. Ramayana VI, II, 39: VI 32.9.30.
205. Ramayana II 39.29.
206. Kapadia, K.M.: *Marriage and Family in India* (2nd Ed), Oxford University, London, 1958, p. 61.
207. Datt, N.K.: *Origin and Growth of caste in India*. Vol. I. Firma. Calcutta, 1968, p. 249.
208. Rugveda X, 102.11.

209. *Ibid.*, X, 40.2.
210. Sengupta, N: *Evolution of Hindu Marriage*, Popular Parkashan, Bombay, 1965, p. 140.
211. Rugveda I. 116.13; 117.24; VI 62.7; X.39.7; cf X 65,12.
212. Upadhyaya, B.S. *Women in Rugveda*, S. Chand and Co., New Delhi, 1974, pp. 108-109.
213. Kane. P.V.: *History of Dharmashastras*, Vol. II. Part. I. Bhandarkar Oriental Research Institute, Poona, 1930, pp. 618-619.
214. Sarkar, S.C.: Some aspects of the early social History of India, Humphery Milford, London, 1928, p. 82.
215. Santi parva. Vol. I, p. 489.
216. Ramayana IV. 208.
217. *Ibid.*, VI 110-20; IV 23.9.
218. *Ibid.*, VI 32.8; III 38.
219. Jayal, S.: *The Status of Women in the Epics*, Motilal Banarsidas, Delhi, 1966, p. 177.
220. Spencer, H.: Sociology. I. Harrison and Sons Ltd., London, 1934, p. 661.
221. Gray, R.E. and Gulliver, P.H.: *The Family Estate in Africa-studies in the Role of Property in Family Structure*, Routledge and Kegan Paul, London, 1964, pp. 21-22.
222. Mahabharat XIII, 55, 7.
223. Altekar, A.S. op. cit., p. 121.
224. Mahabharath XI 25.19.
225. Ramayana II 76.23.
226. Apastrambiya Gruhya Sutra. IV. 2.18.
227. Shankhayana Graha Sutra I,II, 5,2, I 121.
228. Horner, I.B.: *Women Under Primitive Buddhism*, Motilal Banarsidas, Varnasi, 1975, p. 61.
229. Horner, T.B. op. cit., p. 74.
230. *Ibid.*, p. 73.
231. P.T.S. (Ed.) Dhammapada with Commentary on verse 115. Oxford University Press, London, 1915, p. 150.
232. Manu IX 65.
233. Manu V. 157, 158, 160.
234. Vishnu XXV 17 p. 201.
235. Altekar. A.S.: op. cit., p. 156.
236. Alberuni : Ch LXIX as quoted by R.C. Datt, "*History of Civilization in Ancient India*" Vol. III. Vishal Publishers, Delhi, p. 481.
237. Veda Vyasa I 53.
238. Horner, I.B.: op. cit., p. 75.
239. Kane, P.V. op. cit., p. 587.
240. *Ibid.*, p. 593.

241. Manu IX 70.
242. Maine, H.S.: "Early History Institutions" John. Murray, London, 1914, p. 335.
243. Kane. P.V.: op. cit., p. 635.
244. Altekar, A.S. op. cit., pp. 126, 130.
245. Travernier, B.J.: *Travernier Travels in India,* Book III. Bangabasi. Office, Calcutta, 1905, p. 407.
246. Datta, K.K.: Socio-Cultural Background of Modern India. Meenakshi Prakashan, Meerut, 1972, pp. 112-124.
247. Vidyasagar, I.C.: Marriage of Hindu Widow, K.P. Bagchi and Co., Calcutta, 1976, p. 77.
248. Bhattacharya, K.: Institutes of Parasara. Ch. IV. Verse. 27. Asiatic Society of Bengal, Calcutta, 1887, p. 30.
249. Hindu Widow Marriage Act of 1856. in Derrett. J.D. Introduction to Modern Hindu Law, Oxford University Press, Bombay, 1963, pp. 619-622.
250. Kane, P.V. quoted op. cit., p. 706.
251. Brahaspati, in Max Muller Sacred Books of East, Vol. 33, pp. 377-78, Verscs 50-51 and 53.
252. Mitakshara on Yanjavalkya II 135, 136 see para. 39.
253. Kane, P.V. op. cit., pp. 708-709.
254. Vide Moniram V. Kerry ILR 71. A. p. 115.
255. Gour, H.: *The Hindu Code.* Law Publishers, Allahabad, 1971, p. 594.
256. Mitter Dwarikanath. *The position of women in Hindu Law,* D.K. Publishers Mitter Delhi, 1984, pp. 404-405.
257. Mitter, D.: op. cit., p. 414.
258. *Ibid.*, p. 418.
259. Mitter, D.: op. cit., pp. 380-388.
260. Derrett. J.D.: op. cit., pp. 619-622.
261. Gour, H. op. cit., pp. 777-937.
262. Gour, H. op. cit., pp. 958-1974 (i.e. 958-1974).
263. Desai, S.T.: *The Hindu Succession Act, 1956,* in Mulli "Principles of Hindu Law" N.M. Thripathi Private Ltd., Bombay, 1970, pp. 788-789.
264. Desai, S. op. cit., p. 822.
265. *Ibid.*, pp. 830-831.
266. Mitter Dwarikanath. op. cit., p. 432.
267. Hanumanthrayappa. P. and Umamani. K.S.: op. cit., p. 15.
268. Sinha, R.K. and Kanitkar, T.: "Marital dissolution in India" a paper presented at the same National Seminar, p. 1.
269. Rajaraman, T. and Gandhi, E.: Socio-economic and demorgraphic aspects of widowhood in Atnoor and Battagundu Blocks in Tamil Nadu, a paper presented at the same seminar, p. 7.

270. Kamat, A.R. The decline in death rate and its effects on the extent of widowhood, *Sociological Bulletin*, Vol. XII, 1963, p. 18.
271. Hanumanthrayappa *et. al.*, Op. cit., p. 15.
272. Agarwala, S.N.: *Indian Population Problem*, Tata McGraw-Hill, Bombay, 1972, p. 95.
273. Nye, F.I. and Berardo, F.M. op. cit., p. 591.
274. Bankoff, E.A.: op. cit., p. 827.
275. Thekkamalai, S.S.: op. cit., p. 138.
* *Anastasi. A. Psychological testing*, Macmillan Co., Newyork, pp. 428-436, 1961.
276. Merriam, *Webster Dictionary*, 1952, p. 609.
277. Rubin Richard, Frank D., Cyril M. (Eds) *Advance in Behavioural Therapy*, Academic Press, New York, 1969, p. 83.
278. Sinha, Durganand: Towards an Ecological Framework of Deprivation in Durganand Sinha, Tripathi, R.C. and Girishwar, Mishra (Eds) *Deprivation - Its Social roots and Psychological consequences*. Concept Publishers, New Delhi, 1982, p. 25.
279. Hunt, J.Mc.: The Psychological Basis for using pre-school enrichment as an Antidote for Cultural Deprivation. The Mirrill Palmer, *Quarterly of Behaviour and Development*, Vol. 10, No. 2, 1964, pp. 209-243.
280. Adams, A.A.: The Effects of Planned Background Experiences on Economically Disadvantaged kindergarten children (unpublished Doctoral thesis), Missicippi State Univ. 1971.
281. Gordon, E.A. : Review of Compensatory Education. *American Journal of Orthopsychiarty*, Vol. 35, No. 4, 1965, pp. 640-651.
282. Davis, R.E.: Social Deprivation and Cognitive Functioning in lower-class children. *Dissertation Abstracts International*, Vol. 29, (4-13). 1968, pp. 1505-1507.
283. Ojha, A.B.: The Myth of Non-Deprived in Agarwal A.G. (Ed.) *Poverty, Deprivation and Intelligence*, Criterion Publications, New Delhi, 1978, p. 119.
284. *Ibid.*, p. 123.
285. Tripathi, L.R. and Misra, G.: Cognitive activities as a function of Prolonged Deprivation. *Psychological Studies*, Vol. 20, No. 1, 1975, pp. 54-61.
286. Wight, B.W. *et. al.*,: Cultural deprivation, operational definition in terms of language development. *Ame. Jr. of Orthopsychiatry*, 1970, pp. 77-86.
287. Monks F.J. *et. al.*,: *Determinants of Behavioural Development*, Academic Press, New York, 1972, pp. 336-350.
288. Tripathi, L.R. and Misra, G. (1975) op. cit., pp. 54-61.
289. *Ibid.*, pp. 54-61.
290. Nurcombe, B.: Deprivation: An Essay in Definition with Special consideration of the Australian Aboriginals, *Medical Journal of Australia*, Vol. 2, No. 1, 1970, pp. 82-92.

291. Misra, G. and Tripathi, L.B.: Development of an objective Measure of prolonged Deprivation in Agarwala, K.G. (Ed.), op. cit., p. 129.
292. Tripathi, L.B. and Misra, G.: "Some cognitive process as a Functions of Prolonged Deprivation", *Indian Journal of Psychology*, Vol. 59, No. 2, 1976, pp. 129-143.
293. Misra, G.: Motivational Structure and Prolonged Deprivation, *The Indian Journal of Social Work*, Vol. XLIII, No. 1, 1982, p. 24.
294. Misra, G. and Tripathi, L.B.: Prolonged Deprivation and status perception, *The Indian Journal of Social Work*, Vol. XXXIX, No. 2, 1978, pp. 115-116.
295. Psychological Abstracts Index I Vol. 66, 1981, p. 306.
296. Anandalakshmy, A.: "There's a Method to the Measurement" in Durganand Sinha (Ed.) op. cit., p. 37.
297. *Ibid.*, p. 38.
298. Valentine C.A.: The "Culture of poverty" its scientific significance and its implication for action in E.W. Leacock (Ed) *The Culture of Poverty: A Critique*, Simon and Schuster, New York, 1971.
299. Pealtie, L.R.: The structure parameters of emerging life-styles in Venezuela in Leacock (Ed.) *Ibid.*
300. Mussen, P.H., Conger J.J. and Kagan, J.: *Child Development and Personality*, 3rd Ed. Harper and Row, New York, 1969, pp. 357-402.
301. Gordon, E.A. op. cit., pp. 640-651.
302. Whiteman, M. and Deutsch, M.: Social Disadvantage as Related to Intellective and Language Development. In Detusch, M *et. al.*, (Ed) *Social-Class, Race and Psychological Development*, Holt Rinchart, New York, 1968, pp. 86-114.
303. Tannenbaum, A.J.: Some non-intellectual concomitants of Social deprivation. *Israil Annals of Psychiatry and Related Disciplines*, Vol. 7, No. 1, 1969, pp. 9-30.
304. David, Beres in Sparlock. J. Social Deprivation in Childhood and Character Formation. *Journal of the American Psycho Analytic Association*. Vol. 18, 1970, pp. 621-630.
305. Hurlock, E.B.: *Personality Development*, Tata McGraw-Hill, New Delhi, 1976, p. 235.
306. *Ibid.*, p. 235.
307. *Ibid.*, p. 236.
308. *Ibid.*, p. 235.
309. *Ibid.*, p. 236.
310. Geschwender, J.A.: Status inconsistency, Social isolation and individual unrest, *Social Force*, Vol. 46, No. 3, 1968, pp. 477-483.
311. Hurlock, op. cit., p. 235.
312. *Ibid.*, p. 209.
313. *Ibid.*, p. 210.

314. Goode, W.J.: The Theoretical Importance of Love, *Ame. Sociological Review*, Vol. 24, No. 1, 1959, p. 38.
315. Jersild, A.T.: *The Psychology of Adolescence*, 2nd Ed. Macmillan Co., New York, 1963, pp. 177-188.
316. Hurlow, H.F.: The Nature of Love, *American Psychologist*, Vol. 13, No. 4, 1958, pp. 673-685.
317. *Ibid.*, p. 211.
318. Hurlock, op. cit., p. 212.
319. Alexander, I.E. and Adlerstein, A.M.: Affective responses of the concept of death in population of children and early adolescents. *Journal of General Psychology*, Vol. 93, No. 2, 1958, pp. 167-177.
320. Chaubey, N.P., Pandey L.P. and Patni, Rajni: *Deprivation and Human Personality, Current Theory and Research*. IASS, Allahabad, 1986, p. 471.
321. Das. J.P.: Cultural Deprivation and Cognitive competence, *International Review of Research in Mental Retardation*, Vol. 6, No. 2, 1973, pp. 1-53.
322. Wight, D.W., Gloniger, M.F. and Kneene, P.J.: Cultural Deprivation, operation definition in terms of language development. *Ame. Jr. of Orthopsychiatry*, Vol. 6, No. 3, 1972, pp. 326-337.
323. Deutsch, M.: The disadvantaged children and the learning process in Harry A. Passow (Ed.) *Education in Depressed Areas*, Teachers College Press, Columbia Univ., New York, p. 78.
324. Himes, J.S.: Some work-Related cultural deprivations of lower-class Negro youths, *Journal of Marriage and the Family*, Vol. 26, No. 4, 1964, pp. 447-449.
325. Hunt, J. Mc. V., op. cit., pp. 209-243.
326. Samant, C.R.: Construction of the scale of cultural, Deprivation and its application. Unpublished Masters' Thesis, Utkal University.

# TWO

# The Setting

## PART - I

### 2.1 Dharwad

Dharwad is an important city in the north western region of the present Karnataka State and is the headquarter of Dharwad district. The city is spread over a total area of 20.76 square kilometres. It is located at 15.20° to 15.28° North Latitude and from 75.0° to 75.9° East Longitude. The city is situated on the eastern slopes of the ridge of the Western Ghats, on a chain of hillocks at a height of 2,580 feet above the mean sea level. National Highway No. 4 which runs north-west to south-east connects this city with important commercial cities such as of Pune and Mumbai in the north-west and Bangalore in the South-east. Bombay is 724 Kms away towards the north. Bangalore (the state capital) is 427 kms away from the city to the south, and the north-eastern coastal town Karwar is 110 kms away from Dharwad district is spread over an area of 13783 Sq.cm. The district is divided into 17 taluks for administrative purposes.

Dharwad is situated in the transitional belt between the Malenad region (hilly area) and a Maidan area (plain area), hence it is described as a Semi-Malenad region. A daily mean maximum temperature of Dharwad is 37.2°C and a daily mean minimum temperature is 28.8°C. It is recorded that Dharwad experiences a maximum temperature of 36.05°C in the month of April and a minimum temperature of 12.16°C in the month of December. There is a gradual rise in the temperature of this area, between Jan and April. Dharwad city receives an average rainfall of 32.8" and

Dharwad district receives an average rainfall of 27.23", which is lesser than that of Dharwad city alone. The maximum rainfall is from the South west monsoon in the months of June and July. The general wind direction is from the east to west and from west to east with a maximum velocity of 10 miles per hour in the month of July[1]. The climate of the city is pleasant, moderate and salubrious and hence is often described as "Chhota Mahabaleshwar". It is also called a hill station, since it is built on a range of several hills. The surroundings of the city have an excellent, scenic look.

The soil found around Dharwad is of mixed characteristics. On the eastern and northern side Yeribhumi i.e. black soil, is abundant, where *jawar*, wheat and cotton are grown. On the other hand in the southern and western side, the soil is medium red, murrum and mixed which is suitable for paddy crops. This part is more influenced by the wet environment of Malenad region. The district is predominantly agrarian. The major crops grown are *jawar*, paddy along with cotton, chillies, wheat and oil seeds. The staple food of the people in Dharwad district is *jawar*, wheat and paddy.

The rural Dharwad is typical of any village in the state. Most of the houses have mud walls with traditional tiled roofs. The affluent farming community has brick with concrete roof. About 1,173 villages are electrified.

Hubli-Dharwad is the second largest city in Karnataka. Though both the cities are considered a single urban community for administrative purposes, they have retained their own distinct characteristics in the fields of culture and function. The district is culturally rich, specially in folklore. Infact folklore is a way of life for an average ruralite in the district. Dharwad is a well-known educational, cultural and administrative centre whereas Hubli is an industrial and commercial centre and has also recently emerged as an important educational centre. Dharwad being the central district is well connected with its neighbours, Bijapur and Belgaum in the North, Shimoga in the South, Raichur and Bellary in the East and North Canara in the West. This helps for better communication and business. The population of Dharwad was just 27,136 and 27,191 in the years of 1872 and 1881 respectively. While Dharwad district has the population of 29,45,487 according to 1891 Municipal Annual reports, the population of the town was

32,672. During that decade, some of the suburbs of Dharwad which were outside the Municipal limits were included. During the last 11 decades i.e. from 1872 to 1981, the population of Dharwad is continuously increasing, as can be seen from the Table 2.1.

**TABLE - 2.1**
**POPULATION AND PERCENTAGE VARIATION FOR DHARWAD (1872-1981)**

| *Year* | *Total Population* | *Variation* | *Percent Variation* |
|---|---|---|---|
| 1872* | 27,136 | — | — |
| 1881* | 27,191 | + 55 | + 0.2 |
| 1891** | 32,672 | + 5,481 | +20.1 |
| 1901 | 21,230 | –11,442 | –35.0 |
| 1911 | 29,591 | + 8,361 | +39.3 |
| 1921 | 34,220 | + 4,629 | +15.6 |
| 1931 | 40,904 | + 6,684 | +19.5 |
| 1941 | 47,992 | + 7,088 | –17.3 |
| 1951 | 66,571 | +18,579 | +38.7 |
| 1961 | 77,163 | +10,592 | +15.9 |
| 1971*** | 114,216 | +37,053 | +48.0 |
| 1981 | 174,101 | +59,885 | +52.4 |

*Source:* Census Handbook, Dharwad District - 1971 and 1981 Part B Primary Census Abstract.

* Census returns quoted in Gazetteer of Bombay Presidency - 1884 Vol, XXII

** Municipal Annual Report, quoted by MF Karennavar. " A Geographical Analysis of Hubli-Dharwad Region" Unpublished Ph.D. Thesis submitted to Karnataka University, Dharwad - 1967.

*** Excluding the population of surrounding villages like Yettingudda, Kelgeri, Navalur, Tadsinkoppa, Gamangatti, and Amargol which are included in the Ward-wise population figure of Hubli-Dharwad Municipal Corporation.

Note: (i) Population figures for the year 1872, 1881 and 1891 included the population of suburbs of Dharwad

(ii) Populations figures for the year 1901, 1911, 1921 and 1931 has not taken account of the suburbs of Dharwad town which were outside the Municipal limit at the respective years.

(iii) Population figures for certain areas like Athikol, Hosyellapur, Saidupur and Saptapur which are contiguous to Dharwad have not been included in Dharwad town by 1951 and 1961 census.

During the decade 1901-1911 and 1941-1951 the increase in the percentage of population was mainly because of the inclusion of suburban residents in the population of Dharwad. During earlier decades i.e. 1911-21, 1921-31 and 1931-41, the population varied from 15.6 per cent to 19.5 per cent, because the suburban residents were not included. During the decade 1941-1951 there was an increase in the population of Dharwad on account of new extensions which had sprung up around the town. Several such extension areas have come up, because government and private servants prefer to keep their families here for their children's education and also to spend their retired life in Dharwad. This place is therefore, quite often, called "Pensioner's Paradise". The town is the seat of two Universities viz the Karnataka University and the Agricultural University. Besides there are many schools and colleges too.

The population percentage during 1951-61 has come down to 15.9 per cent because of the non-inclusion of the residents of certain suburban areas which were contiguous to Dharwad town by 1951 and 1961 census. The percentage increase in the population for the decade 1961-71 was highest among all the earlier decades. This could have been due to the inclusion of a number of villages around Dharwad city in the corporation area. Another reason could be the migration of people from the surrounding rural area to the urban centre, lured by jobs, education and other amenities that were available in the city.

Table 2.2 gives the sex-wise population distribution and sex-ratio of Dharwad city from 1901 to 1981. In 1901 for 1000 males there were 929 females, whereas during 1981 there were 891 females per 1000 males. The decrease in the sex ratio could perhaps be due to the large number of unmarried male students coming to Dharwad for education and employment.

During the last three decades, the population of Dharwad is increasing on account of its salubrious climate, cultural and intellectual atmosphere and educational institutions. It being the district headquarter, a number of government and semi-government offices have come up. Most government servants, when transferred to Dharwad, prefer to settle down in this place.

Table 2.3 shows the distribution of population by religion in

Karnataka and in Dharwad district. Hindus are more in number in both the areas. Buddhists are lesser in number than Jains.

**TABLE - 2.2**
**DISTRIBUTION OF POPULATION IN DHARWAD CITY BY SEX AND NUMBER OF FEMALES PER 1000 MALES (1901 - 1981)**

| *Year* | *Total Population* | *Males* | *Females* | *Number of Females per 1000 Males* |
|---|---|---|---|---|
| 1901 | 21,230 | 11,002 | 10,228 | 929 |
| 1911 | 29,591 | 15,100 | 14,491 | 959 |
| 1921 | 34,220 | 17,966 | 16,254 | 904 |
| 1931 | 40,904 | 21,556 | 19,348 | 897 |
| 1941 | 47,992 | 24,948 | 23,044 | 923 |
| 1951 | 66,571 | 34,887 | 31,684 | 908 |
| 1961 | 77,163 | 41,077 | 36,086 | 878 |
| 1971 | 1,14,216 | 61,588 | 52,628 | 854 |
| 1981 | 1,74,101 | 92,065 | 82,036 | 891 |

*Source*: Census Handbook - Dharwad District - 1971 and 1981 Part-B, Primary Census Abstract

**TABLE - 2.3**
**STATE AND DISTRICT WISE DISTRIBUTION OF POPULATION BY RELIGION 1981**

| | *Hindus* | *Muslims* | *Christians* | *Jains* | *Buddhists* |
|---|---|---|---|---|---|
| Karnataka | 3,18,52,029 (85.8) | 41,63,691 (11.2) | 7,73,500 (2.1) | 2,84,508 (0.8) | 42,251 (0.1) |
| Dharwad District | 24,17,633 (82.1) | 4,66,617 (15.8) | 28,096 (0.9) | 30,692 (1.0) | 167 (0.005) |

*Source*: As in Table 2.2.

Table 2.4 gives the details regarding caste composition of Karnataka, Dharwad district and Dharwad city. Information about Karnataka and Dharwad collected from the Karnataka Backward Class Commission Report and the information about Dharwad city collected by Demographic Research Centre, Institute of Economic Research, Dharwad, since caste plays an important role in the social system.

**TABLE -2.4**
**CASTE-WISE POPULATION OF KARNATAKA STATE, DHARWAD DISTRICT AND DHARWAD TOWN**

| | *Population* | | |
|---|---|---|---|
| *Caste* | *Karnataka State* | *Dharwad Dist.* | *Dharwad City* |
| Brahmins | 12,69,455 (4.00) | 75,653 (3.00) | 25,000 (20.00) |
| Lingayat | 43,92,699 (15.00) | 7,23,118 (28.00) | 26,250 (21.00) |
| High Caste Hindus | 73,07,613 (24.00) | 1,42,027 (6.00) | 2,500 (2.0) |
| Low Caste Hindus | 92,43,205 (31.00) | 10,86,450 (43.00) | 26,250 (21.00) |
| Harijans (SC) | 39,43,205 (13.00) | 1,33,836 (5.00) | 12,500 (10.00) |
| Muslims | 31,88,640 (11.00) | 3,60,262 (14.00) | 27,500 (22.00) |
| Christians | 6,27,861 (2.0) | 27,742 (1.0) | 5,000 (4.0) |
| Total | 3,00,08,050 (100.00) | 25,44,088 (100.00) | 1,25,000 (100.00) |

Figures in the Brackets show Percentage

(i) Population figures are taken from 'Karnataka Backward class Commission Report' chairman I.G. Havanur, Vol II pp. 6-200, 1975. The commission adopted the 1972 population estimating it from the 1971 consolidated census population.

(ii) Population figures for Dharwad city taken from Demographic Research Centre, Institute of Economic Research, Dharwad.

Dharwad has been, for many years, one of the important educational centres of Karnataka State. Table 2.5 gives the percentage of literacy of Dharwad city and district. In all the three decades the percentage of literacy is higher in Dharwad city than in the district. During 1951 the literacy rate of Dharwad city was 44.90 per cent whereas it rose to 59.79 per cent in 1981 which was actually double the all India literacy rate (29.46 per cent in 1981). Among all the eleven cities in the state, Mangalore (70.18%) stands first in terms of percentage of literacy, Hubli-Dharwad city occupies 8th rank. However, when we compare the literacy rate of only Dharwad city with other cities, it takes the 6th rank, followed by Belgaum (65.81%) and Kolar (65.00%).

### TABLE - 2.5
### LITERACY RATE OF DHARWAD CITY AND DHARWAD DISTRICT

| *Years* | *Percentage of Literacy* | |
|---|---|---|
| | *Dharwad city* | *Dharwad District* |
| 1951 | 44.90 | 25.99 |
| 1961 | 54.30 | 33.35 |
| 1971 | 59.62* | 38.51 |
| 1981 | 59.79 | 42.16 |

*Source*: Census of India, 1961, 1971 and 1981

* Excluding the literacy rate of people living in surrounding villages like Yettingudda, Kelgeri, Navalur, Tadsinkoppa, Gamangatti and Amargol, which are included in ward-wise figures of Hubli-Dharwad.

### TABLE 2.6

**(A) PER CENTAGE DISTRIBUTION OF POPULATION IN DHARWAD CITY BY AGE (1981)** **(B) INCIDENCE OF WIDOW/ER HOOD PER 1000 POPULATION IN DHARWAD CITY (1981)**

| *Age* | *Male* | *Female* | *Total* | *Widowers* | *Widows* | *Total* |
|---|---|---|---|---|---|---|
| 0-9 | 26.35 | 26.70 | 26.56 | — | — | — |
| 10-14 | 13.50 | 14.00 | 13.76 | 0.02 | 0.05 | 0.03 |
| 15-19 | 10.48 | 9.76 | 10.12 | 0.04 | 0.24 | 0.14 |
| 20-24 | 9.64 | 9.02 | 9.33 | 0.12 | 1.13 | 0.63 |
| 25-29 | 7.52 | 7.75 | 7.66 | 0.35 | 2.63 | 1.49 |
| 30-34 | 5.98 | 6.05 | 6.02 | 0.76 | 5.51 | 3.14 |
| 35-39 | 5.38 | 5.43 | 5.41 | 1.22 | 8.07 | 4.65 |
| 40-44 | 4.95 | 4.60 | 4.79 | 2.67 | 17.47 | 10.07 |
| 45-49 | 4.30 | 3.96 | 4.13 | 4.03 | 24.53 | 14.28 |
| 50-54 | 3.72 | 3.76 | 3.74 | 7.19 | 39.88 | 23.54 |
| 55-59 | 2.38 | 2.08 | 2.23 | 8.98 | 48.88 | 28.93 |
| 60-64 | 2.47 | 2.79 | 2.63 | 14.15 | 68.18 | 41.17 |
| 65-69 | 1.24 | 1.39 | 1.31 | 18.10 | 74.53 | 46.32 |
| 70+ | 2.00 | 2.62 | 2.31 | 1.0 | 10.70 | 5.85 |
| Total | 100.00 | 100.00 | 100.00 | 100.00 | 100.00 | |

*Source*: Census of India 1981. Series -9 Karnataka part IV-A Social and Cultural Tables.
Computed from the district level age and marital status distribution tables.

The percentage distribution of population of Dharwad city by sex and age has been given in Table 2.6(A) About 40.32 per cent of the total population fall in the age group of 0-14 years, while about 53.38 per cent of the population come in the age group of 15-59 years. In the latter age groups the remaining 6.25 per cent of the population fall in 60+ age group. In the 15-59 years age group, female population is less than male population while in other age groups, opposite holds good.

The percentage distribution of widowers and widows does not show any significant variation as is seen from Table 2.6(B) But, when we consider the incidence of widow/er hood per 1000 population by age, the true dimensions of the incidence of widow/er hood can be discerned from Table 2.6(B) It is seen that the number of widows being 1.13 per 1000 females is significantly higher at age of 20-24 compared to the corresponding number among males being 0.12. It is seen that the number of widows per 1000 population, in each age group, progressively increases, reaching a peak of 88.63 per cent at the older age of 70+, while the number of widowers remain quite modest being 0.7 per 1000 males up to age 30-34. Of course then there is progressive rise reaching a peak of 25 per 1000 males at the older age of 70+. By and large it is seen that the number of widows per 1000 population in each age group is much higher than the corresponding number for males.

**Social Reform Activities in Dharwad**

Like in the other parts of India, some intellectuals and social reformers tried to give a new definition to traditional Indian values here, so as to defend traditional culture against unfavourable comparison with the west.

The question of widow remarriage and the prohibition of infant marriage enjoyed the attention of both British as well as native Indians. In 1837, the principal Sadar Ameen (Native Judge) of Dharwad opined that the government ought to take positive steps in making it possible for widows, especially virgin widows, to remarry[2]. He observed that widow remarriage was a justifiable act and a logical measure to be taken after the prohibition of the sati system.

He strongly condemned the system of infant marriages which contributed to a large number of child widows. In this context the judge said: "I may venture to say while female infants are permitted to marry, the chances are that scarcely one half or one-third of the males survive to the period of the consummation of such marriages and consequently the number of females destined to perpetual widowhood and the immoral and shameful results are immensely increased"[3].

He further said, "Though a great portion of the higher castes of Hindus may now consider such a measure an innovation on them by gone practices that they may consequently oppose and be very unwilling to express their approbation in the first instance; Yet I have reason to think that several sensible individuals upwardly approve of the measure, but either from shame to appear singular or from fear of persecution, withold the expression of their real sentiments"[4].

The pioneer opinion expressed by the native judge, in fact preceded such similar views which were to become popular in Bengal many years later.

After some years B.M. Malabari, a social reformer of Bombay, had brought the issue to the forefront. The Government again sought the views of yet another native judge of Dharwad for a second time. This Native Judge opined: "It is true that infant marriages have already ruined Indian society to a very great extent and unless put a stop to will do more harm"[5].

The Judge summed up the prevailing sentiments thus: "They are fully aware of the cruelty and hardships of enforced widowhood, and yet they have not the courage of openly declaring their private wishes"[6].

Knowing that a Native Judge was sympathetic to social reform, many native gentlemen from different parts of the country like Pandurang Narayan of Navalgund and Pandit Keshav Vaidya of Bombay discussed this view with him[7].

They implored him to take up the issue and make it more popular and widely known over the District so as to gain more supporters to the cause of social reform and also thus create a favourable climate among the people for reform. Even the social reformer, B.M. Malabari himself wrote to the judge, asking for support and encouragement for enacting a legislation on widow remarriage. The judge also kept himself in touch with the reformist movement in the Madras Presidency. He obtained the article published in Journals and newspapers of Madras to keep abreast of the reform activities.

Many other residents of Dharwad, during the later decades of the nineteenth century, also took a keen interest in reformist ideas. An Assistant Master in the local Kanarese School wrote an article upholding the idea of widow remarriage in 1884[8]. However, Venkat Range Katti, the Principal of Men's Training college at Dharwad, wrote book entitled *Vidhava Vadhava Vapan Anachar* in Marathi (or *Vidhava Mundana Anchar* in Kannada) that had received wide publicity. In the preface of this book, Katti systematically argued that no genuine Smriti ever entertains the idea of shaving of widow's head and their disfigurement. He believed that the custom of tonsure had been followed by Hindu society under the influence of Buddhism where the female monks shaved their heads, wore red clothes and lived an ascetic life. He strengthened his argument by citing evidences from several ancient Hindu texts to prove that disfigurement of widows was only a later development. For example, Parashara and other authorities have ruled that a woman's head should never be shared for any reason whatever. On account of a Prayaschita or atonement for an offence, her hair's end to the length of two fingers cut off. The tonsuring of widows is not a general custom in this country. It is unknown in some parts of the Deccan and in northen India as well as in Malayala.

In fact, Katti offered a prize of Rs 500 in 1889 to any one who proved that tonsure of widows was justified and had the sanction of the Hindu laws and tenets. In this context he said "an appeal is made to our present reformers and men of patriotic feelings to gird up their loins to put down this abominable and unauthorized custom of recent-origin as early as possible"[9].

Akkadas Ganapati Hegde, a reformer, launched a movement for remarriage of widows among the Havyaka section of Brahmanas, which has had some success.

Thus, various enlightened men of Dharwad tried to take up the issues having social relevance, especially questions regarding infant marriage, polygamy, widow remarriage, etc., to create a favourable public opinion to bring about reformation in Hindu society.

Some newspapers of Dharwad also supported this movement. The *Karnatak Wartika* in 1879 gave credit to the British for attempting to reform Hindu society and welcomed their interference in the customs and traditions of the people[10]. The *Karnataka Patra* also carried an article pointing out that the rationality to be found among the English would be of benefit to India[11].

A bold step was taken by various, enlightened, reformist groups of Dharwad, about 150 years ago to bring to an end the evils of widowhood by encouraging the British Government to enact striking legislation on prohibiting infant marriages and encouraging widow marriage in India[12].

## PART- II
## THE SAMPLE

### Profile of The Widows

This chapter specifically focuses upon the background factors pertaining to Hindu Widows. The findings pertaining to their personal characteristics and family background are presented here*. This chapter provides not only a "Profile" of the Hindu Widow, but also an insight into the background factors that may be found relevant in the analysis of their deprivation, attitudes and dispositions.

The background factors are classified under two broad headings.

(a) Personal characteristics.
(b) Family background.

The data regarding personal characteristics of the respondents include:

1. Demographic characteristics
2. Socio-economic characteristics
3. Accommodation and living arrangements
4. Type of employment and reactions
5. Marital life and reactions

The data pertaining to Family background are discussed in the next chapter.

## 2.2 Demographic Characteristics

The personal background factors are examined in the following analysis. This helps us in understanding 'who' these widows are and 'how' they can be identified in terms of a definite set of personal characteristics.

### Age

We may first consider the factor of age. The particulars regarding the age of the respondents at different stages of life are presented in Table 2.7.

**TABLE - 2.7**
**DISTRIBUTION OF WIDOWS BY AGE AT PRESENT, AT MARRIAGE, AND AT WIDOWHOOD**

*Age at Present*

| | *No.* | *Mean* | *SD* |
|---|---|---|---|
| Urban | 150 | 55.89 | 14.09 |
| Rural | 150 | 50.40 | 13.01 |
| 't' value | | | 3.55** |

*Age at Marriage*

| | *No.* | *Mean* | *SD* |
|---|---|---|---|
| Urban | 150 | 13.34 | 5.09 |
| Rural | 150 | 10.34 | 3.98 |
| 't' value | | | 5.00** |

*Age at Widowhood*

| | *No.* | *Mean* | *SD* |
|---|---|---|---|
| Urban | 150 | 41.50 | 13.41 |
| Rural | 150 | 38.11 | 11.34 |
| 't' value | | | 2.36* |

Note: * Significant at 5 per cent level.
** Significant at 1 per cent level.

It may be observed from the table that the mean age, at present, of the urban respondents is 55 (55.89) whereas that of the rural respondents is 50 (50.40). The statistical results show that there is a significant difference between the mean age at marriage at 1 per cent level. The mean age at marriage of the respondents in the urban area is 13 (13.34) as against 10 (10.34) in rural areas.

However, the difference in mean age at marriage between rural and urban widows is found to be significant at 1 per cent level.

Further, the age at widowhood of the urban respondents is 41 (41.50) while that of rural respondents is 38 (38.11). The statistical test also established the significant (at 5 per cent) result between the mean age at widowhood.

For the purpose of further analysis, the respondents are classified into three groups with the class interval of 30 years, as such: less than 30 years, 31-60 years and over 60 years, According to this classification, the data shows that 10 (10.0) per cent of the respondents are below 30; 63 (63.0) per cent are of the ages ranging between 30-60 years, and nearly 27 (27.0) per cent of the respondents are over 60 years of age.

**Duration of Married life, Widowhood and Age difference between the spouses.**

The particulars regarding the duration of married life, widowhood and age difference between the spouses is given in Table 2.8.

**TABLE - 2.8**
**DISTRIBUTION OF WIDOWS BY DURATION OF MARRIED LIFE, DURATION OF WIDOWHOOD AND AGE DIFFERENCE BETWEEN SPOUSES**

*Duration of Married life*

| | *No.* | *Mean* | *SD* |
|---|---|---|---|
| Urban | 150 | 28.39 | 14.4 |
| Rural | 150 | 27.01 | 12.5 |
| 't' value | | | 0.89NS |

*Duration of Widowhood*

| | *No.* | *Mean* | *SD* |
|---|---|---|---|
| Urban | 150 | 12.65 | 6.6 |
| Rural | 150 | 14.20 | 10.6 |
| 't' value | | | 1.49NS |

*Age Difference Between Spouses*

| | *No.* | *Mean* | *SD* |
|---|---|---|---|
| Urban | 150 | 11.25 | 4.3 |
| Rural | 150 | 9.87 | 5.4 |
| 't' value | | | 2.44* |

From the data presented in Table 2.8, we find that the mean duration of married life of urban respondents is 28.39 whereas that of rural respondents is 27.01.

The mean duration of widowhood life of urban and rural respondents is 12.65 and 14.20 respectively.

The mean age difference between the spouses of urban respondents is 9.87 years while that of rural respondents is 11.25 years.

**Place of Origin**

With regard to the respondents' place of origin, the data reveal that a majority of the respondents belonged to the urban and rural areas of Dharwad District, and Taluk, itself while the remaining came from adjacent and other districts. The particulars regarding the respondents' place of origin are presented in Table 2.9.

**TABLE - 2.9**
**DISTRIBUTION OF WIDOWS BY PLACE OF ORIGIN**

| *Place or Origin* | *Urban Per cent* | *Rural Per cent* | *Total Per cent* |
|---|---|---|---|
| Same District | 30.67 | 13.33 | 22.00 |
| Same Taluk | 13.33 | 40.00 | 26.67 |
| Adjacent Districts | 20.00 | 5.33 | 12.67 |
| Adjacent Taluks | 13.33 | 29.34 | 21.33 |
| Other Districts | 6.67 | 2.00 | 4.33 |
| Other Taluks | 14.00 | 10.00 | 12.00 |
| Neighbouring States | 2.00 | - | 1.00 |
| Total | 100.00 | 100.00 | 100.00 |

The data given in the above table reveals that 30.67 per cent of urban respondents come from the same district whereas 40 per cent of the rural respondents come from the same taluk. And about 20 per cent of the urban respondents come from adjacent districts while 29.34 per cent of the rural respondents come from adjacent taluks. Nearly 6 (6.67) per cent of urban respondents come from other districts and in rural area 10 per cent of them come from other taluks. Only about 2 per cent of the urban respondents come from neighbouring states like Maharashtra and Goa.

**Mother Tongue**

In accordance with the findings regarding the place of origin of the respondents, the data with regard to the mother tongue indicates that respondents whose mother tongue is Kannada represent the single largest group in the sample. Table 2.10 represents the distribution of the widows according to their mother tongue.

**TABLE - 2.10**
**DISTRIBUTION OF WIDOWS BY MOTHER TONGUE.**

| *Mother Tongue* | *Urban Per cent* | *Rural Per cent* | *Total Per cent* |
|---|---|---|---|
| Kannada | 86.67 | 93.33 | 90.00 |
| Marathi | 8.00 | 6.67 | 7.33 |
| Konkani | 5.33 | - | 2.67 |
| Total | 100.00 | 100.00 | 100.00 |

The data in Table 2.10 indicates that the respondents with regional language Kannada constitute 86.67 per cent in urban area and 93.33 per cent in rural areas. The Marathi language is the mother tongue of about 8.33 per cent in urban area and 6.67 per cent in rural areas. The remaining 5.33 per cent of the respondents in the urban area come from other linguistic groups such as Konkani.

**2.3 Socio-economic Characteristics**

The socio-economic background of the widows. Given here are the findings pertaining to the respondents' caste affiliation, educational level, occupational status, income, type of family, family size and married life and so forth are presented.

*Caste*

The respondents professing the Hindu religion belong to diverse castes and sub-castes. It is difficult to arrange them in a neat hierarchy. This categorization is made, taking into consideration the position of various castes in relation to the existing caste structure. Generally, for the classification of castes, the accepted criteria are the ritual status of the castes, food habits and the type of occupation, traditionally associated with them. Accordingly, the classification of castes is made into three categories. These being 'high' 'intermediate' and 'low' for the purpose of presentation and analysis of the data. The high castes include Brahmin, Vishwakarma, Gowda Sarsvath and Lingayaths which have relatively high ritual status, vegetarian food habits and are traditionally associated with non-manual occupations. The low-caste category comprises of Scheduled Castes and Scheduled Tribes which are usually on the lower rungs of the hierarchy and have relatively low ritual status, non-vegetarian food habits and are traditionally associated with unclean manual occupations. The 'intermediate' castes include varied castes, which could neither be classified traditionally nor associated with manual occupations. Some of the intermediate castes, due to sanskritization, claim greater proximity to the Brahmin caste, and assume a superior status over the other castes of the same category.

According to this classification, the data reveals that about two-thirds of the urban respondents (73.33 per cent) and nearly 46 (46.67) per cent of the rural respondents come from high castes. The particulars regarding the caste of the respondents are presented in Table 2.11.

**TABLE - 2.11**
**DISTRIBUTION OF WIDOWS BY CASTE**

| *Caste* | *Urban Per cent* | *Rural Per cent* | *Total Per cent* |
|---|---|---|---|
| Low caste | 12.67 | 33.33 | 23.00 |
| Intermediate caste | 14.00 | 20.00 | 17.00 |
| High caste | 73.33 | 46.67 | 60.00 |
| Total | 100.00 | 100.00 | 100.00 |

The table indicates that nearly 12.67 per cent in the urban area and 33.33 per cent of respondents in rural areas belong to 'low' castes, as against 14 per cent and 20 per cent of the intermediate caste respondents from urban and rural areas respectively.

Further, the Lingayat or Veerashaiva caste, which falls into the high caste category, is the dominant caste in this area. Unlike a Brahmin woman, the Lingayat woman especially in the higher subcaste, is prohibited from marrying again after divorce or widowhood. However, the Lingayat woman is not free from the disabilities that the Hindu woman in general is suffering from.

**Education**

The data pertaining to the educational level of the respondents reveal that the majority of the respondents, both before and after widowhood, are illiterate. The particulars regarding the educational level of the respondents are presented in Table 2.12.

**TABLE -2.12**
**EDUCATIONAL LEVEL OF WIDOWS**

| | *Before Widowhood* | | | *After Widowhood* | | |
|---|---|---|---|---|---|---|
| *Educational level* | *Urban Per cent* | *Rural Per cent* | *Total Per cent* | *Urban Per cent* | *Rural Per cent* | *Total Per cent* |
| Illiterate | 49.33 | 88.00 | 68.67 | ·49.33 | 88.00 | 88.00 |
| Literate | 50.67 | 12.00 | 31.33 | 50.67 | 12.00 | 12.00 |
| Total | 100.00 | 100.00 | 100.00 | 100.00 | 100.00 | 100.00 |
| $X^2$ | value | 52.2* | 51.2** | | | |

Calculated $X^2 = 51.2$, table value of $X^2$ with 1 d f at .01 level is 6.63. Hence the difference is significant.

Further, the table shows that, before widowhood, nearly 49 (49.33) per cent of the urban respondents, in comparision to 88 (88.00) per cent of rural respondents, are illiterates. 50.67 per cent of the respondents in the urban area, as against 12 (12.00) per cent of the rural respondents, are literates. It has been learnt from reliable sources that in the urban area, the literate category includes 24 (24.67) per cent of the primary educated and 15 (15.33) per cent of higher secondary educated. Only about 5 (5.33) per cent of the respondents have undergone Matriculation and P. U. C. education. In the rural area 7 (7.33) per cent and 4 (4.67) per cent of respondents have primary and secondary level education respectively. Nearly 6 (6.00) per cent of the urban respondents have higher education, and only 2 (1.33) per cent are postgraduates.

However, it is also significant to note that about 4.7 per cent of the urban respondents continued their education after widowhood. Two women who were only matriculates at the time of widowhood, did their postgraduation subsequently. One graduate woman did postgraduation after widowhood and now she is doing her doctoral degree. She is the highest educated respondent in this study.

## 2.4 Type of Employment and Reactions

The data regarding the occupational status of the respondents is given in Table 2.13.

The data presented in the Table 2.13 reveals that about 60 (60.00) per cent and 44 (44.00) per cent of the respondents in urban areas are housewives both before and after widowhood respectively, whereas only 20 (20.67) per cent and 8 (8.67) per cent of the respondents in rural areas are housewives both before and after widowhood. About 14 (14.67) per cent and 17 (17.33) per cent of the urban respondents are working as land labourers, among them 4 (4.67) per cent are working as maid servants both before and after widowhood respectively while nearly 60 (60.00) per cent and 76 (76.67) per cent of the rural respondents are working as land labourers, before and after widowhood respectively.

TABLE - 2.13
DISTRIBUTION OF WIDOWS BY OCCUPATIONAL STATUS

| | *Before Widowhood* | | | *After Widowhood* | | |
|---|---|---|---|---|---|---|
| *Occupational Status* | *Urban Per cent* | *Rural Per cent* | *Total Per cent* | *Urban Per cent* | *Rural Per cent* | *Total Per cent* |
| House wife | 60.00 | 20.67 | 52.00 | 44.00 | 8.67 | 26.33 |
| Land labourers/ Maid servant | 14.67 | 60.00 | 16.00 | 17.33 | 76.67 | 47.00 |
| Self employed | 14.67 | 16.00 | 17.33 | 20.00 | 11.33 | 15.67 |
| Government employed | 10.66 | 3.33 | 14.67 | 18.67 | 3.33 | 11.00 |
| Total | 100.00 | 100.00 | 100.00 | 100.00 | 100.00 | 100.00 |
| $X^2$ Value | | 75.88** | | | 111.3** | |

Calculated $X^2$ = 75.88 and 111.3, table value of $X^2$ with 3 d f at 0.01 level is 11.34. Hence, the difference is significant.

Further, about 14 (14.67) and 20 (20.00) per cent of the urban respondents are self-employed both before and after widowhood respectively. They have taken up self employment like vegetable selling, delivering milk, tailoring, petty business and soforth. And only 10 (10.67) per cent and 18 (18.67) per cent of the respondents both before and after widowhood, in the urban area, are government employees. They are in class IV, clerical, and teaching jobs.

Hence, with regard to the occupational status of the widows studied, it can be stated that about 1 (1.33) per cent in urban area and 1 (0.67) per cent in rural areas started working just before widowhood, while about 14 (14.67) per cent of the urban respondents and 11 (11.33) per cent of the rural respondents started working only after widowhood due to sheer economic deprivation. Further, 8 (8.33) per cent of the urban respondents, as against 10 (10.00) per cent of the rural, started working within a year of widowhood. While 7 (7.670 per cent of the respondents in urban area, in comparision to 2 (2.00) per cent of the rural respondents started working after one year of widowhood.

**Persons Helped in Getting Employment**

The data pertaining to the persons who had helped in getting job/work is presented in Table 2.14.

**TABLE - 2.14**

**PERSONS HELPED IN GETTING JOB/WORK AFTER WIDOWHOOD**

| *Persons Helped* | *Urban Per cent* | *Rural Per cent* | *Total Per cent* |
|---|---|---|---|
| Parents/Brothers | 40.75 | 55.55 | 46.67 |
| Father-in-law | 7.40 | - | 4.44 |
| Husband's former employer | 37.04 | 27.78 | 33.33 |
| Friends/Neighbours | 14.81 | 16.67 | 15.56 |
| Total | 100.00 | 100.00 | 100.00 |

It is observed from the table that about 40(40.75) per cent of the urban respondents and 55 (55.55) per cent of the rural respondents are helped by their parents/brothers in getting Job/work. About 37 (37.04) per cent of them in urban areas, compared to 27 (27.78) per cent in rural areas, are helped by their husband's former employer. Only one respondent in the urban area has been helped by her father-in-law in securing employment.

**Problems Faced in getting Job/Work**

The data pertaining to the problems faced by the widows in getting job/work is presented in Table 2.15.

The data presented in Table 2.15 reveals that almost all the widows who started working after widowhood faced problems in getting employed. About 40 (40.74) per cent of urban respondents, as against 66 (66.67) per cent of the rural respondents, faced employment problems owing to lack of proper education. About 33 (33.33) per cent of the urban, in comparision to 11 (11.11) per cent of the rural respondents, faced problems owing to lack of proper experience and training, while nearly 25 (25.93) per cent of the respondents in urban area as against 22 (22.22) per cent of the rural respondents faced problems due to lack of proper approach.

**TABLE - 2.15**
**REASONS FOR THE PROBLEMS FACED IN GETTING JOB/WORK**

| *Reasons* | *Urban* *Per cent* | *Rural* *Per cent* | *Total* *Per cent* |
|---|---|---|---|
| Lack of proper education | 40.74 | 66.67 | 51.11 |
| Lack of proper experience and training | 33.33 | 11.11 | 24.44 |
| Lack of proper approach | 25.93 | 22.22 | 24.45 |
| Total | 100.00 | 100.00 | 100.00 |

**Job-Satisfaction**

With a view to assessing job satisfaction among the widows, the respondents were asked as to whether they were satisfied with their present employment. In response to this, about 36 (36.00) per cent of the urban respondents, as against 87 (87.33) per cent of the rural respondents, stated that they were not satisfied with their present employment. The particulars regarding job satisfaction, reasons for job satisfaction or dissatisfaction are presented in Tables 2.16, 2.17 and 2.18.

**TABLE - 2.16**
**DISTRIBUTION OF WIDOWS BY JOB SATISFACTION**

| *Responses* | *Urban* *Per cent* | *Rural* *Per cent* | *Total* *Per cent* |
|---|---|---|---|
| No | 36.00 | 87.33 | 61.67 |
| Yes | 20.00 | 4.00 | 12.00 |
| Not working | 44.00 | 8.67 | 26.33 |
| Total | 100.00 | 100.00 | 100.00 |

It is evident from the data presented in the table that only 20 (20.00) per cent of urban respondents, as against 4 (4.00) per cent of the rural respondents, are satisfied with their present employment, whereas about 36 (36.00) per cent and 87 (87.33) per cent of both rural and urban respondents respectively are not satisfied with their present employment. As such, the findings seem to suggest that a majority of widows are dissatisfied with their present employment.

**TABLE - 2.17**
**REASONS FOR JOB SATISFACTION**

| *Reason* | *Urban Per cent* | *Rural Per cent* | *Total Per cent* |
|---|---|---|---|
| Earning good salary | 30.00 | 33.33 | 30.56 |
| Got expected post/work | 36.67 | 16.66 | 33.33 |
| Convenient timings/work place is at a reasonable distance | 33.33 | 50.00 | 36.11 |
| Total | 100.00 | 100.00 | 100.00 |

It is observed from Table 2.17 that about 30 (30.33) per cent of the urban respondent, in comparison to 33 (33.33) per cent of the rural respondents, have stated that they are earning a good salary, whereas about 36 (36.67) per cent urban and only 16 (16.66) per cent of the rural respondents mentioned that they got expected post/work/convenient timings. And nearly 33 (33.33) per cent of the respondents in urban area and 50 (50.00) per cent of the respondents in rural areas said that their work place is at a reasonable distance.

**TABLE - 2.18**
**REASONS FOR DISSATISFACTION**

| *Reason for Dissatisfaction* | *Urban Per cent* | *Rural Per cent* | *Total Per cent* |
|---|---|---|---|
| Low emoluments | 38.89 | 47.32 | 44.87 |
| Post held is below expectation/ Inconvenient timings/Lack of avenue for promotion/work place is far off. | 22.22 | 3.05 | 8.65 |
| Seasonal/irregular work | 27.78 | 42.75 | 38.38 |
| Sexual harassment by male/ secondary treatment by lady colleagues/friends | 11.11 | 6.88 | 8.10 |
| Total | 100.00 | 100.00 | 100.00 |

Further, the data presented in table 2.18 reveals that about 38 (38.89) per cent of the urban respondents, as against nearly 47 (47.32) per cent of the rural respondents, stated low emoluments as a reason for their dissatisfaction with their present employment. About 27 (27.78) per cent of the urban, in comparision to 42 (42.75) per cent of the rural respondents, mentioned seasonal/irregular work as the cause of their dissatisfaction. While 11 (11.11) per cent in the urban area, as against 6 (6.88) per cent in rural areas, opined sexual harassment by male/secondary treatment by other women as the reason for their dissatisfaction with the present employment.

Thus, with regard to the job satisfaction of the respondents, the findings seem to suggest that a majority of the widows are dissatisfied with their present employment.

*Income*

For the purpose of determining the income of the widows, the annual income of the respondents from their salary/wage is take into account since they do not have any other source of income. As such, the particulars regarding the income of the widows are presented in Table 2.19.

**TABLE - 2.19**

**DISTRIBUTION OF WIDOWS BY INCOME**

| *Income* | *Before Widowhood* | | | *After Widowhood* | | |
|---|---|---|---|---|---|---|
| | *Urban Per cent* | *Rural Per cent* | *Total Per cent* | *Urban Per cent* | *Rural Per cent* | *Total Per cent* |
| Nil | 53.33 | 17.33 | 35.33 | 37.33 | 10.67 | 24.00 |
| Below 1000 | 22.67 | 70.67 | 46.67 | 42.67 | 81.33 | 62.00 |
| 1001-5001 | 13.33 | 8.00 | 10.67 | 6.67 | 4.67 | 5.67 |
| 5001-above | 10.67 | 4.00 | 7.33 | 13.33 | 3.33 | 8.33 |
| Total | 100.00 | 100.00 | 100.00 | 100.00 | 100.00 | 100.00 |
| $X^2$ Value | | 70.66** | | | 49.82** | |

Calculated $X^2$ = 70.66 and 49.89, table value of $X^2$ with 3 d f at 0.01 level is 11.34. Hence, the difference age significant.

Average individual income of the urban widows = 3546.25

Average individual income of the rural widows = 2790.32

The annual income of the respondents in urban area ranges from Rs. 500 to Rs. 24000, whereas in rural areas it ranges from

Rs. 500 to 5,000. However the data presented in Table 2.19 reveals that the proportion of respondents coming from 'nil' to 'high' both before and after widowhood are unequal. About 53 (53.33) per cent of the Urban respondents and 17 (17.33) per cent of the rural respondents before widowhood belonged to nil income group ; whereas 37 (37.33) per cent and 10 (10.67) per cent of the urban and rural respondents respectively belong to nil income group after widowhood since they are dependents on their children.

Further, it is evident from the Table that those who belong to below Rs. 1000 income group constitute a greater proportion, as compared to nil and high income groups. Before widowhood, about 22 (22.67) per cent of the respondents in urban area and 70 (70.67) per cent of the rural respondents belonged to the below - Rs. 1000 income group, as against 42 (42.67) per cent and 81 (81.67) per cent of the respondents in urban and rural areas respectively, after widowhood. As such, before widowhood there were about 10 (10.67) per cent of the urban respondents and 4 (4.00) per cent of the rural respondents who belonged to Rs. 5000 and above income group, while after widowhood nearly 13 (13.33) per cent of the respondents in urban area and only 3 (3.33) per cent of the rural respondents belong to the same group.

### 2.5 Accommodation and Living Arrangement

With regard to the living arrangements of the respondents the data indicates that over three-fourths are living with their children. The remaining respondents are either living independently or with own/husband's relations. The distribution of widows, by their living arrangements is presented in Table 2.20.

It can be observed that about 77 (77.34) per cent of the urban respondents, as against 84 (84.67) per cent of the rural respondents, are living with their children. Nearly 16 (16.67) per cent of the urban respondents, in comparision to 19 (19.33) per cent of the rural, are staying with their minor children; and about 7 (7.00) per cent and 2 (2.00) per cent of the respondents in urban and rural areas respectively, are staying with their daughters, who are married/divorced/widowed. About 5 (5.33) per cent of the respondents in the urban area, as against 4 (4.00) per cent in rural areas, are living independently. Further, about 14 (14.00) per cent of the urban and 6 (6.66) per cent of the rural respondents are living with their own relations, like parents/brothers. And the remaining 3 (3.33) per cent and 4 (4.67) per cent of the respondents in urban and rural areas respectively are living with their deceased husband's kinsmen. However, it is statistically found that there is no significant difference between the urban and rural widows in respect of their living arrangements. Thus, in the view of the above findings it may be stated that a majority of the widows are living with their children. In support of this, it is observed that 81 (81.00) per cent of the respondents expressed their wish to live with their children.

**TABLE - 2.20**

**DISTRIBUTION OF WIDOWS BY LIVING ARRANGEMENTS**

| *Living Arrangement* | *Urban Per cent* | *Rural Per cent* | *Total Per cent* | *$X^2$ Value* |
|---|---|---|---|---|
| Independently | 5.33 | 4.00 | 4.67 | |
| With Children | 77.34 | 84.67 | 81.00 | |
| With own relations | | | | |
| Parents/Brothers | 14.00 | 6.66 | 10.33 | $2.98^{NS}$ |
| With Husband's Kinsmen | 3.33 | 4.67 | 4.00 | |
| Total | 100.00 | 100.00 | 100.00 | |

Calculated $X^2 = 2.98$, Table value of $X^2$ with 3 d f at .05 level is 7.81. Hence, the difference is not significant.

**Type of Accommodation**

With regard to the respondents type of accommodation, the data reveals that about three-fourths of the respondents, both in urban and rural areas, are living in their own houses. The particulars regarding the respondents types of accommodation are presented in the following Table 2.21.

The table shows that about 68 (68.00) per cent of the urban respondents, as against 74 (74.67) per cent of the rural respondents, are living in their own houses. Whereas 14 (14.00) per cent of the urban respondents, in comparision to 4 (4.00) per cent of the rural, are living in rented houses. In rural areas most of the respondents have their own houses whether big or small. About 14 (14.00) per cent of respondents in urban area, and 8 (8.00) per cent in rural areas, are living in their relative's houses, like parents brothers/

in-law's houses. Only 4 (4.00) per cent of the respondents in urban area as against 13 (13.33) per cent of the rural widows are living in Janata House. However, $X^2$ result shows that there is a significant difference between urban and rural respondents with respect to their type of accommodation.

**TABLE - 2.21**

**DISTRIBUTION OF WIDOWS BY TYPE OF ACCOMMODATION**

| *Accommodation* | *Urban Per cent* | *Rural Per cent* | *Total Per cent* | *$X^2$ Value* |
|---|---|---|---|---|
| Janata House | 4.00 | 13.33 | 8.67 | |
| Rented House | 14.00 | 4.00 | 9.00 | |
| Own House | 68.00 | 74.67 | 71.33 | 18.8** |
| Relative's House | 14.00 | 8.00 | 11.00 | |

Calculated $X^2$ =18.8, Table Value of $X^2$ with 3 d f at .01 level is 11.34. Hence, the difference is significant.

**Type of Family**

Table 2.22 represented the particulars regarding the respondents type of family.

**TABLE - 2.22**

**DISTRIBUTION OF WIDOWS BY TYPE OF FAMILY**

| *Type of Family* | *Urban Per cent* | *Rural Per cent* | *Total Per cent* |
|---|---|---|---|
| Joint Family | 4.00 | 10.00 | 7.00 |
| Nuclear Family | 94.67 | 89.33 | 92.00 |
| Alone | 1.33 | 0.67 | 1.00 |
| Total | 100.00 | 100.00 | 100.00 |

About 4 (4.00) per cent of the urban respondents and about 10 (10.00) per cent of the rural respondents belong to joint families; whereas 94 (94.67) per cent of the urban respondents and 89 (89.67) per cent of the rural respondents come from nuclear families. However, the single largest group is of those who come from nuclear families. It is also significant to note that 1 (1.33) per cent of the respondents in urban area and 1 (0.67) per cent of respondents in rural areas have come neither from joint/nor nuclear family.

**Size of the Family**

The size of the respondents' families varied from single to 12 members. However, two-thirds of the respondents both in urban and rural areas come from families with five or more members. Table 2.23 represent the particulars regarding the respondents' family size.

**TABLE - 2.23**
**DISTRIBUTION OF WIDOWS BY FAMILY SIZE**

| *Size of Family* | *Urban Per cent* | *Rural Per cent* | *Total Per cent* |
|---|---|---|---|
| Single Member | 8.00 | 6.00 | 7.00 |
| 2-4 | 25.33 | 19.33 | 22.34 |
| 5-7 | 50.67 | 60.00 | 55.00 |
| 8-10 | 12.00 | 8.00 | 10.33 |
| 11 and above | 4.00 | 6.67 | 5.33 |
| Total | 100.00 | 100.00 | 100.00 |

The data indicates that about 25 (25.33) per cent of the respondents in urban area and 19 (19.33) per cent in rural areas come from the families with 4 or less members; whereas about 66 (66.67) per cent of the urban and 74 (74.67) per cent of the rural respondents come from families with more than 5 members. However, the single largest category is of those who come from the families with 5-7 members. It is also significant to note that about 8 (8.00) per cent of the respondents in urban area and 6 (6.00) per cent of the respondents in rural areas live alone. The average family size in the urban area is 5.84, and in the rural 6.06.

**Details About the Respondents' Marriage and Reactions.**

With a view to ascertain details about their marriage and marital life, the respondents were asked a few questions. The findings pertaining to — the persons who made the mate selections, with/without their consent, married within or outside the kinship relations, background of the respondents' spouses, lead happy/unhappy married life and reasons for their unhappiness are presented in the following Tables.

**Persons Who Made the Selection of Partners**

With regard to the persons who made the selection of partners the data indicates that over two-thirds of the respondents' Fathers made the selection of partners. The distribution of widows, according to the persons who made the mate-selection, is presented in Table 2.24.

**TABLE - 2.24**
**PERSONS WHO MADE THE SELECTION OF PARTNERS**

| *Person Who Made the Selection* | *Urban Per cent* | *Rural Per cent* | *Total Per cent* |
|---|---|---|---|
| Father/Brother/s | 92.00 | 90.00 | 91.00 |
| Maternal Uncle/s | 6.67 | 8.00 | 7.33 |
| Paternal Uncle/s | 1.33 | 2.00 | 1.67 |
| Total | 100.00 | 100.00 | 100.00 |

It can be observed from Table 2.24 that for about 92 (92.00) per cent of urban respondents and 90 (90.00) per cent of the rural respondents, parents made the selection of partners; for about 10 (10.00) per cent of the respondents in urban area and nearly 12 (12.00) per cent of the respondents in rural areas brother/s made the selection of partners. For about 6 (6.67) per cent of the urban respondents, as against about 8 (8.00) per cent of the rural respondents, maternal uncle/s made the selection of the partners. While paternal uncle/s made the selection of partners for only 1 (1.33) per cent and about 2 (2.00) per cent of the respondents in urban and rural areas respectively.

Further, the data indicates that about 90 (90.00) per cent of the urban respondents, in comparision to 98 (98.00) per cent of the rural, states than the selection of partners was made without their consent; whereas about 15 (15.00) per cent of the respondents in urban area, in comparision to 3 (3.00) per cent of the rural, mentioned that the selection of partners was made with their consent.

In the view of the selection of partners within or outside kinship relations, the data indicates, that in the case of 45 (45.00) per cent of the urban respondents, as against 20 (20.00) per cent of the rural respondents, the selection of partners was outside the close kinship relations; whereas in the case of 55 (55.00) per cent of the urban respondents, in comparision to 80 (80.00) per cent of the rural respondents, the selection of partners was within the close kinship relations.

**Background of Respondents Spouses**

With regard to the persons to whom the respondents got married, the data reveals that about 55 (55.00) per cent of the urban respondents, as against 80 (80.00) per cent of the rural respondents, married close relatives; and nearly 45 (45.00) per cent of the urban respondents, in comparison to 20 (20.00) per cent of the rural respondents married spouses who were not related to them. The particulars regarding the persons to whom widows got married to are presented in Table 2.25.

The data indicates that those who married within the close kinship relations seem to have married maternal uncles. The table also shows that about 19 (19.33) per cent of the urban respondents, in comparision to 36 (36.00) per cent of the rural respondents, married maternal uncles. Whereas 24 (24.00) per cent of the urban respondents, as against 40 (40.00) per cent of the rural respondents, married distant relatives. And only 1 (0.67) per cent of respondents in urban areas and 1 (1.33) per cent of the respondents in rural areas married the elder sister's widower.

**TABLE - 2.25**
**BACKGROUND OF RESPONDENTS SPOUSES**

| *Background of Persons* | *Urban Per cent* | *Rural Per cent* | *Total Per cent* |
|---|---|---|---|
| Elder Sister's Widower | 0.67 | 1.33 | 1.00 |
| Brother of Sister in-law | 1.33 | 2.67 | 2.00 |
| Maternal Uncle | 19.33 | 36.00 | 27.67 |
| Distant relative | 24.00 | 40.00 | 32.00 |
| Outsider | 54.67 | 20.00 | 37.33 |
| Total | 100.00 | 100.00 | 100.00 |

**2.6 Reactions Toward Married Life**

With a view to ascertaining marital satisfaction among the widows, the respondents were asked as to whether they were happy during their married life, or to gauge the quality of marital happiness. In response to this, nearly two-thirds of the respondents, in both urban and rural areas expressed happiness with their earlier marital life. The particulars have been presented in Table 2.26.

It is observed from the table that about 17 (17.33) per cent of the urban respondents as against 21 (21.33) per cent of the rural respondents, were not happy with their earlier life; whereas about 82 (82.67) per cent of the urban respondents, in comparison to 78 (78.67) per cent of the rural respondents, were happy with their earlier life. As such the findings seem to suggest that a majority of widows were happy with their earlier marital life.

**TABLE - 2.26**

**DISTRIBUTION OF WIDOWS BY MARITAL SATISFACTION**

| *Marital Satisfaction* | *Urban* *Per cent* | *Rural* *Per cent* | *Total* *Per cent* |
|---|---|---|---|
| Unhappy | 17.33 | 21.33 | 19.33 |
| Happy | 82.67 | 78.67 | 80.67 |
| Total | 100.00 | 100.00 | 100.00 |

**Reasons for Unhappiness**

With a view to assessing the respondents unhappy marital life, a question was posed as to what were the reasons for their unhappiness. The particulars regarding reasons for unhappiness are presented in Table 2.27.

**TABLE - 2.27**

**REASONS FOR UNHAPPY MARRIED LIFE**

| *Reasons* | *Urban* *Per cent* | *Rural* *Per cent* | *Total* *Per cent* |
|---|---|---|---|
| He was not taking proper care of the family | 42.30 | 40.62 | 41.37 |
| He was much older than me | 26.93 | 25.00 | 25.87 |
| He had several bad habits | 30.77 | 34.38 | 32.76 |
| Total | 100.00 | 100.00 | 100.00 |

It is evident from the above table that about 42 (42.30) per cent of the urban respondents, in comparison to 40 (40.62) per cent of the rural respondents, stated that the deceased husbands were not taking proper care of the family. About 26 (26.93) per cent of the respondents in the urban area, as against 30 (30.77) per cent in the rural area, stated that the deceased husbands were much older than themselves. Whereas nearly 30 (30.77) per cent of the urban respondents and 34 (34.38) per cent rural respondents said that the husbands had several bad habits. However, the data regarding for unhappiness seem to suggest that a majority of the deceased husbands were not taking care of the family.

## REFERENCES

1. M.F. Karennavar: The Climate Analysis of Hubli- Dharwad City" *The Indian Geographical Journal*. Vol. XLIII, Nos. 3-4, July-Sept, 1969, p. 51.
2. Letter No. 281 Rao, Bahadur Parsi: Venkatrao, Principal Sadar Ameen to the secretary of Indian Law Commission No. 688, Dafter M, Inamdar MSS.
3. Parsi Venkatrao, Inamdar MSS, op. cit.
4. Letter No. 281 of 1837 Parsi Venkatrao to P.W. Lellyt, acting judge. Letter dated 5th July 1838 from Parsi Venkatrao No. 688 Dafter M. Inamdar MSS.
5. Tirumalrao - Report on Enforced widowhood (p3) dated 30th December, 1884 in response to Government order No. 4164. Packet No. 688, Dafter D. Inamdar MSS.
6. Tirumalrao, op. cit., p. 36.
7. From Paṅdurang Narayan of Navalgund, 3rd Feb. 1885 and From Pandit Narayan Keshav Vaidya of Bombay 5th Feb & 9th May, 1885 packet No. 668, Dafter M. Inamdar MSS.
8. B.M. Malabari to Tirumalrao, Packet 704, Dafter "E" Inamdar MSS.
9. Katti, Venkata Rango: *Vidhava Vapan Anachara*, Poona Oriental Book House, Poona 1889, pp. 9,11. p. Gazetteer of Karnataka State Part II 1883 pp. 494.
10. *Karnataka Wartika*, 23 March, 1879, Bombay, Native Newspaper Report.
11. *Karnataka Patra*, 19 June, 1893, B.N.N.R.
12. Mudbidri, A.G.: Widow Remarriage Dharwad's Initiative, A paper presented at the National Seminar on Widowhood in India. Sponsored by J.S.S. & SDMET Ujire, Dharwad, 1987.

Note: The findings of the present study are presented in the empirical present tenses unless found absolutely to deviate.

THREE

# Family Background

The main aim of discussing the family background is to portray the widow's family condition, which is essential for understanding their problems.

Under this heading, an attempt is made to depict the socio-economic conditions of husbands, children and problems faced by the widows. Hence, the findings pertaining to the respondent's husbands and children are presented here.

The family background of the respondents includes the following components:

(a) Socio-economic characteristics of the deceased husbands.
(b) Property left by the deceased husbands.
(c) Details about the children.
(d) Problems faced by the widows in upbringing the children.

### 3.1 Socio-Economic Characteristics

With regard to the socio-economic status of the deceased husbands, the data pertaining to the age at death, causes of death, treatment received, educational level, occupation and status, income, property left, details about the children, problems faced by the widows in their upbringing and so forth are presented in the following tables.

### Age of Deceased Husbands

We may first consider the factor of age. The particulars regarding the age of the deceased husbands are presented in Table 3.1.

**TABLE - 3.1**
**DISTRIBUTION OF DECEASED HUSBANDS BY AGE AT DEATH**

| *Age at Death* | *Urban Per cent* | *Rural Per cent* | *Total Per cent* | $X^2$ *Value* |
|---|---|---|---|---|
| 0-29 | 11.33 | 7.33 | 9.33 | |
| 30-39 | 12.00 | 20.00 | 16.00 | |
| 40-49 | 22.67 | 26.67 | 24.67 | $8.62^{N.S}$ |
| 50-59 | 25.33 | 28.00 | 26.67 | |
| 60-69 | 16.67 | 10.67 | 13.67 | |
| 70 and above | 12.00 | 7.33 | 9.66 | |
| Total | 100.00 | 100.00 | 100.00 | |

Calculated $X^2 = 8.6$; table value of $X^2$ with 5 d f at .05 level is 11.0g. Hence the difference is not significant.

The data in the above table reveals that the husbands who died in the age-group of 50-59 years constitute the largest single proportion of the total sample, representing about 25 (25.33) per cent in urban area and 28(28.00) per cent in rural areas. However, it is significant to note that about half of the husbands, i.e 48(48.00) per cent and 54 (54.67) per cent from urban and rural areas respectively, died in the age between 40-59 years. It may also be observed from the table that nearly 12 (12.00) per cent in urban area as, against 7(7.33) per cent in rural areas, died at the age of 70 and above . The mean age at death of the urban deceased husbands studied is 48.87 and that of rural is 47.93.

**Cause of Death**

With regard to the causes of death of husbands, the data indicates that over one-thirds died of diseases and the remaining died of either old age or accident/snake bite/suicide/murder. The distribution of deceased husbands according to the causes of death is presented in Table 3.2.

It can be observed from the table that about 72 (72.67) per cent of the husbands in urban as well as in rural areas died of one or the other ailments whereas, about 27 (27.33) per cent of respondent's husbands in urban and rural areas died of accident, old age, snake bite/murder, suicide etc. Nearly 21 (21.33) per cent of the respondents in urban area, as against 8 (8.67) per cent in rural areas, died of heart-attack. And about 18 (18.00) per cent of the urban men in comparison to 21 (21.33) per cent in rural areas, died of prolonged illness. Nearly 4 (4.67) per cent of the deceased men in the urban area, as against 7 (7.33) per cent in the rural areas, died of old age. Thus, in the view of above findings it may be stated that a majority of the husbands died of some sickness or disease. The results establish that there is a significant difference between the urban and rural husbands in respect of cause of their deaths.

**TABLE - 3.2**
**DISTRIBUTION OF DECEASED HUSBANDS BY CAUSES OF DEATH**

| *Causes of Death* | *Urban Per cent* | *Rural Per cent* | *Total Per cent* | *$X^2$ Value* |
|---|---|---|---|---|
| Heart attack | 21.33 | 8.67 | 15.00 | |
| Paralysis | 6.67 | 4.00 | 5.33 | |
| Cholera | 6.00 | 8.00 | 7.00 | |
| Typhoid | 10.00 | 10.00 | 10.00 | |
| Asthama/Jaundice | 10.66 | 20.67 | 15.67 | 15.90* |
| Prolonged illness | 18.00 | 21.33 | 19.67 | |
| Accident | 4.67 | 3.33 | 4.00 | |
| Old age | 4.67 | 7.33 | 6.00 | |
| Others* | 18.00 | 16.67 | 17.33 | |
| Total | 100.00 | 100.00 | 100.00 | |

Calculated $X^2$ =15.90; table value of $X^2$ with 8 d f at .05 level is 15.51
Hence, the difference is significant.
* Suicide, snake bite, Murder etc.

The deceased husbands of the respondents suffered from illness from less than one week to 15 months. Nearly 18 (18.00) per cent of the urban husbands, as against 10 (10.00) per cent rural, suffered less than a week. About 54 (54.6) per cent of the urban husbands, in comparison to 62 (62.7) per cent of rural husbands, were ill for more than six months.

Further, with regard to the deceased husbands' "place of death", the data reveals that nearly 52 per cent of the respondents in urban areas, and 73 per cent in rural areas, died in their homes/ residences. About 20 per cent and 10 per cent of the respondents, in urban and rural areas respectively, breathed their last in private nursing homes. Whereas, about 18 per cent and 17 per cent of the respondents, from urban and rural areas, died in Government hospitals.

**Nature of Treatment**

In consonance with the findings regarding the causes of death of the husbands, the data, regarding the treatment received, indicates that a large number of husbands had not received treatment. Table 3.3 pertains to the distribution of the deceased husbands by treatment received.

**TABLE - 3.3**
**DISTRIBUTION OF DECEASED HUSBANDS BY TREATMENT RECEIVED**

| *Treatment Received* | *Urban Per cent* | *Rural Per cent* | *Total Per cent* | *$X^2$ Value* |
|---|---|---|---|---|
| No | 51.33 | 78.67 | 65.00 | |
| Yes | 48.67 | 21.33 | 35.00 | 24.62** |
| Total | 100.00 | 100.00 | 100.00 | |

Calculated $X^2$ =24.62; table value of $X^2$ with 1 d f at .01 level is 6.63. Hence the difference is significant.

It can be observed from the table that about 51 (51.33) per cent of the urban respondent's husbands, as against 78 (78.67) per cent of the rural, had not received treatment. While nearly 48 (48.67) per cent of the respondent's husbands in the urban area, in comparison to 21 (21.33) per cent in rural areas had received treatment before their death. But, the respondents opined that, it had not been adequate. However, it is statistically found, that there is a significant difference between the urban and rural deceased husbands, in respect of the treatment received.

**Reasons for not Receiving Treatment**

Table 3.4 provides the particulars regarding the reasons for not receiving treatment.

The data, presented in table 3.4, reveals that about 52 (52.67) per cent of the urban deceased husbands, as against 25 (25.33) per cent of the rural, had not received treatment due to lack of proper medical treatment at their place, and were unable to bear the higher expenses. In the case of 21 (21.33) per cent of urban husbands in comparison to 38 (38.00) per cent of the rural, the sickness had advanced to a stage where no time was left to take the treatment.

And about 7 (7.33) per cent of the urban husbands and 12 (12.00) per cent of rural husbands had not received treatment owing to strenuous job/tension in the family. Thus, the findings of the present study seem to suggest that a majority of the deceased husbands had not received proper treatment before their death.

**TABLE - 3.4**
**REASONS FOR NOT RECEIVING TREATMENT**

| *Causes of Death* | *Urban Per cent* | *Rural Per cent* | *Total Per cent* |
|---|---|---|---|
| No time was left to take the treatment | 21.33 | 38.00 | 19.67 |
| Lack of proper medical treatment at your place unable to bear higher expenses | 52.67 | 25.33 | 53.00 |
| Negligence on the part of doctors/patients. | 11.33 | 18.00 | 10.67 |
| Strenuous Job | 3.33 | 6.67 | 5.00 |
| Tension in the family | 4.00 | 5.33 | 4.66 |
| Not applicable | 7.34 | 6.67 | 7.00 |
| Total | 100.00 | 100.00 | 100.00 |

**Educational Level of Deceased Husband**

The data pertaining to the educational level of the respondents deceased husbands reveals that nearly one-fourth in the urban area, and about one-third in the rural areas were illiterates. The particulars regarding the educational level of the deceased husbands are presented in Table 3.5.

**TABLE - 3.5**
**DISTRIBUTION OF DECEASED BY EDUCATIONAL LEVEL**

| *Educational Level* | *Urban Per cent* | *Rural Per cent* | *Total Per cent* | *$X^2$ Value* |
|---|---|---|---|---|
| Illiterate | 26.67 | 76.67 | 50.67 | |
| Primary | 14.67 | 13.33 | 14.00 | |
| Secondary | 19.33 | 6.67 | 13.00 | 100.26** |
| S.S.L.C and Higher Education | 39.33 | 3.33 | 21.33 | |

Calculated $X^2$ =100.26; table value of $X^2$ with 3 d f at .01 level is 11.34. Hence the difference is significant.

The table indicates that about 26 (26.67) per cent husbands in urban area, as against 76 (76.67) per cent of in rural areas, were illiterate. Whereas, about 39 (39.33) per cent of the deceased husbands in urban area, in comparison to 3 (3.33) per cent of them in rural areas, had higher education. In the urban area, in the higher educated category, about 20 (20.0) per cent of the deceased husbands had passed S.S.L.C. and about 12 (12.0) per cent were graduates, the remaining 7 (7.3) per cent having post-graduate and professional degrees. The data seems to suggest that at all educational levels, the urban deceased husbands had relatively higher educational qualifications than the rural counterparts.

However, the statistical results show that the difference between the urban and rural husbands is highly significant in respect of their educational level.

**Occupation**

The occupations followed by the husbands of widows are discussed under family background, with a view that this information may provide a more direct index of the socio-economic conditions in which the widows spent their earlier life. The information pertaining to the husband's occupation is of importance in depicting the social background as it is one of the factors that determines one's social origin. Hence, particulars regarding the occupations followed by the respondent's husband was collected. The data pertaining to the actual occupations carried on by husbands of the respondents are presented in Table 3.6.

The data in the Table 3.6 reveals that about 16 (16.00) per cent of the urban deceased husbands as against 47 (47.33) per cent of the rural deceased husbands were land labourers. Whereas nearly 18 (18.67) per cent of the husbands in urban area, in comparison to 30 (30.00) per cent of their rural counterparts, were actual cultivators. It is also observed from the table that nearly 48 (48.66) per cent of the urban respondent's husbands, as against 4 (4.67) per cent of the rural respondent's husbands, were Government/private employees. And about 6 (6.67) per cent of them in urban area, and nearly 3 (3.33) per cent in the rural, were *hamals*/auto drivers. As such it can be stated that nearly half of the deceased husbands in the urban area, and more than one-fourth of them in rural areas, carried on unskilled occupations. In this context, the data seems to suggest that the occupational status of the respondents and their deceased husbands are incompatible. It is also significant to note that most of them, both in urban and rural areas, were working at the time of their death.

**TABLE - 3.6**
**DISTRIBUTION OF DECEASED HUSBANDS BY OCCUPATIONAL STATUS**

| *Occupational Status* | *Urban Per cent* | *Rural Per cent* | *Total Per cent* | *$X^2$ Value* |
|---|---|---|---|---|
| Actual cultivator | 18.67 | 30.00 | 24.33 | |
| Big/petty businessman | 6.67 | 4.00 | 5.33 | |
| Land labourer | 16.00 | 47.33 | 31.67 | 90.06** |
| Artisan | 3.33 | 10.67 | 7.00 | |
| Govt/Private employee | 48.66 | 4.67 | 26.67 | |
| Others | 6.67 | 3.33 | 5.00 | |
| Total | 100.00 | 100.00 | 100.00 | |

Calculated $X^2$ = 90.06; table value of $X^2$ with 5 d f at .01 level is 15.09. Hence the difference is significant.

However, the $X^2$ value establish that there is significant difference between the urban and rural deceased husbands in respect of their occupational status.

**Income**

In order to determine the family income, the annual income of the respondents, husbands family, from all sources, is taken into account. On the basis of income so determined, the deceased husbands families are classified into three types of families with 'low' , 'medium' and 'high' income. The families with an annual income of less than Rs.5000 are classified as families with 'low' income and those with Rs. 5000 to 20,000 as 'medium' and lastly those with an annual income more than Rs. 20,000 as 'high' income families. As such, the particulars regarding family income are presented in Table 3.7.

The annual family income of the deceased husbands ranges from Rs. 500 to Rs. 25,000. However, the data presented in Table 3.7 reveals that the proportion of husbands coming from 'high'

(Rs.20001 - above) 'medium' (Rs.5000-10000) and 'low' (Rs.1001-2000) income families are unequal. There are about 44 (44.67) per cent in the urban area as against 80 (80.00) per cent of the deceased husbands in rural areas, who come from 'low' income families. In comparison, about 18 (18.00) per cent and 8 (8.66) per cent of the husbands in urban and rural areas respectively, come from 'medium,' income families. Nearly 37 (37.33) per cent of them in urban area, as against 3 (3.33) per cent of the deceased husbands in rural areas come from 'high' income families. It is evident from the above table that a majority of the deceased husbands come from 'low' income families. Moreover, nearly 50 (50.00) per cent of husbands were the only earning members in their families. However, the difference between the urban and rural deceased husbands, in respect of their annual income level is found to be statistically significant.

**TABLE - 3.7**

**DISTRIBUTION OF DECEASED HUSBANDS BY INCOME**

| *Income* | *Urban Per cent* | *Rural Per cent* | *Total Per cent* | *$X^2$ Value* |
|---|---|---|---|---|
| Below-1000 | 10.67 | 16.67 | 13.67 | |
| 1001-2000 | 26.67 | 44.67 | 35.67 | |
| 2001-5000 | 7.33 | 26.67 | 17.00 | 77.16** |
| 5001-10000 | 8.67 | 5.33 | 7.00 | |
| 10001-20000 | 9.33 | 3.33 | 6.33 | |
| 20001 and above | 37.33 | 3.33 | 20.33 | |
| Total | 100.00 | 100.00 | 100.00 | |

Calculated $X^2$ =77.16; table value of $X^2$ with 5 d f at .01 level is 15.09. Hence the difference is significant.

**Other Earning Members**

The data pertaining to the other earning members in their families indicated that, in the case of nearly 50 per cent of the families, the deceased husbands were the only bread winners. In the remaining families there were normally one or two earning members in addition to such husbands. However, it is also significant to note that in case of more than three fourths (88 per cent) of families, the deceased husbands were the heads of their families who managed their family affairs.

**3.2 Property Left by the Deceased Husbands**

The main aim underlying discussion of the property left by the deceased husbands, is to ascertain how many widows possess a degree of economic security. This background factor pertains to the socio-economic conditions of the respondents family in which they are living at present.

Under this heading data pertaining to the savings, moveable and immoveable property are presented in the following tables.

**Savings**

The data pertaining to the savings left by the deceased husbands indicate that more than three fourths of the urban deceased husbands, as against 96 (96.00) per cent of the rural deceased husbands, left no savings at all. Table 3.8 represents the particulars regarding the respondent's husband's saving.

**TABLE - 3.8**
**SAVINGS LEFT BY THE DECEASED HUSBANDS**

| *Savings* | | *Urban Per cent* | *Rural Per cent* | *Combined Per cent* | *$X^2$ Value* |
|---|---|---|---|---|---|
| 1. Bank savings | No | 83.33 | 96.67 | 90.00 | |
| | Yes | 16.67 | 3.33 | 10.00 | 14.82** |
| 2. Insurance | No | 77.33 | 96.67 | 87.00 | |
| | Yes | 22.67 | 3.33 | 13.00 | 24.51** |
| 3. Provident fund | No | 77.33 | 96.67 | 87.00 | |
| | Yes | 22.67 | 3.33 | 13.00 | 24.51** |
| 4. Jewellery (in totals) | Nil | 41.33 | 84.67 | 63.00 | |
| | 1-4 | 22.00 | 8.67 | 15.33 | 62.66** |
| | 5-9 | 12.67 | 3.33 | 8.00 | |
| | 10+ | 24.00 | 3.33 | 13.67 | |
| Total (all columns) | | 100.00 | 100.00 | 100.00 | |

(1) Calculated $X^2 = 14.82$; table value of $X^2$ with 1 d f at .01 level is 6.63. Hence the difference is significant.

(2) & (3) Calculated $X^2 = 24.51$; table value of $X^2$ with 1 d f at .01 level is 6.63. Hence the difference is significant. .01 level is 6.63. Hence, the differences is significant.

(4) Calculated $X^2 = 62.66$; table value of $X^2$ with 3 d f at .01 level is 11.34. Hence the difference is significant.

The Bank savings of the deceased husbands range from Rs 500 to Rs 8000. However, the data in the above table reveals that in the urban area only about 16 (16.67) per cent of the respondent's husbands, as against only (3.33) per cent of the husbands in rural areas, had left any bank savings. Whereas about 83 (83.33) per cent of them from the urban area and 96 (96.67) per cent in rural areas had no bank savings at all. The statistical results establish that there is a significant difference between the urban and rural men in respect of their bank savings.

Further, it is also evident from the table that in the urban area about 22 (22.67) per cent of the husbands, as against only 3 (3.33) per cent in rural areas, had left savings through both insurance and provident fund. It is also significant to note that the husbands who had left savings in rural areas were either school teachers or police constables. It is therefore found that there is a significant difference between the urban and rural deceased husbands in respect of their savings through insurance and provident fund.

With regard to the gold left by the respondents, husbands, it is found that about 41 (41.33) per cent of them in the urban area had left behind no gold jewellery, whereas in rural areas this figure ran up to as much as 85 ( 84.67) per cent. About 58 (58.67) per cent urban husbands, in comparison to only 15 (15.33) per cent rural based husbands, had left gold jewellery of about 4 to 10 *totas*. However, the statistical test shows that there is a significant difference between urban and rural deceased husbands in respect of the gold earned.

**Property**

In collecting the data pertaining to the property left by the deceased husbands, information regarding the house and land was sought. The particulars regarding the property of the respondents' husbands are presented in Table 3.9.

**House**

It can be observed from the table that about 39 (39.33) per cent of the urban husbands and 24 (24.67) per cent of the rural husbands had no houses. Whereas, only 4 (4.67) per cent of the deceased husband's in the urban area and about 50 (50.67) per cent of them in rural areas had thatched houses. And about 8(8.00) per cent in the urban area, and 10(10.00) per cent in rural areas had *Kachcha* houses, as against 21 (21.33) per cent in urban and 11 (11.33) per cent in rural areas who had semi-*pakka* houses. The remaining 26(26.67) per cent of urban deceased husbands in comparison to 3(3.33) per cent in rural areas, had pakka houses. In view of this, it may be stated that deceased husbands, who had *pakka* houses, were fewer in number compared to those who had semi-*pakka* and thatched houses. Therefore, it is statistically found that there is a significant difference between the urban and rural deceased husbands in respect of the houses left by them at the time of their death.

**TABLE - 3.9**

**PROPERTY LEFT BY THE DECEASED HUSBANDS**

| *House and Land* | *Urban Per cent* | *Rural Per cent* | *Combined Per cent* | *$X^2$ Value* |
|---|---|---|---|---|
| 1. House | | | | |
| Nil | 39.33 | 24.67 | 32.00 | |
| Thatched | 4.67 | 50.67 | 27.67 | 94.54 |
| Kachcha | 8.00 | 10.00 | 9.00 | |
| Semi Pakka | 21,33 | 11.33 | 16.33 | |
| Pakka | 26.67 | 3.33 | 15.00 | |
| 2. Land (acres) | | | | |
| Nil | 72.67 | 50.00 | 61.33 | |
| 0-4 | 3.33 | 9.33 | 6.33 | |
| 5-9 | 3.33 | 12.00 | 7.67 | 21.02 |
| 10-19 | 6.67 | 6.00 | 6.33 | |
| 20 and above | 14.00 | 22.67 | 18.34 | |
| Total | 100.00 | 100.00 | 100.00 | |

(1) Calculated $X^2$ = 95.54, table value of $X^2$ with 4 d f at .01 level is 13.28. Hence, the difference is significant.

(2) Calculated $X^2$ = 21.02; table value of $X^2$ with 4 d f at .01 level is 13.28. Hence the difference is significant.

## Land

In case of the land left by the respondents' husbands, the data suggests that in the urban area about three fourths (72.67), and in the rural nearly half (50.00), of the deceased husbands had no lands at all. About 13 (13.33) per cent urban, as against 27(27.333) per cent rural, husbands had left behind land ranging from 1 to 19 acres. The remaining 14 (14.00) per cent husbands in the urban area, in comparison to 22 (22.67) per cent in the rural, had left land ranging from 20 to 40 acres. Thus, with regard to landed property, the findings seem to suggest that the landless husbands constitute a significant proportion of the deceased husbands in both urban and rural areas. However, the $X^2$ results establish that there is a significant difference between the urban and rural deceased husbands in respect of the landed property owned by them at the time of their death.

### 3.3 Details about the children

Under this, information is obtained regarding the personal characteristics of the respondent's children. Characteristics like age, educational level, marital status, occupation and income are presented. The particulars regarding the above components are presented in the tables below.

#### Age

The age distribution of the respondents' children is shown in Table 3.10.

**TABLE - 3.10**

**NO. OF CHILDREN BORNE BY THE WIDOWS**

| *Children* | *Male* | | *Female* | | *Total* | |
|---|---|---|---|---|---|---|
| *Age (Yrs.)* | *Urban Per cent* | *Rural Per cent* | *Urban Per cent* | *Rural Per cent* | *Male Per cent* | *Female Per cent* |
| 0-19 | 18.14 | 25.36 | 21.52 | 26.55 | 21.70 | 23.88 |
| 20-39 | 52.10 | 61.72 | 51.48 | 59.71 | 56.84 | 55.36 |
| Over 40 | 29.76 | 12.92 | 27.00 | 13.74 | 21.56 | 20.86 |
| Total | 100.00 | 100.00 | 100.00 | 100.00 | 100.00 | 100.00 |
| $X^2$ | | 18.3** | | 11.98** | | |

Calculated $X^2$ = 18.3; and 11.98 table value of $X^2$ with 2 d f at .01 level is 9.21. Hence there is a significant difference.

It may be observed from the table that the respondents' male children who fall in the age-group of 20-39 constitute the largest single proportion in urban and rural areas representing about 52 (52.10) per cent and 61 (61.72) per cent respectively. While about 18 (18.14) per cent of the urban children and nearly 25 (25.36) per cent of the children in rural areas are of the age between 0-19 years. It is also observed that about 29 (29.76) per cent of urban children in comparison to 12 (12.92) per cent of the children in rural areas are of the age over 40. The median age of the urban respondent's male children is 32.23 and that of rural respondent's male children is 27.98.

Further, the table reveals that nearly 51(51.48) per cent of female children in the urban area, in comparison to 59 (59.71) per cent in rural areas, are between 20-39 years of age and constitute the largest single proportion. And about 21 (21.52) per cent of the female children in urban area, as against 26 (26.55) per cent in rural areas fall in the age-group of 0-19 years. And the remaining 27(27.00) per cent in urban area and 13 (13.74) per cent in rural areas are of the age over 40. The median age of the urban female children studied is 31.07 and that or rural female is 27.86.

**Education**

The particulars regarding the educational level of the respondents' children are presented in Table 3.11.

**TABLE 3.11**
**EDUCATIONAL LEVEL OF CHILDREN**

| *Educational Level* | *Male* | | *Female* | | *Total* | |
|---|---|---|---|---|---|---|
| | *Urban Per cent* | *Rural Per cent* | *Urban Per cent* | *Rural Per cent* | *Male Per cent* | *Female Per cent* |
| Illiterate | 9.30 | 55.02 | 27.00 | 68.72 | 31.84 | 56.65 |
| Primary | 11.16 | 21.53 | 19.83 | 16.11 | 16.27 | 18.08 |
| Secondary | 14.42 | 10.53 | 13.93 | 8.53 | 12.50 | 11.39 |
| S.S.L.C. | 34.88 | 7.18 | 22.36 | 4.27 | 21.23 | 13.84 |
| Higher education | 30.24 | 5.74 | 16.88 | 2.37 | 18.16 | 16.04 |
| Total 215 | 100.00 | 100.00 | 100.00 | 100.00 | 100.00 | 100.00 |
| $X^2$ value | | 74.51* | | 92.84** | | |

Calculated $X^2$ = 74.51; and 92.84 table value of $X^2$ with 4 d f at .01 level is 13.28. Hence there is a significant difference.

The data reveals among the respondents' male children, in the urban areas, about 90(90.00) per cent, and in rural areas about 45 (45.00) are educated. Among females about 73 (73.00) per cent in urban areas and about 31 (31.84) per cent in rural areas are educated. About 9 (9.30) per cent of the male children in urban area and 55 (55.02) per cent in rural areas, in comparison to 27 (27.06) per cent in urban areas and 68 (68.72) per cent of the female children in rural areas are illiterates. The data also reveals that numbei of educated male and female children decreases as the educational level progresses in rural areas. And the graduation, postgraduation and professional degrees and diplomas are taken to represent high educational level, the data suggests that in rural areas there are only graduates and diploma holders. The data also suggests that both male and female children in urban areas are relatively higher educated than their rural counterparts.

**Discontinuation of Education**

With regard to the discontinuation of education the data reveals that about 29 (29.33) per cent of the urban children, as against 11 (11.33) per cent of rural children, stopped education due to their father's death. The particulars regarding the respondent's children's discontinuation of education and reasons for the same are presented in Table 3.12.

**TABLE - 3.12**

**DISCONTINUATION OF EDUCATION AMONG CHILDREN**

| *a. Discontinuation of Education* | *Urban Per cent* | *Rural Per cent* | *Total Per cent* | |
|---|---|---|---|---|
| No. | 49.34 | 20.00 | 34.67 | |
| Yes. | 29.33 | 11.33 | 20.33 | |
| Didn't go at all | 10.00 | 48.00 | 29.00 | |
| Not discontinued | 11.33 | 20.67 | 16.00 | |
| *b. Reasons* | *Per cent* | *Per cent* | *Per cent* | $X^2$ |
| To look after agriculture | 20.46 | 35.29 | 24.59 | |
| To continue family business | 13.64 | 29.42 | 18.03 | 6.24** |
| Started working | 65.90 | 35.29 | 57.38 | |
| | 100.00 | 100.00 | 100.00 | |

Calculated $X^2$ = 72.00; and 6.24 table value of $X^2$ with 2 d f at .05 level is 5.99. Hence there is a significant difference.

The table shows that about 49 (49.34) per cent of respondents in the urban areas, in comparison to 20 (20.00) per cent in rural areas reported that their children did not discontinue their education; whereas in the case of 10 (10.00) per cent of the respondents in urban areas, and 48 (48.00) per cent in rural areas the problem of discontinuing their education did not arise at all. About 29 (29.33) per cent of the urban respondents, as against 11 (11.33) per cent of the rural respondents, said that their children discontinued education after their father's death. However, the $X^2$ results show that there is a significant difference between urban and rural children in respect of discontinuation of their education.

Further it can be observed that about 65 (65.90) per cent of the urban children, as against about 35 (35.29) per cent of the rural children, started working in order to support their families. Whereas about 20 (20.46) per cent in urban areas and 35 (35.29) per cent in rural areas started looking after their agriculture. And the remaining 13 (13.64) per cent in urban areas, as against 29 (29.42) per cent in rural areas joined their family business by discontinuing their education. It can be said that a majority of the children started working in order to support the family income.

It is found that there is a significant difference between the urban and rural children in respect of the reasons for discontinuing their education.

**Marital Status**

With regard to the marital status of the respondent's children, the data indicates that in urban and rural areas over three-fourth of males and females are married and the remaining children are either unmarried or divorced/widowed. The distribution of the urban and rural children according to their marital status is presented in Table 3.13

**TABLE - 3.13**
**DISTRIBUTION OF CHILDREN BY MARITAL STATUS**

| *Marital Status* | *Male* | | *Female* | | *Total* | |
|---|---|---|---|---|---|---|
| | *Urban Per cent* | *Rural Per cent* | *Urban Per cent* | *Rural Per cent* | *Male Per cent* | *Female Per cent* |
| Married | 53.95 | 61.72 | 68.77 | 84.83 | 57.78 | 76.4 |
| Unmarried | 46.00 | 38.28 | 30.0 | 14.22 | 42.3 | 22.5 |
| Divorced/ widowed | - | - | 1.3 | 1.0 | - | 1.1 |
| Total | 100.00 | 100.00 | 100.00 | 100.00 | 100.00 | 100.00 |

It can be observed from the table that about 54 (53.95) per cent of the urban male children are married as against 61(61.72) per cent of their rural counterparts. Whereas in urban areas about 46 (46.00) per cent of the male children, in comparison to 38 (38.28) per cent in rural areas are unmarried.

Further, in urban areas, about 68 (68.77) per cent of female children, as against 84 (84.83) per cent in rural areas, are married while nearly 29 (29.95) per cent urban female children, in comparison to about 14 (14.22) per cent in rural areas, are unmarried. And only 1 (1.23) per cent of female children in urban and 1 (0.95) per cent in rural areas, are either divorced or widowed. Thus, in view of the above findings, it may be stated that greater number of female children are married than, the male children due to their familial responsibilities.

Further, about 15 (15.33) per cent of the urban respondents as against 3 (3.33) per cent of rural respondents prefer their daughter's marriage only after completion of their studies, whereas about 10 (10.0) per cent and 9 (9.33) per cent of the respondents in urban and rural areas respectively, prefer their daughter's marriage before the completion of their studies.

It is observed that almost all the respondents who have unmarried daughters face problems in getting them married off. About 5 (5.33) per cent of the urban respondents, as against about 4 (4.67) per cent of the rural respondents, state that the dowry demands are beyond their means. While nearly 2 (2.00) per cent and about 4 (4.00) per cent in the urban and rural mention that they do not receive any help to carry out marriage negotiations. About 18 (18.00) per cent of the urban respondents and nearly (3.33) per cent of the rural respondents say that they are not finding an alliance for their daughters and that they are also facing financial problems.

**Occupation**

The particulars regarding the respondents' children's occupation are presented in Table 3.14.

The data in this regard reveals that about 35 (35.81) per cent of the urban male children, as against 8 (8.62) per cent of their rural counterparts are government servants. While about 25 (25.12)

the rural respondents, state that their children behave as they like whereas, 8 (8.00) per cent of the respondents in urban areas and 20 (20.67) per cent in the rural areas say that their children hardly listen to them. About 4 (4.67) per cent and nearly 12 (12.00) per cent in the urban and the rural areas respectively mention that their married children stay separately. While 4 (4.00) per cent of the respondents in urban areas and 7 (7.33) per cent of the respondents in rural areas complain that their children are not helping them in taking care of other minor children. In view of this, it may be stated that more rural widows noticed changes in their children's behaviour as compared to the urban widows. However, the difference between the urban and rural widows in respect of stating that instances of changes occur, are found to be statistically significant.

**Reasons for changes**

The data regarding the reasons for change in children's activities indicate that a majority of the respondents state that it is difficult to have a check over the children's activities without male members. The particulars regarding the reasons for changes in children's activities are presented in Table 3.21.

**TABLE.- 3.21**

**REASONS FOR CHANGE IN CHILDREN'S ACTIVITIES**

| *Reasons* | *Urban Per cent* | *Rural Per cent* | *Total Per cent* | *$X^2$ Value* |
|---|---|---|---|---|
| Due to lack of adequate finance unable to satisfy their needs | 4.67 | 4.00 | 4.33 | |
| It is difficult to have a check over their activities without a male member | 14.00 | 34.67 | 24.33 | 34.82** |
| Bad companions | 6.67 | 18.67 | 12.67 | |
| Not changed/not having issues | 74.66 | 42.66 | 58.67 | |
| Total | 100.00 | 100.00 | 100.00 | |

It can be observed from Table 3.21 that about 6 (6.67) per cent of the urban respondents as against 18 (18.67) per cent of the rural respondents state that a vicious circle of friends and companions is the reason for the change in their children's activities. About 14 (14.00) per cent and 34 (34.67) per cent of the respondents in urban and rural areas respectively say that without a male member in the family, it is difficult to have a check over the children's activities. And the remaining 4 (4.67) per cent of the urban respondents and 4 (4.00) per cent of the rural respondents mention that the reason for the change in their children's activities is that they are unable to satisfy the latter's needs due to lack of adequate finance. As such the data seems to suggest that the absence of male member in the family is one of the important reasons for the change in children's activities. The statistical results show that there is a significant difference between the urban and rural widows in respect of stating reasons for the change in their children's activities.

### Decision Making by Widows

With a view to ascertaining the decision-making capacity of the widows, the respondents were asked as to whether they make decisions regarding children's education and matrimonial matters. In response to this, about over one-fourth (30.67) per cent in urban area and over half of the respondents in rural areas state that they consult close relatives while making decisions. The particulars regarding the decisions making by widows are presented in Table 3.22.

**TABLE - 3.22**
**DECISION MAKING BY WIDOWS**

| *Decision Making* | *Urban Per cent* | *Rural Per cent* | *Total Per cent* | *$X^2$ Value* |
|---|---|---|---|---|
| Consult close relatives | 30.67 | 54.00 | 42.33 | |
| Consult close friends | 4.00 | 6.00 | 5.00 | |
| Consult adult children | 12.67 | 4.67 | 8.66 | 22.63** |
| Herself | 3.33 | 3.33 | 3.67 | |
| Do not make decisions/ not having issues | 49.33 | 32.00 | 40.67 | |
| Total | 100.00 | 100.00 | 100.00 | |

(a) Calculated $X^2$ = 34.84; table value of $X^2$ with 3 d f at .01 level is 11.34. Hence, the difference is significant.

(b) Calculated $X^2$ = 22.63; table value of $X^2$ with 4 d f at .01 level is 13.28. Hence, the difference is significant.

It is observed from Table 3.22 that an absolute minority of 3 (3.33) per cent or urban respondents and 3 (3.33) per cent of the respondents, from rural areas state that they make decisions independently. About 30 (30.67) per cent of the urban respondents and 54 (54.00) per cent of the rural respondents say that they consult relatives. About 12 (12.67) per cent of the respondents in urban area and 4 (4.67) per cent of the respondents in rural areas consult adult children, whereas nearly 4 (4.00) per cent in urban area and 6 (6.00) per cent of the respondents in rural areas mention that they consult close friends, while making decisions about their children's education and matrimonial matters. And the remaining 49 (49.33) per cent of the respondents in urban area, in comparison to 32 (32.00) per cent in the rural areas, state that they do not make any decision regarding their children's future since their children got married before research is undertaken and working and living happily with their own families. In this group, as mentioned earlier, a few respondents are childless widows. Thus, the findings seem to suggest that a large number of widows consult either close relatives, adult children or close friends while taking decisions. However, the differences between the urban and rural widows in respect of their decision-making is found to be statistically significant.

FOUR

# Deprivation

In this chapter an attempt is made to study the deprivation faced by widows. The main focus in this chapter has been on the economic deprivation, social deprivation, emotional deprivation and cultural deprivation. However, the reasons for such deprivations and the effects of widowhood on the health of the widows have also been dealt with.

The main objective of this chapter is to measure the deprivation level of the widows in the fields mentioned above. The deprivation level is analysed in relation to area, caste, age and occupation variables. These variables may be of obvious importance in the analysis of the deprivation faced by the widows in their life.

With this view in mind, relevant questions pertaining to the respondents' deprivation have been included in the interview schedule. The responses to these questions, which throw light on the problems faced by the widows, are analysed and discussed in this chapter.

### 4.1 Economic Deprivation

To begin with, we may consider the economic deprivation of widows. To elicit data pertaining to widows' economic deprivation a series of statements were included in the interview schedule. The respondents were requested to mention 'No' or 'Yes' with each of the statements. In all, there are six such statements in the schedule and the responses to these statements are scored according to the following procedure to ascertain the deprivation level of the widows.

The responses denoting positive answers are assigned the score 1.

The responses denoting negative answers are assigned the score 0.

The following items are included to evaluate the economic deprivation of the respondents and the scoring pattern is as follows:

| *Economic Deprivation* | *Never* | *Sometimes* | *Often* |
|---|---|---|---|
| (1) Money | 0 | 1 | 2 |
| (2) Food/clothing/shelter | 0 | 1 | 2 |
| (3) Employment of self | 0 | 1 | 2 |
| (4) Employment of children | 0 | 1 | 2 |
| (5) Education of children | 0 | 1 | 2 |
| (6) Marriage of children | 0 | 1 | 2 |

## The Deprivation Level and the Variables

Under this section the different variables such as area, caste, age and occupation and their association with the deprivation level of the respondents have been discussed. Table 4.1(A) provides the particulars regarding the economic deprivation of the widow, in relation to their localities.

**TABLE - 4.1 (A)**
**AREA AND ECONOMIC DEPRIVATION**

| *Area* | *N* | *Score* | *Per cent* | *'t' value* |
|---|---|---|---|---|
| Urban | 150 | 6.43 | 53.6 | |
| Rural | 150 | 6.78 | 56.5 | $1.86^{NS}$ |
| Combined | 300 | 6.60 | 55.0 | |

*Note*: N.S. : Not Significant
* : Significant at 0.05 level
** : Significant at .01 level

The data pertaining to the area of the widow and their deprivation in the economic field is presented in Table 4.1(A). The data indicates that about 54 (53.6) per cent of the urban respondents faced economic deprivation. Though it seems rural respondents are more deprived, the statistical results establish that there is no significant difference between the urban and rural respondents with respect to economic deprivation.

However, the economic deprivation seems to be associated with all the caste categories. The particulars pertaining to this are presented in Table 4.1(B).

**TABLE - 4.1 (B)**
**CASTE AND ECONOMIC DEPRIVATION**

| *Caste* | *N* | *Score* | *Per cent* | *'t' value* |
|---|---|---|---|---|
| Upper caste (UC) | 180 | 6.56 | 54.7 | 0.67[NS] |
| Intermediate caste (IC) | 53 | 6.70 | 55.8 | 0.33[NS] |
| Lower caste | 67 | 6.64 | 55.3 | 0.45[NS] |
| Combined | 300 | 6.60 | 55.0 | |

Caste is a composite variable consisting of three broad caste groups as explained in material and method chapter.

On review of Table 4.1(B) it could be noticed that about 54 (54.7) per cent of upper caste respondents, in comparison to about 55 (55.8) per cent of intermediate caste respondents, faced economic deprivation. And about 55 (55.3) per cent of the lower caste respondents faced economic deprivation. Thus, in view of the above findings, we may suggest that there is no difference between the caste groups. The widows of the three caste groups faced economic deprivation.

However, the 't' test is not significant in all the three combination of caste groups. Thus the test implies that the caste status of the respondents is not relevant with reference to deprivation level in the economic field.

**TABLE - 4.1 (C)**
**AGE AND ECONOMIC DEPRIVATION**

| *Age Years* | *N* | *Score* | *Per cent* | *'t' value* | |
|---|---|---|---|---|---|
| Below 30 | 31 | 7.00 | 58.3 | 2.35* | (1 & 2) |
| 30-60 | 189 | 6.61 | 55.1 | 2.21* | (1 & 3) |
| 60 and above | 80 | 6.44 | 53.7 | 0.68 NS | (2 & 3) |
| Combined | 300 | 6.60 | 55.0 | | |

In view of the importance of age as a variable in determining one's deprivation, to begin with, we may consider the relationship between the age of the widows and their economic deprivation. The data pertaining to this is presented in Table 4.1(C).

The data reveals that about 58 (58.3) per cent of the respondents who fall in the below 30 years age group faced economic deprivation. About 55 (55.1) per cent of the respondents who fall in the age-group of 30-60 years, in comparison to 53 (53.7) per cent of the respondents who are of the age group over 60 faced economic deprivation. As such, the data seems to suggest that in terms of age, young and middle aged widows faced more economic deprivation than the widows of the older age group.

However, the 't' test of significance also indicates a significant difference between the respondents of different age groups with respect to the economic deprivation of the widows.

We may next consider the economic deprivation of widows in terms of their working and non-working status. The data pertaining to this is presented in Table 4.1(D).

**TABLE - 4.1 (D)**

**OCCUPATION AND ECONOMIC DEPRIVATION**

| *Caste* | *N* | *Score* | *Per cent* | *'t' value* |
|---|---|---|---|---|
| Working | 176 | 6.59 | 54.9 | $0.15^{NS}$ |
| Non working | 124 | 6.62 | 55.2 | |
| Combined | 300 | 6.60 | 55.0 | |

A detailed examination of Table 4.1(D) reveals that about 54 (54.9) per cent of working respondents, as against 55 (55.2) per cent of non-working respondents, faced economic deprivation. As such widows of both groups faced economic deprivation

The 't' test results reveal that there is no significant difference between the working and non working respondents with respect to the economic deprivation level. Thus, it is implied that there is no association between occupation of the respondents and economic deprivation level.

The data presented in Table 4.1(E) reveal that among widows whose husbands income was nil about 49 (49.19) per cent of the urban widows found the expenses on their children's education and marriage most difficult to meet, whereas, 45 (45.00) per cent of the rural widows found the expenses on the livelihood most difficult to meet.

**TABLE - 4.1 (E)**
**HUSBAND'S INCOME AND ECONOMIC DEPRIVATION**

| *Area* | *Income* | *Expenses Found Most Difficult to Meet* | | | *Total* | *$X^2$value* |
|---|---|---|---|---|---|---|
| | | *Liveli-hood* | *Education/ Marriage* | *Others*** | | |
| Urban | Nil | 26.22 | 49.19 | 24.59 | 100.00 | |
| | Below 10,000 | 33.89 | 28.82 | 37.29 | 100.00 | 10.47* |
| | Above 10,000 | 6.67 | 50.00 | 43.33 | 100.00 | |
| Rural | Nil | 45.00 | 30.00 | 25.00 | 100.00 | |
| | Below 10,000 | 56.78 | 12.71 | 30.51 | 100.00 | 10.43* |
| | Above 10,000 | 16.67 | 25.00 | 58.33 | 100.00 | |
| Combined | | 38.67 | 28.76 | 32.66 | 100.00 | |

** Agriculture. Medical, give and take with relatives and friends, etc.

The widows whose husbands income was below Rs. 10,000, about 37 (37.29) per cent of the urban widows found the expenses on agriculture, medical and give and take with relative and friends as difficult to meet while, in rural area 56 (56.78) per cent of the widows found the expenses of livelihood difficult to meet.

The widows whose husband's income was above Rs. 10,000, 50 (50.00) per cent of the urban widows found the expenses on the children's education and marriage as difficult to meet while about 58 (58.33) per cent of the rural widows found expenses on agriculture, medical and give and take as most difficult to meet.

The hypothesis for the study is that the income of the husband has an influence on widow's level of economic deprivation is not rejected.

Next we may consider whether the husband's age at death has any influence on the economic deprivation of widows.

It may be observed from Table 4.1(F) that among the widows' whose husbands died before 40 years of age, about 34 (34.29) per cent of the urban widows faced problems of their children's education and marriage while about 41 (41.46) per cent of the rural widows faced the problems of livelihood.

Among the widows whose husbands died between 40 and 59 years of age, about 37 (37.50) per cent of the urban widows faced the problem of their children education and marriage whereas, in rural areas about 31 (31.70) per cent of the widows faced the problem of livelihood.

**TABLE - 4.1 (F)**
**HUSBAND'S AGE AND ECONOMIC DEPRIVATION PROBLEMS FACED**

| *Area* | *Husband's Age (yrs) at Death* | *Finance* | *Liveli- hood* | *Employ- ment* | *Educa tion & Marriage* | *Others** | *Total* | *$X^2$ Value* |
|---|---|---|---|---|---|---|---|---|
| Urban | Less than 40 | 14.28 | 22.86 | 17.14 | 34.29 | 11.43 | 100 | |
| | 40-59 | 5.66 | 33.33 | 13.89 | 37.50 | 9.72 | 100 | $9.5^{NS}$ |
| | 60 and above | 16.28 | 30.23 | 6.98 | 18.60 | 27.91 | 100 | |
| Rural | Less than 40 | 24.39 | 41.46 | 9.76 | 14.63 | 9.76 | 100 | |
| | 40-59 | 20.73 | 31.70 | 15.86 | 14.63 | 17.08 | 100 | $15.45^{NS}$ |
| | 60 and above | 33.34 | 14.81 | 22.22 | 22.22 | 7.41 | 100 | |
| Combined | | 17.3 | 30.67 | 14.00 | 23.67 | 14.33 | 100 | |

* Luxury items, Give and take with friends and relatives.

Next, among the widows whose husbands died at the age of 60+, about 30 (30.23) per cent of the widows faced the problem of livelihood while about 33 (33.34) per cent of the rural widows faced financial problems.

The hypothesis put for the study is that husbands age at death has an influence on the economic deprivation of widows is rejected.

Further, the particulars pertaining to the respondents' efforts to overcome the problems are presented in Table 4.2.

It may be observed from the Table 4.2 that about 42 (42.67) per cent of the urban respondents, as against 50 (50.67) per cent of the rural respondents, have reported that their children started working, while about 24 (24.67) per cent of the urban respondents in comparison to 32 (32.00) per cent of the rural respondents have stated that they started working. And about 14 (14.00) per cent of the respondents in urban area and 10 (10.67) per cent of the rural respondents have mentioned that they incurred loans.

**TABLE - 4.2**
**EFFORTS MADE TO OVERCOME THE PROBLEMS**

| *Efforts Made* | *Urban Per cent* | *Rural Per cent* | *Total Per cent* | *$x^2$ Value* |
|---|---|---|---|---|
| Sold land/house | 3.33 | 3.33 | 3.33 | |
| Incurred loans | 14.00 | 10.67 | 12.33 | |
| Started working | 24.67 | 32.00 | 28.34 | 14.66* |
| Given up entertainments and luxuries | 15.33 | 3.33 | 9.33 | |
| Children started working | 42.67 | 50.67 | 46.67 | |
| Total | 100.00 | 100.00 | 100.00 | |

Calculated $X^2$ = 14.66; table value of $X^2$ with 2 d f at .05 level is 13.28. Hence, the difference is significant.

Thus, it is evident from the data that a significant majority of the respondent's children started working. However, the $X^2$ value establish that there is a significant difference between the urban and rural widows with respect to the efforts made to overcome the problems.

We may next consider the debt taken by the widows, amount borrowed and their opinion towards debt. The data presented in Table 4.3(A) indicates that about 25 (25.67) per cent of the respondents have incurred debt.

**TABLE - 4.3**
**(A) DEBT TAKEN BY WIDOWS**

| *Debt taken* | *Urban %* | *Rural %* | *Total %* | *$X^2$ Value* |
|---|---|---|---|---|
| No | 81.33 | 67.33 | 74.33 | |
| Yes | 18.67 | 32.67 | 25.67 | 7.68** |
| Total | 100.00 | 100.00 | 100.00 | |

Calculated $X^2$ = 7.68; table value of $X^2$ with 1 d f at .01 level is 6.63. Hence, the difference is significant.

**(B) AMOUNT BORROWED**

| *Amount Borrowed* | *Urban %* | *Rural %* | *Total %* | *$X^2$ Value* |
|---|---|---|---|---|
| Below 5000 | 28.57 | 81.67 | 62.33 | |
| 5001-above | 71.43 | 18.33 | 37.67 | 21.56** |
| Total | 100.00 | 100.00 | 100.00 | |

Calculated $X^2$ = 21.56; table value of $X^2$ with 1 d f at .01 level is 6.63. Hence, the difference is significant.

### (C) PURPOSE FOR AMOUNT BORROWED

| *Purpose of Borrowing* | *Urban %* | *Rural %* | *Total %* | *$X^2$ Value* |
|---|---|---|---|---|
| For food & clothes | 21.43 | 22.45 | 22.08 | |
| For marriage | 35.71 | 34.69 | 35.06 | |
| For agriculture | 17.86 | 32.66 | 27.27 | 20.36** |
| For business | 25.00 | 10.20 | 15.59 | |
| Total | 100.00 | 100.00 | 100.00 | |

Calculated $X^2$ = 20.36; table value of $X^2$ with 3 d f at .01 level is 11.34. Hence, the difference is significant.

### (D) OPINION TOWARDS DEBT

| *Opinion towards Debt* | *Urban %* | *Rural %* | *Total %* | *$X^2$ Value* |
|---|---|---|---|---|
| Likely to repay | 28.57 | 12.25 | 18.18 | |
| Will become very difficult | 50.00 | 48.97 | 49.36 | 8.77** |
| May continue as it is | 21.43 | 38.78 | 32.46 | |
| Total | 100.00 | 100.00 | 100.00 | |

Calculated $X^2$ = 8.77; table value of $X^2$ with 2 d f at .01 level is 5.99. Hence, the difference is significant.

It may be observed from the table that about 18(18.67) per cent of the respondents in urban area, as against 32 (32.67) per cent of the rural respondents have incurred debt in order to overcome their economic problems. In view of the above findings we may state that the proportion of those who have taken debt is lower than those who have not done so. However, there is significant difference between the urban and rural widows with respect to the debt taking itself.

Further, the data in Table 4.3(B) indicates that about 71(71.43) per cent of the urban respondents borrowed Rs.5000, in comparison to 81 (81.67) per cent of the rural respondents who borrowed below Rs 5000. Thus, with regard to the amount borrowed we may say that a majority of the widows borrowed not more than Rs.5000. However. a significant difference is found between the urban and the rural widows with respect to the amount borrowed.

Table 4.3(D) also reveals that a majority of the respondents reported that it would become very difficult to repay the debt. About 50 (50.00) per cent of the respondent in urban and 48 (48.97) per cent in the rural area have stated so, whereas, about 21

(21.43) per cent of the urban respondents and 38 (38.78) per cent of rural respondents have reported that the debt taking might continue. Thus, it may be said that only about 18 (18.18) per cent of the respondents have stated that they are likely to repay their debts. However, the difference between the urban and rural widows is found to be statistically significant.

Further the Table 4.3(C) shows that about 35 (35.71) per cent and 34 (34.69) per cent of the respondents, from urban and rural areas respectively, have reported that they borrowed money for the marriage of their children, while above 17 (17.86) per cent of the urban respondents and 32 (32.66) per cent of the rural respondents mentioned that they borrowed for agricultural purposes. As such, the data seems to suggest that a majority of the respondents borrowed money for conducting the marriage of their children. However, the difference between the urban and rural widows is found to be statistically significant. Further, it is of significance to note that the expenses on necessities were difficult to meet. The particulars regarding this are presented in Table 4.4.

**TABLE - 4.4**
**EXPENSES FOUND MOST DIFFICULT TO MEET**

| *Items of Expenses* | *Urban %* | *Rural %* | *Total %* | *$X^2$ value* |
|---|---|---|---|---|
| Food, cloth, shelter | 25.33 | 52.00 | 38.67 | |
| Education of the children | 14.00 | 6.00 | 10.00 | |
| Marriage of the children | 27.33 | 10.00 | 18.67 | 35.12** |
| Agriculture | 6.67 | 12.67 | 9.66 | |
| Medical | 10.67 | 7.33 | 9.00 | |
| Others* | 16.00 | 12.00 | 14.00 | |
| Total | 100.00 | 100.00 | 100.00 | |

* House rent, daughter's delivery and other expenses.
Calculated $X^2$ = 35.12; table value of $X^2$ with 5 d f at .o1 level is 15.09. Hence the difference is significant.

It is evident from the Table 4.4 that about 27 (27.33) per cent of the respondents in urban area, in comparison to 10 (10.00) per cent of the rural respondents, have stated that the expenses of the children's marriage are found to be most difficult to meet. Whereas in urban area, about 25 (25.33) per cent of the respondents, as against 52 (52.00) per cent of the rural respondents, have mentioned that expenses on food, clothing and shelter are found to be most difficult to meet. Thus, with regard to expenses, it may be said that a significant majority (38.67) of the respondents found the expenses on food, clothing and shelter most difficult to meet. The $X^2$ value shows that there is a significant difference between the urban and rural widows with respect to the expenses found to be difficult to meet.

We may next consider how many destitute widows are receiving the widow-pension instituted by the Government of Karnataka and how many are aware of this scheme as shown in Table 4.5.

**TABLE - 4.5**
**WIDOWS RECEIVING WIDOW PENSION**

| *Widow Pension* | *Urban %* | *Rural %* | *Total %* |
|---|---|---|---|
| No | 84.67 | 82.00 | 83.33 |
| Yes | 15.33 | 18.00 | 16.67 |
| Total | 100.00 | 100.00 | 100.00 |

The data presented in the above table reveals that about 15 (15.33) per cent of the urban respondents, as against 18(18.00) per cent of the rural, are beneficiaries of this scheme. Thus, it may be said that about 16 (16.67) per cent of the respondents who are destitutes are receiving this pension.

Further, the data suggests that about 86 (86.00) per cent of the urban respondents, as against 78 (78.00) per cent the rural respondents, are aware of this social security scheme.

**4.2 Social Deprivation**

Under this heading the social deprivation of the widows is focused upon. The main purpose behind this is to ascertain how widows are treated by the members of their families, both before and after widowhood, change in the frequency of kinsmens' and friends' visits, and vice versa, leisure time activities and adjustment to such situations. In other words, an attempt has been made to know, how the social activities of the widows are narrowed down, which may in turn speak of social support rendered by the people and the social deprivation faced by the widows.

The responses to each of the questions relating to social deprivation are scored as follows:

As example:

(1) How were you looked after by your family members before widowhood.

| | |
|---|---|
| (1) Bad | 0 |
| (2) Indifferent | 1 |
| (3) Well | 2 |

(2) How are you looked after by your family members after widowhood.

| | |
|---|---|
| (1) Bad | 0 |
| (2) Indifferent | 1 |
| (3) Well | 2 |

(3) Did your family members respect you before widowhood.

| | |
|---|---|
| (1) Never | 0 |
| (2) Sometimes | 1 |
| (3) Often | 2 |

(4) Do your family members respect you after widowhood.

| | |
|---|---|
| (1) Never | 0 |
| (2) Sometimes | 1 |
| (3) Often | 2 |

The data pertaining to the respondents social deprivation are presented in Table 4.6(A).

**TABLE - 4.6 (A)**
**AREA AND SOCIAL DEPRIVATION**

| *Area* | *N* | *Before* | | *After* | | *'t' Value* |
|---|---|---|---|---|---|---|
| | | *Score* | *Per cent* | *Score* | *Per cent* | |
| Urban | 150 | 5.38 | 53.8 | 5.89 | 58.9 | 2.62** |
| Rural | 150 | 4.63 | 46.3 | 5.16 | 51.6 | 3.70** |
| Combined | 300 | 5.01 | 50.1 | 5.52 | 55.2 | 4.09 |
| 't' value | | | 4.12** | | 4.59** | |

Note: NS: Not significant

*: Significant at .05 level.

**: Significant at .01 level.

The data pertaining to the area of the widows and their deprivation in the social field is presented in the above table.

Before widowhood, about 53 (53.8) per cent of the urban respondents in comparision to 46 (46.3) per cent of the rural respondents, faced social deprivation whereas, after widowhood, the same situation was faced by about 58 (58.9) per cent of the urban respondents as against 51 (51.6) per cent of rural respondents.

Further, it may be observed that a greater number of urban respondents than rural respondents faced social deprivation. And the percentage of both urban and rural respondents has gone up after widowhood.

The test value reveals that there is a significant difference in respect of all categories. It can be inferred from the findings in the table that there is a positive effect of widowhood on social life of the widows in both the areas. The hypothesis put for study that there is a difference in the social deprivation level of rural and urban widows is not rejected.

Further, it may be of significance to know how the widows belonging to different caste categories faced social deprivation. The data pertaining to this is presented in Table 4.6(B).

**TABLE - 4.6 (B)**

**CASTE AND SOCIAL DEPRIVATION**

| *Caste* | | *Before* | | *After* | | *'t' Value* |
|---|---|---|---|---|---|---|
| | *N* | *Score* | *Per cent* | *Score* | *Per cent* | |
| Upper caste (UC) | 180 | 5.23 | 52.3 | 5.91 | 59.1 | 4.24** |
| Intermediate caste (IC) | 53 | 5.17 | 51.7 | 5.43 | 54.3 | 0.86NS |
| Lower caste (LC) | 67 | 4.27 | 42.7 | 4.54 | 45.4 | 1.04NS |
| Combined | 300 | 5.01 | 50.1 | 5.52 | 55.2 | 4.09** |
| 't' value | UC & IC | | 0.24* | | 2.06* | |
| | IC & LC | | 3.14** | | 3.23** | |
| | UC & LC | | 4.38** | | 6.44** | |

Note: Same as for Table 4.6(A).

Observation of the above table reveals that prior to widowhood about 52 (52.3) per cent of the upper caste respondents, as against 51 (51.7) per cent of the intermediate caste and 42 (42.7) per cent of the lower caste respondents, faced social deprivation. Whereas, after widowhood, about 59 (59.1) per cent of the upper caste respondents, in comparison to 54 (54.3) per cent of the intermediate caste and 45 (45.4) per cent of the lower caste respondents, faced social deprivation.

The data indicates that in case of upper caste respondents the percentage has gone up after widowhood. While in both intermediate and lower castes there is not much difference in this percentage. In terms of intercaste categories there are differences between them both before and after widowhood.

However, the 't' test of significance indicates that there is a significant difference in the upper caste after widowhood, while it is not so in other castes. But in case of intercaste categories there is significant difference between them. Therefore, it implies that there is significant association between intercaste categories and social deprivation.

Further, the social deprivation faced by widows belonging to different age groups is presented in Table 4.6(C).

**Age and Social Deprivation**

It is clear from Table 4.6(C) that prior to widowhood about 54 (54.3) per cent of the respondents below 30 years of age, in comparison to 49 (49.0) per cent of the respondents in the 30-60 years age group, and 50 (50.9) per cent of the respondents of 60 years and above, faced deprivation. After widowhood, however, about 53 (53.6) per cent of the respondents below 30 years, as against 53 (53.7) per cent in the age group of 30-60 years and 59 (59.4) per cent of 60 and above, faced social deprivation.

**TABLE - 4.6 (C)**
**AGE AND SOCIAL DEPRIVATION**

| *Age (Years)* | | | *Before* | | *After* | | *'t' Value* |
|---|---|---|---|---|---|---|---|
| | | *N* | *Score* | *Per cent* | *Score* | *Per cent* | |
| Below 30 | (1) | 31 | 5.43 | 54.3 | 5.36 | 53.6 | 0.19** |
| 31-60 | (2) | 189 | 4.90 | 49.0 | 5.37 | 53.7 | 2.75** |
| 60 and above | (3) | 80 | 5.09 | 50.9 | 5.94 | 59.4 | 3.83** |
| Combined | | 300 | 5.01 | 50.1 | 5.52 | 55.2 | 4.09** |
| | | 1 & 2 | | $1.64^{NS}$ | | $0.04^{NS}$ | |
| 't' value | | 2 & 3 | | $0.96^{NS}$ | | 2.88** | |
| | | 1 & 3 | | $1.01^{NS}$ | | 2.21** | |

Note: Same as in Table 4.6(A).

The table shows that in all the age groups, the percentage has gone up after widowhood. Whereas, in case of inter-age groups; there is not much difference between, before and after widowhood. But the difference is seen between the age groups of 30-60 and 60 and above, and below 30 years.

However, the statistical results show that in all the age groups, there is significant difference both before and after widowhood, while there is no significant difference between the different age-groups in case of before widowhood. But after widowhood the difference is significant only between the 31-60 years group and 60 and above age group.

Further, the data pertaining to the social deprivation is related to the occupational status as shown in Table 4.6(D) in order to know to what extent the variable is associated with the social deprivation of the respondents. It is clear from Table 4.6(D) that about 49 (49.5) per cent of working respondents, as against 50 (50.9) per cent of the non-working respondents, faced social deprivation before widowhood, whereas about 54 (54.8) per cent of the working widows in comparison to 55 (55.8) per cent of the non-working widows faced social deprivation after widowhood.

**TABLE - 4.6 (D)**

**OCCUPATION AND SOCIAL DEPRIVAT'ON**

| *Occupation* | | *Before* | | *After* | | *'t' Value* |
|---|---|---|---|---|---|---|
| | N | *Score* | *Per cent* | *Score* | *Per cent* | |
| Working | 176 | 4.95 | 49.5 | 5.48 | 54.8 | 3.04** |
| Non-working | 124 | 5.09 | 50.9 | 5.58 | 55.8 | 2.66** |
| Combined | 300 | 5.01 | 50.1 | 5.52 | 55.2 | 4.09** |
| 't' value | | | $0.73^{NS}$ | | $0.61^{NS}$ | |

The findings indicate that in both the groups there is an increase in the percentage of widows. There is not much difference between the working and non-working groups both in the case of before and after widowhood.

The 't' test of significance also indicates that there is a significant difference between the respondents who faced social deprivation before and after widowhood. But there is not much difference between the working and non-working widows with respect to social deprivation.

Further, the data pertaining to the frequency of visits by the kinsmen of both sides and the widows, both before and after widowhood, in relation to the variables as mentioned before, is discussed in Table 4.7(A) in order to know the extent of decrease in the frequency of visits after widowhood.

**TABLE 4.7 (A)**
**AREA OF FREQUENCY AFTER WIDOWHOOD**

| *Area* | | *Before Widowhood* | | *After Widowhood* | | *'t' Value* |
|---|---|---|---|---|---|---|
| | *N* | *Score* | *Per cent* | *Score* | *Per cent* | |
| Urban | 150 | 5.80 | 72.5 | 3.49 | 43.6 | 11.16** |
| Rural | 150 | 5.83 | 72.9 | 3.77 | 47.1 | 9.51** |
| Combined | 300 | 5.82 | 72.7 | 3.63 | 45.4 | 14.64 |
| 't' value | | | 0.14NS | | 1.38NS | |

**Area and Frequency of Visits.**

The data pertaining to the area of the widows and the frequency of kinsmen's visits and widow's visits is presented in the above table.

It may be observed that before widowhood about 72 (72.5) per cent of the urban respondents, in comparison to 72 (72.9) per cent of the rural respondents, reported that the kinsmen used to visit them frequently and vice versa. Whereas, after widowhood, this figure dropped to about 43 (43.6) per cent for the urban respondents as against 47 (47.1) per cent for the rural respondents.

Hence, the data seems to suggest that after widowhood there is a decrease in the frequency of kinsmen's and widows' visits to each other, both in urban and rural areas. But there is not much difference between the two areas.

The test value reveals that there is a significant difference between, before, and after widowhood in both the areas. It can be inferred from the findings in the table that there is a positive effect of widowhood on the frequency of kinsmen's and widow's visits to each other.

We may next consider the relationship between caste and frequency of visits. The data pertaining to this are provided in the following table.

**Caste and Frequency of Visits**

The data presented in Table 4.7(B) indicates that before widowhood about 75 (75.8) per cent of the upper caste respondents as against 66 (66.2) per cent of the intermediate caste and 69 (69.7) per cent of the lower caste respondents reported that kinsmen used to visit them and vice-versa. While after widowhood this figure dropped to about 46 (46.0) per cent for the upper caste respondents, in comparison to 42 (42.5) per cent for the intermediate and 45 (45.9) per cent for the lower caste respondents. Thus, with regard to the frequency of the kinsmen's and widow's visits, the findings suggest that after widowhood, in all the caste categories, the frequency of visits between both the categories has decreased and there is much difference before and after widowhood. In terms of intercaste categories this difference is not very significant, except, prior to widowhood between upper and intermediate castes.

TABLE - 4.7 (B)

CASTE AND FREQUENCY OF VISITS

| *Caste* | | *Before Widowhood* | | *After Widowhood* | | *'t' Value* |
|---|---|---|---|---|---|---|
| | *N* | *Score* | *Per cent* | *Score* | *Per cent* | |
| Upper caste (UC) | 180 | 6.06 | 75.8 | 3.68 | 46.0 | 12.77** |
| Intermediate caste (IC) | 53 | 5.30 | 66.2 | 3.40 | 42.5 | 5.40** |
| Lower caste (LC) | 67 | 5.58 | 69.7 | 3.67 | 45.9 | 5.60** |
| Combined | 300 | 5.82 | 72.7 | 3.63 | 45.4 | |
| 't' value | UC & IC | | 2.59** | | 1.04NS | |
| | IC & LC | | 0.80NS | | 0.79NS | |
| | UC & LC | | 1.73NS | | 0.04NS | |

However, the 't' test of significance indicates that there is a significant difference before and after widowhood in all the caste categories. However, this is not significant between the caste categories except between the upper and intermediate castes. Therefore, it implies that there is a significant association between the caste and frequency of visits.

We may further consider the frequency of visits in terms of the different age groups. The relevant data is presented in Table 4.7(C).

**TABLE - 4.7 (C)**
**AGE AND FREQUENCY OF VISITS**

| *Age (Years)* | | *No.* | *Before Widowhood* Score | Per cent | *After Widowhood* Score | Per cent | *'t' Value* |
|---|---|---|---|---|---|---|---|
| Below 30 | (1) | 31 | 6.10 | 76.3 | 3.39 | 42.4 | 6.33** |
| 31-60 | (2) | 189 | 5.92 | 74.0 | 3.86 | 48.3 | 11.09** |
| 60 and above | (3) | 80 | 5.46 | 68.3 | 3.16 | 39.5 | 7.71** |
| Combined | | 300 | 5.82 | 72.7 | 3.63 | 45.4 | 14.64** |
| 't' value | | 1 & 2 | | 0.56NS | | 1.39NS | |
| | | 2 & 3 | | 1.71NS | | 3.10** | |
| | | 1 & 3 | | 1.71NS | | 0.63NS | |

**Age and Frequency of Visits**

It is observed from the above table that before widowhood about 76 (76.3) per cent of the urban respondents who fall in the age group of below 30 years, as against 74 (74.0) per cent of the respondents of 31-60 years age group and 68 (68.3) per cent in the post-60 years age group, reported that kinsmen used to visit them and vice versa. After widowhood this figure dropped to about 42 (42.4) per cent for the respondents in the below-30 years age group in comparison to 48 (48.3) per cent for the respondents of 31-60 years age group and 39 (39.5) per cent for the respondents of 60 and above age group.

Table 4.7(C) suggests that in all the age groups the frequency of the kinsmen's and widows' visits to each other has come down and there is much difference before and after widowhood. There is not much difference between the inter age groups, except in case of post-widowhood between 31-60 years age group and 60 and above.

However, the difference before and after widowhood in all other age groups is found to be statistically significant, while there is no significant difference between the different age groups both before and after widowhood. After widowhood the difference between the 31-60 age group and 60 and above age group is found to be statistically significant.

Further, we may consider the relationship between the occupational status of the widows and frequency of visits. The data pertaining to this are presented in Table 4.7(D).

**TABLE - 4.7 (D)**
**OCCUPATION AND FREQUENCY OF VISITS**

| *Occupation* | | *Before Widowhood* | | *After Widowhood* | | *'t' Value* |
|---|---|---|---|---|---|---|
| | *No.* | *Score* | *Per cent* | *Score* | *Per cent* | |
| Working | 176 | 5.77 | 72.1 | 3.80 | 47.5 | 10.23** |
| Non-working | 124 | 5.89 | 73.6 | 3.39 | 42.4 | 10.63** |
| Combined | 300 | 5.82 | 72.7 | 3.63 | 45.4 | 14.64 |
| 't' value | | | 0.53NS | | 2.00* | |

## Occupation and Frequency of Visits

We may observe from the above table that before widowhood 72 (72.1) per cent of the working respondents, as against 73 (73.6) per cent of the non-working respondents, said that kinsmen used to visit them and vice-versa. Whereas, after widowhood, this figure dropped to about 47 (47.5) per cent for the working respondents in comparison to 42 (42.4) per cent for the non-working respondents.

As such, we may suggest that in both the groups, the frequency of visits between respondents and kinsmen has decreased and the difference before and after widowhood is found to be significant.

The 't' test of significance also indicates that there is a significant difference before and after widowhood in both the groups. While before widowhood the difference is not significant between the working and non-working groups, in contrast, after widowhood, this difference is statistically found to be significant.

We may first consider the frequency of visits between widows and friends before widowhood. The data pertaining to this is provided in Table 4.8(A).

It can be observed from the table that the proportion of respondents who visited their friends sometimes is about 52 (52.00) per cent among urban respondents, whereas it is about 70 (70.67) per cent among rural respondents. In the case of friends visits to the respondents, about 36 (36.67) per cent of the urban respondents as against 20 (20.00) per cent of the rural respondents reported that they did so some times.

Further, the proportion of those who visited their friends often is about 44 (44.00) per cent among urban respondents while it is only about 26 (26.00) per cent among rural respondents. On the contrary in case of friend's visits to the respondents, about 54 (54.66) per cent of the urban respondents in comparison to 74 (74.00) per cent of rural respondents stated that their friends visited often.

### TABLE - 4.8 (A)
### FREQUENCY OF VISITS BETWEEN WIDOWS AND FRIENDS BEFORE WIDOWHOOD

| | *Widows Visit to Friends* | | | *Friends Visit to Widows* | | |
|---|---|---|---|---|---|---|
| *Frequency of Visits* | *Urban Per cent* | *Rural Per cent* | *Total Per cent* | *Urban Per cent* | *Rural Per cent* | *Total Per cent* |
| Never | 4.00 | 3.33 | 3.33 | 8.67 | 6.00 | 7.33 |
| Some times | 52.00 | 70.67 | 61.67 | 36.67 | 20.00 | 28.33 |
| Often | 44.00 | 26.00 | 35.00 | 54.66 | 74.00 | 64.34 |
| Total | 100.00 | 100.00 | 100.00 | 100.00 | 100.00 | 100.00 |
| $X^2$ value | | | 11.28** | | | 12.4** |

Calculated $X^2 = 11.28$; table value of $X^2$ with 2 d f at .01 level is 9.21. Hence the difference is significant.
Calculated $X^2 = 12.4$; table value of $X^2$ with 2 d f at .01 level is 9.21. Hence the difference is significant.

Thus, the findings suggest that a majority of the widows visited their friends sometimes, while a significant majority of the friends visited the respondents.

However, in both the cases, the difference between urban and rural widows, with respect to their visits to one another, is found to be statistically significant.

We may next consider the frequency of visits between widows and friends after widowhood as shown in Table 4.8(B).

The data presented in Table 4.8(B) reveals that the proportion of respondents who visited their friends sometimes is about 52 (52.00) per cent among the urban respondents, whereas it is about 40 (40.00) per cent among the rural respondents. While friends' visits to the respondents is about 64 (64.67) per cent in case of the urban respondents in comparison to 38 (38.67) per cent for rural respondents. Further, about 32 (32.67) per cent of urban respondents, in comparison to 53 (53.33) per cent of rural respondents have reported that they visit their friends often, while about 20 (20.00) per cent of the urban respondents as against 54 (54.66) per cent of the rural respondents have stated that their friends visit them often.

## TABLE - 4.8 (B)
## FREQUENCY OF VISITS BETWEEN WIDOWS AND FRIENDS AFTER WIDOWHOOD

| Frequency of visits | *Widows Visit to Friends* Urban Per cent | Rural Per cent | Total Per cent | *Friends Visit to Widows* Urban Per cent | Rural Per cent | Total Per cent |
|---|---|---|---|---|---|---|
| Never | 15.33 | 6.67 | 11.00 | 15.33 | 6.67 | 11.00 |
| Sometimes | 52.00 | 40.00 | 46.00 | 64.67 | 38.67 | 51.67 |
| Often | 32.67 | 53.33 | 43.00 | 20.00 | 54.66 | 37.33 |
| Total | 100.00 | 100.00 | 100.00 | 100.00 | 100.00 | 100.00 |

Calculated $X^2$ = 31.86; table value of $X^2$ with 2 d f at .01 level is 9.21. Hence, the difference is significant.

Calculated $X^2$ = 39.06; table value of $X^2$ with 2 d f at .01 level is 9.21. Hence, the difference is significant.

Thus, with regard to the frequency of visits after widowhood the findings suggest that in both the cases the frequency rate has come down in comparison to pre-widowhood days.

However, in both the cases, the difference between the urban and rural widows with respect to their visits to each other is found to be statistically significant.

The changes noticed by the widows in their friends is presented in Table 4.8(C).

Table 4.8(C) reveals that about 46 (46.67) per cent of urban respondents, as against 26 (26.67) per cent of rural respondents, noticed a change in their friends.

Further, it may be observed that about 42 (42.86) per cent of the urban respondents have reported that their friends do not invite them for any social and religious functions, whereas about 62 (62.50) per cent of the rural respondents have stated that their friends do not invite them to gossip.

Thus, with regard to the change noticed by the widows in their friends we may conclude that about 36 (36.67) per cent of the respondents noticed a change in their friends and about 36 (36.36) per cent of the respondents complained that their friends do not invite them for any functions.

However, in support of this it may be stated that the difference between the urban and rural widows is statistically significant.

**TABLE - 4.8 (C)**
**CHANGES NOTICED IN FRIENDS**

| *Changes Noticed* | *Urban %* | *Rural %* | *Total %* |
|---|---|---|---|
| No | 53.33 | 73.33 | 63.33 |
| Yes | 46.67 | 26.67 | 36.67 |
| Total | 100.00 | 100.00 | 100.00 |
| **IN WHAT WAY** | | | |
| Do not invite me for any function | 42.86 | 25.00 | 36.36 |
| Do not invite me for gossiping | 14.28 | 62.50 | 31.82 |
| Treat indifferently | 42.85 | 12.50 | 31.82 |
| Total | 100.00 | 100.00 | 100.00 |
| $X^2$ value | 28.32** | | |

Calculated $X^2$ =28.32; table value of $X^2$ with 2 d f at .01 level is 9.21. Hence, the difference is significant.

### 4.3 Emotional Deprivation

We may next consider the emotional deprivation. Questions aimed at eliciting responses that could be taken as indicative of the widows emotional deprivation are included in the interview schedule. Four such questions are taken to ascertain the emotional deprivation of widows and the responses to these questions are scored according to the procedure mentioned below:

(1) How frequently do you feel that you are more unhappy and restless than before

(1) Never 0
(2) Sometimes 1
(3) Often 2

(2) How frequently do you lose your temper

(1) Never 0
(2) Sometimes 1
(3) Often 2

(3) How frequently do you suffer from sleepless nights/feel scared at night

(1) Never 0
(2) Sometimes 1
(3) Often 2

(4) How frequently do you feel lonely even when you are with the members of your family.

(1) Never 0
(2) Sometimes 1
(3) Often 2

The following table provides particulars regarding the emotional deprivation of the widows in relation to their residential area.

**TABLE - 4.9 (A)**

**AREA AND EMOTIONAL DEPRIVATION**

| *Area* | *N* | *Score* | *Per cent* | *'t' Value* |
|---|---|---|---|---|
| Urban | 150 | 5.34 | 69.5 | |
| Rural | 150 | 5.56 | 66.8 | 1.21NS |
| Combined | 300 | 5.45 | 68.1 | |

It is obvious from the above table that about 69 (69.5) per cent of the urban respondents and 66 (66.8) per cent of the rural respondents faced emotional deprivation.

It is clear from the table that there is not much difference between the urban and rural widows with respect to this factor.

The calculated 't' value is found not to be significant with respect to the emotional deprivation of urban and rural widows. And the hypothesis that there is no significant difference in the emotional deprivation of rural and urban widows is rejected.

However, the emotional deprivation of the widows seems to be inversely associated with the caste status. The data pertaining to this is presented in Table 4.9(B).

**TABLE - 4.9 (B)**

**CASTE AND EMOTIONAL DEPRIVATION**

| *Caste* | *N* | *Score* | *Per cent* | *'t' value* |
|---|---|---|---|---|
| Upper caste (UC) | 180 | 5.50 | 68.8 | 0.51NS (1 & 2) |
| Intermediate caste (IC) | 53 | 5.38 | 67.3 | 0.04NS (2 & 3) |
| Lower caste (LC) | 67 | 5.37 | 67.1 | 0.64NS (3 & 1) |
| Combined | 300 | 5.45 | 68.1 | |

From the table it is clear that about 68 (68.8) per cent of the upper caste respondents, in comparison to 67 (67.3) per cent of the intermediate caste respondents and 67 (67.1) per cent of the lower caste respondents faced emotional deprivation.

It may be observed from the table that in all the inter caste categories there is not much difference between them with respect to the emotional deprivation. Further, the 't' value is found not to be significant.

We may next consider the relationship between the age of the widows and their emotional deprivations. The data pertaining to this is presented in Table 4.9(C).

**TABLE - 4.9 (C)**

**AGE AND EMOTIONAL DEPRIVATION**

| *Age* | *N* | *Score* | *Per cent* | *'t' value* |
|---|---|---|---|---|
| Below 30 | 31 | 5.71 | 71.4 | 0.69NS (1 & 2) |
| 31-60 | 189 | 5.52 | 69.0 | 1.48NS (2 & 3) |
| 60 and above | 80 | 5.18 | 64.8 | 1.63NS (3 & 1) |
| Combined | 300 | 5.45 | 68.1 | |

The data in the above table reveals that about 71 (71.4) per cent of the respondents in the below-30 years age-group, as against 69 (69.0) per cent of the respondents of 31-60 years age group and about 64 (64.8) per cent the respondents who fall in the age-group of 60 years and above faced emotional deprivation.

It is clear from the data that in so far as experiencing emotional deprivation is concerned there is not much difference among the widows belonging to different age-groups. However, the test of significance was applied and it was found to be not significant.

We may next consider the emotional deprivation of the widows in terms of their occupational status. The relevant data is given in Table 4.9(D).

**TABLE - 4.9 (D)**

**OCCUPATION AND EMOTIONAL DEPRIVATION**

| *Occupation* | *N* | *Score* | *Per cent* | *'t' value* |
|---|---|---|---|---|
| Working | 176 | 5.35 | 66.9 | 1.28NS |
| Non-working | 124 | 5.59 | 69.8 | |
| Combined | 300 | 5.45 | 68.1 | |

It is revealed from the data in Table 4.9(D) that about 66 (66.9) per cent of the working respondents as against 69 (69.8) per cent of the non-working respondents faced emotional deprivation.

It is clear from the table that there is not much difference between the working and non-working widows in this respect. Further, the 't' value is found to be not significant. The particulars regarding the reasons for emotional deprivation are presented in Table 4.10. The data presented in the table indicates that about 33 (33.33) per cent of the urban respondents in comparison to 51 (51.33) per cent of the rural respondents reported a feeling of insecurity as one of the reasons. Whereas about 27 (27.33) per cent and 21 (21.33) per cent of the respondents in both urban and rural areas respectively stated socio-economic condition as the reason. And about 14 (14.67) per cent of the urban respondents as against 10 (10.67) per cent of the rural respondents mentioned increased worries as the reason for their emotional deprivation.

**TABLE - 4.10**

**REASONS FOR EMOTIONAL DEPRIVATION**

| *Reasons* | *Urban %* | *Rural %* | *Total %* | *$X^2$ Value* |
|---|---|---|---|---|
| Feeling of insecurity | 33.33 | 51.33 | 42.33 | |
| Fear of what happens next | 12.67 | 11.33 | 12.00 | 11.72** |
| Increased worries | 14.67 | 10.67 | 12.67 | |
| Socio-economic conditions | 27.33 | 21.33 | 24.33 | |
| Poor Health/old age | 12.00 | 5.34 | 8.67 | |
| Total | 100.00 | 100.00 | 100.00 | |

Calculated $X^2$ = 11.72; table value of $X^2$ with 4 d f at .05 level is 9.49. Hence the difference is significant.

Hence, the data seems to suggest that, for a significant majority of widows, a feeling of insecurity is the cause for their emotional deprivation. However, it may be stated that the difference between the urban and rural widows with respect to reasons for emotional deprivation is found to be statistically significant.

We may now consider the state of health of the widows. The data pertaining to this is presented in Table 4.11(A).

The table shows that about 86 (86.00) per cent of the

respondents possessed good health before widowhood while only 40 (40.33) per cent of them did so after widowhood.

**TABLE - 4.11 (A)**
**HEALTH STATUS OF WIDOWS**

| | *Before Widowhood* | | | *After Widowhood* | | | $X^2$ *Value* |
|---|---|---|---|---|---|---|---|
| *Health of the Widows* | *Urban* % | *Rural* % | *Total* % | *Urban* % | *Rural* % | *Total* % | |
| Worse/worst | 7.33 | 20.67 | 14.00 | 54.00 | 65.33 | 59.67 | |
| Good/same as before | 92.67 | 79.33 | 86.00 | 46.00 | 34.67 | 40.33 | 10.06* |
| Total | 100.00 | 100.00 | 100.00 | 100.00 | 100.00 | 100.00 | |

Calculated $X^2$ = 10.06; table value of $X^2$ with 1 d f at .01 level is 6.63. Hence, the difference is significant.

In urban area about 92 (92.67) per cent of the respondents, in comparison to about 79 (79.33) per cent of the rural respondents, were healthy, while only 7 (7.33) per cent and 20 (20.67) per cent of the respondents, both in urban and rural areas, had bad health before widowhood. Whereas after widowhood about 46 (46.00) per cent of the urban respondents, as against 34 (34.67) per cent of the rural respondents, had good health and only 54 (54.00) per cent of urban respondents and 65 (65.33) per cent of the rural respondents have bad health.

Hence, the data seems to suggest that a woman's health is affected by widowhood and almost all the widows are suffering from either minor or major ailments. The $X^2$ value establishes that there is a significant difference between the urban and rural widows with respect to their state of health.

The data pertaining to the sufferings faced by the widows is presented in Table 4.11(B). It may be observed that about 34 (34.67) per cent of the urban respondents as against 65 (65.34) per cent of the rural respondents suffered from general dissatisfaction. And about 33 (33.33) per cent and 13 (13.33) per cent of respondents from urban and rural areas respectively suffered from depression. Only about 11 (11.33) per cent of the urban respondents in comparison to 5 (5.33) per cent of the rural respondents suffered from headache.

**TABLE - 4.11(B)**
**SUFFERINGS FACED BY WIDOWS**

| *Reasons* | *Urban %* | *Rural %* | *Total %* | *$X^2$ Value* |
|---|---|---|---|---|
| Headache | 11.33 | 5.33 | 8.33 | |
| Loss of weight | 11.33 | 10.00 | 10.67 | |
| Falling of hair | 9.34 | 6.00 | 7.67 | 31.38** |
| Depression | 33.33 | 13.33 | 23.33 | |
| General dissatisfaction | 34.67 | 65.34 | 50.00 | |
| Total | 100.00 | 100.00 | 100.00 | |

Calculated $X^2$ = 31.38; table value of $X^2$ with 4 d f at .01 level is 13.28. Hence, the difference is significant.

Thus, with regard to sufferings faced by the widows, the findings seem to suggest that a majority of the widows both in urban and rural areas suffered from general dissatisfaction. However, the difference between the urban and rural widows with respect to the suffering faced is found to be statistically significant.

Further, it may be observed from the table that over three-fourths of the widows experienced humiliation in life. The particulars pertaining to the instances of humiliation are presented in Table 4.12.

**TABLE - 4.12**
**INSTANCES OF HUMILIATION**

| *Reasons* | *Urban %* | *Rural %* | *Total %* | *$X^2$ value* |
|---|---|---|---|---|
| Taunting | 28.00 | 44.00 | 36.00 | |
| Ill-treatment | 34.00 | 28.67 | 31.33 | |
| Beating | 8.67 | 10.00 | 9.33 | 10.98** |
| Starving | 15.33 | 8.00 | 11.67 | |
| Treat Warmly | 14.00 | 9.33 | 11.67 | |
| Total | 100.00 | 100.00 | 100.00 | |

Calculated $X^2$ = 10.98; table value of $X^2$ with 4 d f at .05 level is 9.49. Hence, the difference is significant.

The data in Table 4.12 reveals that about 34 (34.00) per cent of the urban respondents are ill-treated while about 44 (44.00) per cent of the rural respondents faced being taunted by the family member, especially from daughters-in-law. Moreover, about 8 (8.67) per cent of the urban respondents, in comparison to 8 (8.00) per cent of the rural respondents are beaten up and made to starve. The data also seems to suggest that about 14 (14.00) per cent of the urban respondents and 9 (9.33) per cent of the rural respondents are treated warmly by the members of their families. Thus, with regard to the instances of humiliation the findings indicate that a significant majority of the respondents are ill-treated. However, it is statistically established that there is a significant difference between the urban and rural widows in respect of the humiliation faced by them.

We may next consider the persons who quarrel with widows and the frequency of such quarrels. The relevant data is presented in Table 4.13.

**TABLE - 4.13**

**PERSONS QUARRELING WITH WIDOWS**

| | *Before Widowhood* | | | *After Widowhood* | | |
|---|---|---|---|---|---|---|
| *Persons* | *Urban Per cent* | *Rural Per cent* | *Total Per cent* | *Urban Per cent* | *Rural Per cent* | *Total Per cent* |
| Mother-in-law | 40.00 | 26.67 | 33.33 | 4.67 | 6.67 | 5.67 |
| Sister-in-law | 11.33 | 6.67 | 9.00 | 6.00 | 3.33 | 4.67 |
| Brother-in-law | 7.33 | 9.33 | 8.33 | 7.33 | 14.00 | 10.67 |
| Co-sisters | 8.67 | 21.33 | 15.00 | 7.33 | 13.33 | 10.33 |
| Daughter-in-law | 15.33 | 10.67 | 13.00 | 48.67 | 36.00 | 42.33 |
| Sons | 10.67 | 20.00 | 15.34 | 21.33 | 23.34 | 22.33 |
| Not Quarrelled | 6.67 | 5.33 | 6.00 | 4.67 | 3.33 | 4.00 |
| Total | 100.00 | 100.00 | 100.00 | 100.00 | 100.00 | 100.00 |
| $X^2$ | | 19.9** | | | 10.66NS | |
| | | *Frequency of Quarrel* | | | | |
| Never | 13.33 | 5.33 | 9.33 | 4.67 | 8.67 | 6.67 |
| Sometimes | 72.67 | 66.00 | 69.33 | 82.67 | 66.67 | 74.67 |
| Often | 14.00 | 28.67 | 21.34 | 12.66 | 24.66 | 18.66 |
| $X^2$ Value | | 10.98** | | | 8.52 | |

(a) Calculated $X^2 = 19.9$; table value of $X^2$ with 6 d f at .01 level is 16.81. Hence, the difference is significant.

(b) Calculated $X^2 = 10.66$; table value of $X^2$ with 6 d f at .05 level is 12.59. Hence, the difference is significant.

(c) Calculated $X^2 = 10.98$; table value of $X^2$ with 2 d f .01 level is 9.21. Hence, the difference is significant.

(d) Calculated $X^2 = 8.52$; table value of $X^2$ with 2 d f at .05 level is 5.93. Hence, the difference is significant.

From the data in Table 4.13, before widowhood we find that about 40 (40.00) per cent of the urban widows, as against 26

(26.67) per cent of the rural widows, have reported that the mother-in-law quarrelled with them. About 15 (15.33) per cent of the urban respondents, in comparison to 10 (10.67) per cent of rural respondents, have stated that daughters-in-law quarrelled with them. And nearly 10 (10.67) per cent of the urban widows and 20 (20.00) per cent of the rural widows have reported that the sons quarrelled with them.

Further, in terms of frequency of quarrels, the data seems to suggest that a higher proportion of respondents, both in urban (72.67) and rural (66.00) areas had quarrelled sometimes. In urban areas about 14 (14.00) per cent and in rural areas nearly 29 (28.67) per cent of the respondents have quarrelled frequently. And only 13 (13.33) per cent of the urban respondents and 5 (5.33) per cent of the rural respondents never quarrelled with any one of the persons mentioned in the table, because they stay away from or they are on good terms with, the members of their families.

Thus, with regard to the persons who quarrelled with the women before widowhood we may conclude that a majority of the widows report that the persons mentioned in the table quarrelled with them. As such a majority of the respondents said that they had quarrelled with them sometimes. However, the statistical results show that there is a significant difference between the urban and rural widows in respect of the persons who quarrelled with them and in the frequency of quarrels.

We may further consider the persons who quarrelled with the widows after widowhood. It is obvious from the table that nearly 49 (48.67) per cent of the urban respondents as against 36 (36.00) per cent of the rural respondents reported that daughters-in-law quarrelled with them. About 21 (21.33) per cent and 23 (23.34) per cent of respondents from urban and rural areas respectively stated that sons quarrelled with them. And only 4 (4.67) per cent of the urban respondents as against 3 (3.33) per cent of the rural respondents reported that they did not quarrel with any one, because they are staying alone.

Thus, with regard to the frequency of quarrels about 82 (82.67) Per cent of the urban respondents, in comparision to 66 (66.67) per cent of the rural respondents quarrelled sometimes. About 12 (12.66) per cent of the respondents in urban area and nearly 25 (24.66) per cent of the respondents in rural areas quarrelled frequently and nearly 4 (4.67) per cent of the urban respondents in comparison to about 9 (8.67) per cent of the rural respondents did not quarrel with the persons mentioned in the table at all, because they are living alone.

Therefore, it can be inferred, that the proportion of widows who reported that the daughter-in-law and sons quarelled with them is higher after widowhood than before. Among those who have quarrelled with widows, a significant majority of them quarrelled sometimes. The difference between the urban and rural widows with respect to the persons who quarrelled with them, and frequency of quarrels, is found to be statistically significant.

Further, it may be of significance to know why the widows say time and again : Widows should not live after widowhood ? In order to elicit relevant data pertaining to this statement, the widows were asked to state the reasons. Table 4.14 represents the reasons stated.

**TABLE - 4.14**
**REASONS STATED FOR THE QUESTION WHY WIDOWS SHOULD NOT LIVE?**

| *Reasons* | *Urban %* | *Rural %* | *Total %* | *$X^2$ value* |
|---|---|---|---|---|
| Difficult to manage family without bread winner | 58.00 | 78.67 | 68.33 | |
| Strict religious taboos attached | 17.34 | 6.67 | 12.00 | 15.58** |
| Loss of Status | 19.33 | 11.33 | 15.34 | |
| Should not die | 5.33 | 3.33 | 4.33 | |
| Total | 100.00 | 100.00 | 100.00 | |

Calculated $X^2$ = 15.58; table value of $X^2$ with z d f at .01 level is 11.34. Hence, the difference is significant.

It may be observed from the table that a majority of the respondents both from urban and rural areas expressed the feeling that widows should not live after the death of their spouse. The reasons given by the widows are presented in the table.

It is evident from the table that about 58 (58.00) per cent of the urban respondents, as against 78 (78.67) per cent of the rural respondents, have reported that it is difficult to manage the family without the bread winner/husband. About 17 (17.34) per cent of the urban respondents, in comparison to 6 (6.67) per cent of rural respondents, have offered the strict religious taboos attached to widowhood as the reason, and about 19 (19.33) per cent of the urban respondents and 11 (11.33) per cent of the rural respondents have mentioned loss of status as the reason. Only 5 (5.33) and 3 (3.33) per cent of the respondents in urban and rural areas respectively expressed that widows should not die.

Thus, with regard to the reasons stated by the widows, it may be said that a significant majority of the widows, both from urban and rural areas, are of the opinion that they faced several problems in managing the family. However, the $X^2$ value establish that there is a significant difference between the urban and rural widows in respect of the statement of the reason.

Further, it is of significance to know to whom widows talk when they are unhappy. The particulars regarding the persons with whom the respondents talk when they were unhappy are presented in Table 4.15.

**TABLE - 4.15**

**PERSONS TO WHOM WIDOWS TALK**

| *Persons* | *Urban %* | *Rural %* | *Total %* | *$X^2$ value* |
|---|---|---|---|---|
| No one | 6.00 | 3.33 | 4.67 | |
| Friends/Neighbours | 32.00 | 24.67 | 28.33 | |
| Relatives | 18.00 | 12.00 | 15.00 | 20.26** |
| Siblings | 20.00 | 44.00 | 32.00 | |
| Family members | 24.00 | 16.00 | '20.00 | |
| Total | 100.00 | 100.00 | 100.00 | |

Calculated $X^2$ = 20.26; table value of $X^2$ with 4 d f at .01 level is 13.28. Hence the difference is significant.

It is obvious from the table that a striking majority 95 (95.33) per cent of the respondents from both urban and rural areas talk to one or the other persons when they feel unhappy.

The findings suggest that during distress about 20 (20.00) per cent of the urban respondents as against 44 (44.00) per cent of rural respondents talk to their siblings. About 32 (32.00) per cent of the respondents in urban area in comparison to 25 (24.67) per cent in rural areas talk to their friends/neighbours about their problems. The proportion of widows in urban and rural areas who talk to their family members are 24 (24.00) per cent and 16 (16.00) per cent respectively. And only 6 (6.00) per cent of the urban respondents and nearly 3 (3.33) per cent of the rural respondents do not talk to any one about their unhappiness/problems. In view of the above findings we may state that the proportion of those who talk to their friend is high in urban area while in rural areas it is high among those who talk to their siblings.

It is significant to know that the proportion of widows who talk to their relatives about their unhappiness is low both in urban and rural areas. However, the difference between the urban and rural widows with respect to the persons to whom they talk during unhappy situations is found to be statistically significant. The proportion of widows who talk to their relatives about their unhappiness is low both in urban and rural areas. However, the difference between the urban and rural widows with respect to the persons with whom they talk during unhappy situations is found to be statistically significant.

Further, we may consider the insecurities felt by the widows. The data pertaining to this is presented in Table 4.16. The table shows that almost all the widows both in urban and rural areas felt one or the other type of insecurity.

**TABLE - 4.16**
**INSECURITY FELT BY WIDOWS**

| *Insecurities* | *Urban %* | *Rural %* | *Total %* | *$X^2$ value* |
|---|---|---|---|---|
| Social insecurity | 16.00 | 20.00 | 18.00 | |
| Emotional insecurity | 46.67 | 20.00 | 33.33 | |
| Economic insecurity | 37.33 | 60.00 | 48.67 | 24.56** |
| Total | 100.00 | 100.00 | 100.00 | |

Calculated $X^2$ = 24.56; table value of $X^2$ with 2 d f at .01 level is 9.21. Hence, the difference is significant.

The data reveals that in urban area about 46 (46.67) per cent of the respondents as against 20 (20.00) per cent of rural respondents felt emotional insecurity, while about 37 (37.33) and 60 (60.00) per cent of the respondents in both urban and rural areas respectively felt economic insecurity. And only about 16 (16.00) per cent of urban respondents in comparison to 20 (20.00) per cent of the rural respondents felt social insecurity.

Thus, with regard to the kind of insecurities felt by the widows we may conclude that about 48 (48.67) per cent of the widows felt economic insecurity. As such, almost all the widows seem to suggest that a woman's life becomes insecure after the death of the husband. However, the difference between the urban and rural widows with respect to the insecurities felt is found to be statistically significant.

Further, it may be of significance to know, on what occasions the widows remember their deceased husbands. The particulars pertaining to the occasions on which widows remember their husbands is given in Table 4.17. A majority of the respondents both in urban and rural areas do remember their husbands on one or the other occasion.

**TABLE - 4.17**

**OCCASIONS ON WHICH WIDOWS REMEMBER THEIR HUSBANDS**

| *Reasons* | *Urban %* | *Rural %* | *Total %* | *$X^2$ Value* |
|---|---|---|---|---|
| Family celebrations | 36.66 | 28.00 | 32.33 | |
| Birth/death day | 18.67 | 4.00 | 11.34 | |
| When someone resembles him/sees a couple | 8.67 | 10.00 | 9.33 | |
| When see articles/persons places associated with him | 16.00 | 20.67 | 18.33 | 25.7** |
| Family crisis | 10.67 | 24.00 | 17.33 | |
| Do not remember | 9.33 | 13.33 | 11.34 | |
| Total | 100.00 | 100.00 | 100.00 | |

Calculated $X^2$ = 25.7; table value of $X^2$ with 5 d f at .01 level. Hence the difference is significant.

It may be observed from the table that nearly 37 (36.66) per cent of the urban respondents as against 28 (28.00) per cent of the rural respondents remember their husbands on the occasions of family celebrations. About 16 (16.00) per cent of the urban respondents remember their deceased husbands when they see articles/persons/places associated with him whereas the corresponding proportion among rural respondents is about 20 (20.67) per cent. And nearly 11 (10.67) per cent of the respondents in urban areas as against 24 (24.00) per cent of the respondents in rural areas remember their husbands on the occasions of family crisis. Only 9 (9.33) per cent of the urban respondents in comparison to about 13 (13.33) per cent of the rural respondents have reported that they do not remember their deceased husbands at all, because their husbands were not good or because of their short married life.

However, there is significant difference between the urban and rural widows in respect of the occasions on which they remember their deceased husbands.

## 4.4 Cultural Deprivation

We may next consider the cultural deprivation. Questions aimed at eliciting responses that could be taken as indicative of the cultural deprivation are included in the schedule. The responses to these questions are scored according to the procedure mentioned below.

As example:

(1) How frequently did you perform daily prayers

| | |
|---|---|
| (1) Never | 0 |
| (2) Sometimes | 1 |
| (3) Often | 2 |

(2) How frequently did you go to the temple.

| | |
|---|---|
| (1) Never | 0 |
| (2) Sometimes | 1 |
| (3) Often | 2 |

(3) How frequently did you go to listen to epics and puranas.

| | |
|---|---|
| (1) Never | 0 |
| (2) Sometimes | 1 |
| (3) Often | 2 |

(4) How frequently did you visit any pilgrim centers.

| | |
|---|---|
| (1) Never | 0 |
| (2) Once | 1 |
| (3) Twice-thrice | 2 |

The particulars regarding the widow's cultural deprivation in terms of their residence are presented in Table 4.18(A).

An observation of the data from the Table 4.18(A) indicates that before widowhood about 41 (41.8) per cent of the respondents in urban area as against 48 (48.6) per cent of rural respondents faced cultural deprivation, whereas, after widowhood, 50 (50.9) per cent of the urban respondents in comparison to 65 (65.1) per cent of rural respondents did so.

**TABLE - 4.18 (A)**
**AREA AND CULTURAL DEPRIVATION**

| Area | N | Before Widowhood Score | Before Widowhood Per cent | After Widowhood Score | After Widowhood Per cent | 't' Value |
|---|---|---|---|---|---|---|
| Urban | 150 | 5.02 | 41.8 | 6.11 | 50.9 | 4.89** |
| Rural | 150 | 5.83 | 48.6 | 7.81 | 65.1 | 7.93** |
| Combined | 300 | 5.43 | 45.2 | 6.96 | 58.0 | 8.69** |
| 't' value | | 3.46** | | 7.11** | | |

The inference that can be drawn from an examination of the table is that there is an increase in the percentage of both the urban and the rural respondents after widowhood and there is also a significant difference between the urban and the rural widows both before and after widowhood.

The cultural deprivation of the respondents is subjected to 't' test of significance in order to verify the significance of the difference between the urban and the rural respondents and both before and after widowhood. The test infers significant association between these variables. Therefore, it implies that the rural widows faced cultural deprivation more than their urban counterparts both before and after widowhood. Further, it may be of significance to know the relationship between the caste status of the widows and cultural deprivation. The data pertaining to this is presented in Table 4.18(B).

**TABLE - 4.18 (B)**
**CASTE AND CULTURAL DEPRIVATION**

| Caste | N | Before Widowhood Score | Before Widowhood Per cent | After Widowhood Score | After Widowhood Per cent | 't' Value |
|---|---|---|---|---|---|---|
| Upper caste (UC) | 180 | 5.82 | 48.5 | 7.53 | 62.8 | 7.61** |
| Intermediate caste (IC) | 53 | 5.38 | 44.8 | 6.64 | 55.3 | 3.37** |
| Lower caste (LC) | 67 | 4.42 | 36.8 | 5.67 | 47.2 | 3.79** |
| Combined | 300 | 5.43 | 45.2 | 6.96 | 58.0 | 8.69** |
| 't' value | UC & IC | | 1.33NS | | 3.13** | |
| | IC & LC | | 2.46* | | 3.12** | |
| | UC & LC | | 4.84** | | 6.75** | |

An examination of the results in the above table indicates that before widowdood about 48 (48.5) per cent of the upper caste respondents, in comparison to 44 (44.8) per cent of the intermediate caste and 36 (36.8) per cent of the lower caste respondents, faced cultural deprivation, while this figure increased to about 62 (62.8) per cent for the upper caste respondents as against about 55 (55.3) per cent for the intermediate caste and 47 (47.2) per cent for lower caste respondents after widowhood.

An insight into the table reveals that in all the three caste categories the percentage of the respondents has gone up after widowhood and there is also a significant difference between the castes, both before and after widowhood.

The cultural deprivation of the respondents belonging to different caste categories is subjected to 't' test of significance. The test results establish that there is a significant difference in all the caste categories both before and after widowhood. It is observed that before widowhood there is not much difference between the upper and intermediate caste. But in all other inter caste categories the difference is significant both before and after widowhood. Hence, the test of significance establishes the relation between caste and cultural deprivation. It also implies the higher the caste the greater the cultural deprivation. The hypothesis that caste has influence on the level of cultural deprivation is not rejected.

We may next consider the relationship between age and the cultural deprivation of the widows. The particulars regarding the cultural deprivation of the widows are presented in Table 4.18(C).

**TABLE - 4.18 (C)**
**AGE AND CULTURAL DEPRIVATION**

| Age | | N | *Before Widowhood* | | *After Widowhood* | | *'t' Value* |
|---|---|---|---|---|---|---|---|
| | | | *Score* | *Per cent* | *Score* | *Per cent* | |
| Below 30 | (1) | 31 | 5.39 | 44.9 | 6.52 | 54.3 | 2.34** |
| 30-60 | (2) | 189 | 5.25 | 43.8 | 6.65 | 55.4 | 6.43** |
| 60 and above | (3) | 80 | 5.85 | 48.7 | 7.85 | 65.4 | 5.79** |
| Combined | | 300 | 5.43 | 45.2 | 6.96 | 58.0 | 8.69 |
| 't' value | | 1 & 2 | | 0.36 NS | | 0.36NS | |
| | | 2 & 3 | | 2.12* | | 4.07** | |
| | | 1 & 3 | | 1.07NS | | 3.26** | |

It may be observed from the data presented in Table 4.18(A) that before widowhood about 45 (44.9) per cent of the respondents who fall in the age-group of below 30 years as against 44 (43.8) per cent of the respondents of 30-60 years age group and 48 (48.7) per cent of the respondents of 60 and above, faced cultural deprivation. Whereas after widowhood about 54 (54.3) per cent of the respondents of below 30 years age group as against 55 (55.4) per cent of the respondents of 30-60 years age group and 65 (65.4) per cent of the respondents of 60 and above faced cultural deprivation.

A detailed examination of the table reveals that in all the age groups the percentage has increased after widowhood. But in case of pre-widowhood, the difference is high only between the 30-60 age group and 60 and above age-group and not between the other age groups. While after widowhood the difference between the below 30 age group and 30-60 years age -group is not much but significant in other age-groups.

However, the 't' test infers that there is a significant difference in all the age groups, both before and after widowhood. It can be inferred from the findings in the table that there is a positive effect of widowhood in all the age groups.

Further, it may be of significance to look at the cultural deprivation faced by the widows belonging to working and non-working groups. The data pertaining to this is presented in Table 4.18(D).

**TABLE - 4.18 (D)**

**OCCUPATION AND CULTURAL DEPRIVATION**

| *Occupation* | *N* | *Before Widowhood* *Score* | *Per cent* | *After Widowhood* *Score* | *Per cent* | *'t' Value* |
|---|---|---|---|---|---|---|
| Working | 176 | 5.28 | 44.0 | 6.88 | 57.3 | 6.56** |
| Non-working | 124 | 5.64 | 47.0 | 7.07 | 58.9 | 5.80** |
| Combined | 300 | 5.43 | 45.2 | 6.96 | 58.0 | 8.69** |
| 't' value | | | 1.53NS | | 0.75NS | |

A close observation of the above table brings to light the fact that before widowhood about 44 (44.0) per cent of the working respondents as against 47 (47.0) per cent of the non-working respondents faced cultural deprivation, whereas after widowhood about 57 (57.3) per cent of the urban respondents in comparision to 58 (58.9) per cent of the rural respondent faced cultural deprivation.

The data reveals that in the working and non-working groups, the percentage has gone up after widowhood. But there is not much difference between these two groups both before and after widowhood.

The test results reveal that in both the groups there is a significant difference before and after widowhood. While between these two groups, the difference is not significant both before and after widowhood. The findings suggest that there is a positive effect of widowhood on both the groups.

We may further consider the reasons given by the widows for their religious activities. The particulars pertaining to the respondents' reasons for doing daily prayers are presented in Table 4.19(A).

**TABLE - 4.19**

**(A) REASONS FOR OBSERVING RELIGIOUS PRACTICES**

| | *Before Widowhood* | | | *After Widowhood* | | |
|---|---|---|---|---|---|---|
| *Doing Daily Prayers* | *Urban* % | *Rural* % | *Total* % | *Urban* % | *Rural* % | *Total* % |
| No belief in such things | 3.33 | 5.33 | 4.33 | 8.00 | 16.00 | 12.00 |
| Belief in such things | 82.00 | 90.00 | 86.00 | 73.33 | 79.33 | 76.33 |
| For purification of the soul and self satisfaction | 14.67 | 4.67 | 9.67 | 18.67 | 4.67 | 11.67 |
| Total | 100.00 | 100.00 | 100.00 | 100.00 | 100.00 | 100.00 |
| $X^2$ value | | 12.2** | | | 16.94** | |

**(B) GOING TO TEMPLE**

| | | | | | | |
|---|---|---|---|---|---|---|
| No belief in such things | 5.33 | 9.33 | 7.33 | 12.67 | 28.00 | 20.33 |
| Belief in such things | 49.33 | 73.33 | 61.33 | 60.00 | 56.67 | 58.33 |
| Lack of time and interest | 45.34 | 17.34 | 31.34 | 27.33 | 15.33 | 21.34 |
| Total | 100.00 | 100.00 | 100.00 | 100.00 | 100.00 | 100.00 |
| $X^2$ value | | 27.42** | | | 13.86** | |

**(C) LISTENING TO EPICS AND PURANAS**

| | | | | | | |
|---|---|---|---|---|---|---|
| Not interested | 40.67 | 87.33 | 64.00 | 58.67 | 73.33 | 66.00 |
| Interested | 41.33 | 7.34 | 24.33 | 36.67 | 15.33 | 26.00 |
| Lack of time and interest | 18.00 | 5.33 | 11.67 | 4.66 | 11.34 | 8.00 |
| Total | 100.00 | 100.00 | 100.00 | 100.00 | 100.00 | 100.00 |
| $X^2$ value | | 71.44** | | | 19.72** | |

**(D) VISITING PILGRIMAGE CENTERS**

| | | | | | | |
|---|---|---|---|---|---|---|
| No belief in such things | 17.33 | 21.33 | 19.33 | 22.00 | 26.67 | 24.33 |
| Belief in such things | 56.00 | 38.00 | 47.00 | 47.33 | 33.33 | 40.33 |
| Financial stringency and old age | 26.67 | 40.67 | 33.67 | 30.67 | 40.00 | 35.34 |
| Total | 100.00 | 100.00 | 100.00 | 100.00 | 100.00 | 100.00 |
| $X^2$ value | | 10.2** | | | 6.14* | |

**(E) CELEBRATING FESTIVALS**

| | | | | | | |
|---|---|---|---|---|---|---|
| Not observing religious practices | | | | 8.67 | 10.00 | 9.33 |
| Observing religious practices | 90.00 | 82.00 | 82.00 | 68.67 | 50.00 | 59.33 |
| Financial stringency | 10.00 | 18.00 | 18.00 | 22.66 | 40.00 | 31.34 |
| Total | 100.00 | 100.00 | 100.00 | 100.00 | 100.00 | 100.00 |
| $X^2$ value | | 13.00** | | | 11.72** | |

**(F) OBSERVING FASTS**

| | | | | | | |
|---|---|---|---|---|---|---|
| No belief in such things | 23.33 | 8.00 | 15.67 | 33.33 | 13.33 | 23.33 |
| Belief in such things | 70.67 | 78.67 | 74.67 | 48.00 | 72.00 | 60.00 |
| Creates problems for employed woman | 6.00 | 13.33 | 9.66 | 8.67 | 8.00 | 8.33 |
| Old age/ill health | - | - | - | 10.00 | 6.67 | 8.34 |
| Total | 100.00 | 100.00 | 100.00 | 100.00 | 100.00 | 100.00 |
| $X^2$ Value | | 16.04** | | | 21.08** | |

(1) For a,b,c,f calculated $X^2$ = 12.2, 16.94, 27.42, 13.86, 71.44, 19.72, 16.04, 21.08; table value of $X^2$ with 2 d f at .01 level is 9.21. Hence the difference is significant.

(2) (d) Calculated $X^2$ =10.2; 6.14; table value of $X^2$ with 2 d f at .01 level, .05 level are 9.21; 5.99 respectively. Hence, the difference is significant.

(3) (e) Calculated $X^2$ =13.00; 11.72; table value of $X^2$ with 1 d f at 2 df respectively at .01 level are 6.63; 9.21. Hence, the difference is significant.

It may be observed from the table that before widowhood about 82 (82.00) per cent of the urban respondents as against 90 (90.00) per cent of the rural respondents have reported that they used to perform daily prayers whereas after widowhood about 73 (73.3) per cent of the urban respondents in comparision to 79 (79.33) per cent of the rural respondents did so. As such, the data seem to suggest that though a significant majority of the respondents have belief in daily prayers there is also a significant decrease in religious activities. However, the difference between the urban and rural widows is found to be statistically significant, both before and after widowhood.

**Reasons for Going to Temple**

The data presented in Table 4.19(B) reveals that before widowhood about 49 (49.33) per cent of the urban respondents in comparison to 73 (73.33) per cent of the rural respondents have mentioned that they went to temples, but after widowhood about 60 (60.00) per cent of the urban respondents in contrast to about 56 (56.67) per cent of the rural respondents did so. In the view of above findings we may suggest that after widowhood, the proportion of those who go to temples has gone up in urban area, while it has decreased among those who have stated they have no time and interest. However, both before and after widowhood, the difference between the urban and the rural widows is found to be statistically significant.

**Reasons for Listening to Epics and Puranas**

The data presented in Table 4.19(C) indicates that before widowhood about 40 (40.67) per cent of the urban respondents, as against 87 (87.33) per cent of the rural respondents, have reported that they were not interested in listening to Epics and Puranas. About 58 (58.67) per cent of the urban respondents in comparison to 73 (73.33) per cent of the rural respondents have stated that they are not interested in listening to Puranas and Epics after widowhood. While, on the whole, the findings suggest that the proportion of those who are interested in listening to Epics and Puranas has increased after widowhood. However, the $X^2$ value establishes that there is a significant difference between the urban and the rural widows with respect to the reasons for listening to Epics and Puranas.

**Reasons for Visiting Pilgrimages**

The particulars regarding the respondents' reasons for visiting places of pilgrimage are presented in Table 4.19(D).

It may be observed from the table that before widowhood 56 (56.00) per cent of the urban respondents in comparison to 38 (38.00) per cent of the rural respondents have reported that they believed in the practice of visiting pilgrimage centers. After widowhood, however, only about 47 (47.33) per cent of the urban respondents as against 33 (33.33) per cent of rural respondents stated that their beliefs still continued. There is therefore an increase in the proportion of widows who do not have belief in such practices. The table also reveals that after widowhood about 35 (35.34) per cent of the respondents have mentioned that due to financial stringency they are unable to visit any place of pilgrimage. However, the statistical results show that there is a significant difference between the urban and rural widows, both before and after widowhood.

**Reasons for Celebrating festivals**

Table 4.19(E) shows that before widowhood about 90 (90.00) per cent of the urban respondents as against 82 (82.00) per cent of the rural respondents stated that they celebrated festivals; whereas after widowhood this figure dropped to about 68 (68.67) per cent for the urban respondents in comparison to 50 (50.00) per cent for the rural respondents. The proportion of those who stated, that they were unable to observe festivals due to financial stringency has gone up after widowhood. And about 9 (9.33) per cent of the respondents have stated that they do not observe the festivals. However, the $X^2$ value shows that there is a significant difference between the urban and rural widows with respect to celebrating festivals.

**Reasons for Observing Fasts**

It is evident from Table 4.19(F) that before widowhood about 70 (70.67) per cent of the urban respondents as against 78 (78.67) per cent of the rural respondents reported that they had believed in rituals like observing fasts whereas after widowhood this figure dropped to about 48 (48.00) per cent of the urban respondents in comparison to 72 (72.00) per cent of rural respondents. Thus, with regard to the findings we may suggest that the proportion of widows who lost belief in such things has gone up after widowhood. The proportion is higher in urban areas than in the rural areas. However, the difference between the urban and the rural widows is found to be statistically significant.

Further, we may consider the changes that occur in the food habits of widows. The data pertaining to the changes observed in food habits of the respondents is presented in table 4.20(A) .

**TABLE - 4.20 (A)**
**CHANGES OBSERVED IN FOOD HABITS**

| | *Before Widowhood* | | | *After Widowhood* | | |
|---|---|---|---|---|---|---|
| *Food* | *Urban* % | *Rural* % | *Total* % | *Urban* % | *Rural* % | *Total* % |
| Simple | 46.67 | 66.67 | 56.67 | 66.67 | 78.67 | 72.67 |
| Good | 33.33 | 18.00 | 25.67 | 20.00 | 11.33 | 15.67 |
| Rich | 20.00 | 15.33 | 17.66 | 13.33 | 10.00 | 11.66 |
| Total | 100.00 | 100.00 | 100.00 | 100.00 | 100.00 | 100.00 |
| $X^2$ value | | 15.9** | | | 15.76** | |

It may be observed from the table that before widowhood about 46 (46.67) per cent of the urban respondents in contrast to 66 (66.67) per cent of the rural respondents have stated that they used to eat simple food. While about 66 (66.67) per cent of the urban respondents in comparison to 78 (78.67) per cent of rural respondents have reported that they eat simple food after widowhood. Thus, with regard to the changes observed in food habits the findings indicate that the proportion of those eating simple food has gone up after widowhood. However, the $X^2$ value shows that there is a significant difference between the urban and rural widows.

Further, the data presented in Table 4.20(B) indicates that before widowhood about 46 (46.67) per cent of the urban respondents as against 66 (66.67) per cent of the rural respondents stated that they were not economically sound. Whereas about 66 (66.67) per cent of the urban respondents in comparison to 78 (78.67) per cent of rural respondents have reported that they are economically unsound/should take simple food.

**TABLE - 4.20 (B)**
**REASONS FOR THE CHANGE**

| Reasons | *Before Widowhood* Urban % | Rural % | Total % | *After Widowhood* Urban % | Rural % | Total % |
|---|---|---|---|---|---|---|
| Economically unsound/should take simple food | 46.67 | 66.67 | 56.67 | 66.67 | 78.67 | 72.67 |
| Economically sound/interested | 40.00 | 28.00 | 34.00 | 18.67 | 13.33 | 16.00 |
| Not interested | 13.33 | 5.33 | 9.33 | 14.66 | 8.00 | 11.33 |
| Total | 100.00 | 100.00 | 100.00 | 100.00 | 100.00 | 100.00 |

Calculated $X^2$ = 15.69; table value of $X^2$ with 2 d f at .01 level is 9.21. Hence the difference is significant.
Calculated $X^2$ = 15.76; table value of $X^2$ with 2 d f at .01 level is 9.21. Hence the difference is significant.

We may next consider the changes noticed in the widows' pattern of dressing. The particulars regarding the changes observed in dressing pattern of the respondents are presented in Table 4.21(A).

It can be observed from the above table that before widowhood about 53 (53.33) per cent of the urban respondents reported that they used to wear simple clothes while about 27 (27.33) per cent of the urban respondents in comparison to 18 (18.00) per cent of the rural respondents stated that they used to wear good clothes. After widowhood these figures changed to about 61 (61.33) per cent of the urban and 76 (76.67) per cent of the rural respondents wearing simple clothes and about 26 (26.67) per cent of the urban respondents and 13 (13.33) per cent of the rural respondents wearing good clothes. As such we may suggest that the proportion of those wearing simple clothes has gone up after widowhood.

## TABLE - 4.21 (A)
## DRESSING PATTERN BEFORE AND AFTER WIDOWHOOD

| Clothes | *Before Widowhood* | | | *After Widowhood* | | |
|---|---|---|---|---|---|---|
| | *Urban* % | *Rural* % | *Total* % | *Urban* % | *Rural* % | *Total* % |
| Simple | 53.33 | 70.00 | 61.67 | 61.33 | 76.67 | 69.00 |
| Good | 27.33 | 18.00 | 22.67 | 26.67 | 13.33 | 20.00 |
| Costly | 19.34 | 12.00 | 15.66 | 12.00 | 10.00 | 11.00 |
| Total | 100.00 | 100.00 | 100.00 | 100.00 | 100.00 | 100.00 |
| $X^2$ value | | 8.54* | | | 9.46** | |

Calculated $X^2$ = 9.461; table value of $X^2$ with 2 d f at .01 level is 9.21. Hence the difference is significant.

## TABLE - 4.21 (B)
## REASONS FOR THE CHANGE

| Reasons | *Before Widowhood* | | | *After Widowhood* | | |
|---|---|---|---|---|---|---|
| | *Urban* % | *Rural* % | *Total* % | *Urban* % | *Rural* % | *Total* % |
| Economically not sound/should wear simple only | 53.33 | 70.00 | 61.67 | 61.33 | 76.67 | 69.00 |
| Economically sound and started working | 38.67 | 16.67 | 27.67 | 13.33 | 6.67 | 10.00 |
| Lost interest | 8.00 | 13.33 | 10.66 | 25.34 | 16.67 | 21.00 |
| Total | 100.00 | 100.00 | 100.00 | 100.00 | 100.00 | 100.00 |

Calculated $X^2$ = 8.54; table value of $X^2$ with 2 d f at .05 level is 5.99. Hence the difference is significant.

Further, the data presented in Table 4.21(B) indicates that before widowhood about 53 (53.33) per cent of the urban respondents, in contrast to 70 (70.00) per cent of the rural respondents, stated that they were economically not sound. Whereas about 38 (38.67) per cent of the urban and 16 (16.67) per cent of the rural respondents mentioned that they were economically sound. But after widowhood about 61 (61.33) per cent of the urban respondents as against 76 (76.67) per cent of the rural respondents have reported that they are economically not sound/should wear simple clothes only whereas about 25 (25.34) per cent of the urban respondents and 16 (16.66) per cent of the rural respondents have stated that they have lost interest. As such we may state that the proportion of those using simple clothes has gone up after widowhood. However, statistically significant difference is found between the urban and rural widows with respect to the dressing pattern.

We may further consider the using of the "Saubhagya" signs by the widows. The particulars are provided in the Table 4.21(C).

**TABLE - 4.21 (C)**
**SAUBHAGYA SIGNS USED AFTER WIDOWHOOD**

| *Saubhagya Signs* | *Urban %* | | *Total %* | *Rural %* | | *Total %* |
|---|---|---|---|---|---|---|
| | *No* | *Yes* | | *No* | *Yes* | |
| Kumkun | 96.67 | 3.33 | 100.00 | 98.67 | 1.33 | 100.00 |
| Mangal sutra | 98.67 | 1.33 | 100.00 | 100.00 | - | 100.00 |
| Flowers | 98.67 | 1.33 | 100.00 | 100.00 | - | 100.00 |

The data in the table suggests that about 3 (3.33) per cent of the urban respondents and 1 (1.33) per cent of the rural respondents are using black kumkum (only one widow is using red kumkum). Of the urban respondents about 1 (1.33) per cent are using Mangal Sutra and another 1 (1.33) per cent wearing flowers whereas in the rural areas no one is either using a Mangal Sutra or wearing flowers.

Further, the data representing the reasons for using or not using ornaments is given in Table 4.22.

The data in Table 4.22 indicates that before widowhood about 40 (40.00) per cent and 66 (66.67) per cent of the respondents in urban and rural areas respectively did not use ornaments whereas after widowhood about 49 (49.33) per cent of the respondents in urban areas and 74 (74.00) per cent of the respondents in rural areas are not using ornaments, due to poverty only. Before widowhood nearly 27 (26.67) per cent and about 11 (11.33) per cent of the respondents in urban and rural areas respectively used ornaments because they were economically sound, while about 33 (33.33) per cent of the respondents in urban areas and 22 (22.00) per cent of the respondents from rural areas used minimum ornaments because they belonged to medium income group. After widowhood about 17 (17.33) per cent and 13 (13.34) per cent of the respondents, in urban and rural areas were not using ornaments because they had lost interest/people did not like it. About 13 (13.34) per cent and nearly 4 (3.33) per cent of the respondents in urban and rural areas respectively used ornaments because they were economically sound/interested.

**TABLE - 4.22**
**REASONS FOR NOT USING ORNAMENTS**

| *Reasons* | *Before Widowhood* | | | *After Widowhood* | | |
|---|---|---|---|---|---|---|
| | *Urban* % | *Rural* % | *Total* % | *Urban* % | *Rural* % | *Total* % |
| Due to poverty not used/using | 40.00 | 66.67 | 56.33 | 49.33 | 74.00 | 61.67 |
| Not using because lost interest | - | - | - | 17.33 | 13.34 | 15.33 |
| Minimum ornaments wed/using | 33.33 | 22.00 | 27.67 | 20.00 | 9.33 | 14.67 |
| Used/Using because economically sound/interested | 26.67 | 11.33 | 16.00 | 13.34 | 3.33 | 8.33 |
| Total | 100.00 | 100.00 | 100.00 | 100.00 | 100.00 | 100.00 |
| $X^2$ value | | 11.38** | | | 22.98** | |

Calculated $X^2$ = 11.39; table value of $X^2$ with 2 d f at .01 level is 9.21. Hence, the difference is significant.
Calculated $X^2$ = 22.98; table value of $X^2$ with 3 d f at .01 level is 11.34. Hence, the difference is significant.

Hence, the data seems to suggest that a majority of the respondents both in urban and rural areas are not using ornaments after widowhood due to poverty.

However, it may be stated that the difference between urban and rural respondents with respect to the reasons for not using ornaments is found to be statistically significant.

We may next consider the socio-religious functions attended by widows both in urban and rural areas. The data seem to suggest that a majority of the respondents both in urban and rural areas do not attended socio-religious functions. The data pertaining to this is provided in Table 4.23.

**TABLE - 4.23 (A)**
**RELIGIOUS FUNCTIONS ATTENDED**

| *Socio-Religious Function* | | *Urban* % | *Rural* % | *Total* % | $X^2$ *Value* |
|---|---|---|---|---|---|
| (a) Laxmi, Gauri, Tulsi, | No | 70.67 | 53.33 | 62.00 | |
| Satyanarayana Pujas | Yes | 29.33 | 46.67 | 38.00 | 8.98** |
| Offered flowers akshata | No | 70.67 | 53.33 | 62.00 | |
| along with others | Yes | 29.33 | 46.67 | 38.00 | 8.98** |
| Whether you Accepted | No | 70.67 | 53.33 | 62.00 | |
| | Yes | 29.33 | 46.67 | 38.00 | 8.98** |
| Allowed to offer flowers, | No | 70.67 | 53.33 | 62.00 | |
| akshata to the god | Yes | 29.33 | 46.67 | 38.00 | 8.98** |
| (b) Invited for Haldi, | No | 80.00 | 64.00 | 72.00 | |
| kumkum | Yes | 20.00 | 36.00 | 28.00 | 9.5** |
| Seated along with | No | 81.33 | 66.00 | 73.67 | |
| others | Yes | 18.67 | 34.00 | 26.33 | 9.06** |

(a) Calculated $X^2 = 8.98$; table value of $X^2$ with 1 d f at .01 level is 6.63. Hence, the difference is significant.
(b) Calculated $X^2 = 9.5$; table value of $X^2$ with 1 d f at .01 level is 6.63. Hence the difference is significant.

The data reveals that nearly 70 (70.67) per cent of the urban respondents and about 53 (53.33) per cent of the rural respondents did not attend religious functions like Laxmi, Gauri, Tulsi and Satyanarayan Pujas. About 29 (29.33) per cent and 46 (46.67) per cent of the respondents from urban and rural areas respectively attended the religious functions held at the houses of their close relatives and friends.

Further, the findings suggest that these widows were offered flowers and akshata along with others. All of them accepted and were allowed to offer flowers and akshata to the deity. However, the difference between the urban and rural respondents in respect of their attending religious functions is found to be statistically significant.

Further, we may consider the socio-religious functions attended by the widows. The data presented in Table 4.23(A) indicates that a high proportion of widows are not invited for such functions. Those who attended such functions were invited by close relatives/friends.

It may be observed from the table that about 80 (80.00) per cent of the urban respondents and 64 (64.00) per cent of the rural respondents were not invited for religious functions, whereas over 18 (18.67) per cent of the respondents in urban areas and 34 (34.00) per cent of the respondents in rural areas were invited for such functions by their close relatives and friends.

Among those who attended such functions about 18 (18.67) per cent of the urban respondents in comparison to 34 (34.00) per cent of the rural respondents reported that they had been seated along with others. In view of the above findings we may state that the proportion of widows who have been invited for socio-religious functions is low. However, there is a significant difference between the urban and rural widows in respect of attending socio-religious functions.

**TABLE 4.23 (B)**
**SOCIAL FUNCTION ATTENDED**

| *Socio-Religious Function* | | *Urban* % | *Rural* % | *Total* % | $X^2$ *Value* |
|---|---|---|---|---|---|
| (c) Attended naming | No | 62.00 | 77.33 | 69.67 | |
| ceremony | Yes | 38.00 | 22.67 | 30.33 | 8.32** |
| Allowed to touch the | No | 77.33 | 77.33 | 69.67 | |
| baby | Yes | 22.67 | 22.67 | 30.33 | 8.32** |
| Applied nama to the | No | 93.33 | 80.00 | 86.67 | |
| baby | Yes | 6.67 | 20.00 | 13.33 | 11.52** |
| (d) Attended marriage | No | 57.33 | 74.67 | 66.00 | |
| ceremony | Yes | 42.67 | 25.33 | 34.00 | 10.02** |
| Gone near to bride | No | 76.00 | 92.00 | 62.00 | |
| and groom | Yes | 24.00 | 8.00 | 38.00 | 14.32** |
| Handed over the | No | 76.00 | 92.00 | 80.67 | |
| present yourself | Yes | 24.00 | 8.00 | 19.33 | 14.32** |

(c) Calculated $X^2 = 8.32$ &11.52; table value of $X^2$ with 1 d f at 0.01 level is 6.63. Hence the difference is significant.

(d) Calculated $X^2 = 10.02$ & 14.32; table value of $X^2$ with 1 d f at 0.01 level is 6.63. Hence, the difference is significant.

Further, we may consider the naming ceremony attended by the widows. It is obvious from Table 4.23(B) that about 62 (62.00) per cent of the urban respondents and 77 (77.33) per cent of the rural respondents attended naming ceremonies. All those respondents who attended the ceremony touched the baby also. But only 6 (6.67) per cent of the respondents in urban area as compared to 20 (20.00) per cent of respondents in rural areas applied *nama* to the baby. In this context we may say that widows attend socio-religious functions but they do not take an active part in such functions. However, the statistical results establish that there is a significant difference between the urban and the rural widows in respect of attending naming ceremonies and taking part in it.

With regard to the widows attending marriages it may be observed from the data presented in Table 4.23(B) that over 42 (42.67) per cent of the urban respondents as against 25 (25.33) per cent of the rural respondents attend the marriage ceremonies while about 57 (57.33) per cent of the urban respondents as compared to 74 (74.67) per cent of the rural respondents do not do so.

Among those who attended the marriage ceremony about 24 (24.00) per cent of the urban respondents and only 8 (8.00) per cent of the rural respondents go near the bride and groom and hand over the gifts/presents themselves because they attend only marriage ceremonies of close relatives and friends.

Thus, with regard to the attending to marriage ceremony by the widows it may be said that a significant majority of the widows both from urban and rural areas do not attend the marriage ceremony. However, the $X^2$ value establishes that there is a significant difference between the urban and rural widows in respect of attending the marriage ceremonies.

It is significant to know the reactions of the widows towards invitations for socio-religious functions. Particulars regarding this are presented in Table 4.24.

It is evident from the Table 4.24 that about 59 (59.33) per cent of the urban respondents as against 72 (72.00) per cent of the rural respondents have reported that they do not attend the marriage ceremony but they send their children or other family members. About 11 (11.33) per cent and 12 (12.66) per cent of the respondents of urban and rural areas respectively reported that they attended marriage ceremonies and about 12 (12.67) per cent of the respondents in urban areas as compared to 4 (4.67) per cent of the respondents in rural areas have said that they believed a widow should not attend such ceremonies.

**TABLE - 4.24**

**REACTIONS TOWARD INVITATION**

| *Socio-Religious Function* | *Urban* % | *Rural* % | *Total* % | $X^2$ *Value* |
|---|---|---|---|---|
| I attend | 11.33 | 12.66 | 12.00 | |
| Do not feel like attending | 12.00 | 4.67 | 8.33 | |
| I do not attend but send my children | 59.33 | 72.00 | 65.67 | 12.52* |
| Believe a widow should not attend | 12.67 | 4.67 | 8.67 | |
| Lack of time and interest | 4.67 | 6.00 | 5.33 | |
| Total | 100.00 | 100.00 | 100.00 | |

Calculated $X^2$ = 12.52; table value of $X^2$ with 4 d f at .05 level is 9.49. Hence the difference is significant.

Thus, with regard to the reactions towards the invitations for attending socio-religious functions the findings indicate that about 12 (12.00) per cent of the respondents attend such functions voluntarily. Whereas about 65 (65.67) per cent of the respondents send their children or the other members of the family. However, there is a significant difference between the urban and the rural widows with respect to the reaction towards invitation for socio-religious functions.

Further, an attempt has been made to see whether the widows observe practices imposed upon them due to widowhood strictly or not. The particulars regarding practices observed due to widowhood and practices observed against taboos for the widows are presented in Tables 4.25(A) and (B).

It is evident from the Table 4.25(A) that about 52 (52.00) per cent of the urban respondents as against 79 (79.33) per cent of the rural respondents are not using *chikki* bangles, kumkum, flowers and Mangal Sutra. About 14 (14.00) per cent of the respondents in urban area and nearly 7 (6.67) per cent of the respondents in rural areas eat one meal late in the day and at night one fruit, milk or *aralittu*. It is also observed that about 13 (13.34) per cent of the urban widows is comparison to 4 (4.00) per cent of the rural respondents shaved their heads (which is prevalent among orthodox Brahmins).

**TABLE - 4.25 (A)**

**PRACTISES OBSERVED DUE TO WIDOWHOOD**

| *Socio-Religious Function* | *Urban* % | *Rural* % | *Total* % | $X^2$ *Value* |
|---|---|---|---|---|
| Wear simple clothes | 13.33 | 6.00 | 9.67 | |
| Not enter kitchen & cook auspicious food/enter marriage Pandal | 7.33 | 4.00 | 5.67 | |
| Eat one meal late in the day, at night one fruit/milk/aralittu | 14.00 | 6.67 | 10.33 | 25.56** |
| Not wear chikki bangles/kumkum/flowers, Mangla sutra | 52.00 | 79.33 | 65.67 | |
| Cut hair | 13.34 | 4.00 | 8.66 | |
| Total | 100.00 | 100.00 | 100.00 | |

(a) Calculated $X^2$ = 25.56; table value of $X^2$ with 4 d f at 0.01 level is 13.28. Hence, the difference is significant.

**TABLE - 4.25 (B)**

**PRACTISES OBSERVED AGAINST TABOOS OF WIDOWHOOD**

| *Practices Observed against Taboos* | *Urban* % | *Rural* % | *Total* % | $X^2$ *Value* |
|---|---|---|---|---|
| Wear all types, all colour clothes | 13.33 | 4.00 | 8.67 | |
| Eat all types of food just like others | 23.33 | 23.00 | 25.67 | |
| Cook auspicious food, participate in poojas, enter marriage Pandal | 7.33 | 23.33 | 15.33 | 49.44** |
| No cutting of hair | 16.00 | 3.33 | 9.67 | |
| Using ornaments | 26.67 | 13.34 | 20.00 | |
| Observing practices strictly | 13.34 | 28.00 | 20.66 | |
| Total | 100.00 | 100.00 | 100.00 | |

Calculated $X^2$ = 49.44; table value of $X^2$ with 5 d f at .01 level is 15.09. Hence the difference is significant.

The statistical result shows that there is a significant difference between the urban and rural widows with respect to the practices observed due to widowhood.

From the data presented in Table 4.25(B) it is found that about 26 (26.67) per cent of the respondents in urban areas in comparison to 13 (13.34) per cent of the respondents in rural areas are using ornaments like chain, gold and glass bangles earrings, nose-ring, etc. And about 7 (7.33) and 23 (23.33) per cent of the respondents from urban and rural areas respectively cook auspicious food, participate in religious rituals. Nearly 23 (23.33) per cent of the respondents in urban area and 28 (28.00) per cent of respondents in rural areas reported that they eat all types of foods just as others eat.

However, the $X^2$ value establish that there is a significant difference between the urban and rural widows with respect to the practices observed against taboos of widowhood.

FIVE

# Reactions and Views

In this chapter an attempt is made to study the help received, the reactions and views of widows. The main focus has been on the help in widowhood, reactions towards widowhood and death, views on status of Hindu widows, marriage and type of family preferred, future plans, and suggestions for the welfare of the widows.

The responses to the questions that throw light on the reactions and views are analysed and discussed in this chapter.

### Help in Widowhood

To begin with, we may consider under this heading the persons who helped widows, kind of help received, persons to share widows' responsibilities, persons approached by widows in difficulties, persons sharing household work, persons taking care of widows now.

### Source and Nature of Help

The following Tables 5.1(A) and (B) indicate the source and nature of help received by the respondents.

It is observed from the table that all the respondents who had received help in the urban and the rural areas had received it from their relatives, friends and neighbours. And about 36 (36.67) per cent of the urban respondents as against 28 (28.67) per cent of the rural widows had received help from sons/daughters, brothers/sisters, and parents, whereas about 20 (20.00) per cent of the respondents in urban area and about 31 (31.33) per cent of the respondents in rural areas had received help from their in-laws.

And about 20 (20.00) per cent of the urban and 16 (16.67) per cent of the rural respondents who had received help from neighbours/friends. The statistical results establish that there is no significant difference between the urban and the rural widows in respect of the persons who help widows.

**TABLE - 5.1 (A)**

**PERSONS WHO HELPED WIDOWS AND KIND OF HELP RECEIVED**

| *Persons Who Help* | *Urban* % | *Rural* % | *Total* % | *$X^2$ Value* |
|---|---|---|---|---|
| Parents | 14.67 | 11.33 | 13.00 | |
| In-Laws | 8.67 | 12.00 | 10.33 | |
| Brothers/Sisters | 20.00 | 31.33 | 25.67 | 7.12NS |
| Sons/daughters | 36.66 | 28.67 | 32.67 | |
| Neighbours | 13.33 | 10.67 | 12.00 | |
| Friends | 6.67 | 6.00 | 6.33 | |
| Total | 100.00 | 100.00 | 100.00 | |

**TABLE - 5.1 (B)**

**KIND OF HELP RECEIVED**

| *Kind of Help* | *Urban* % | *Rural* % | *Total* % | *$X^2$ Value* |
|---|---|---|---|---|
| Food/Clothing/Shelter | 45.33 | 39.33 | 42.33 | |
| Money | 20.67 | 21.33 | 21.00 | |
| Job | 13.33 | 6.67 | 10.00 | 16.8** |
| Education | 14.00 | 3.33 | 8.67 | |
| Shopping | 3.33 | 7.34 | 5.33 | |
| Land Cultivation | 3.33 | 22.00 | 12.67 | |
| Total | 100.00 | 100.00 | 100.00 | |

(a) Calculated $X^2 = 7.12$; table value of $X^2$ with 5 d f at .05 level is 11.09. Hence, the difference is not significant.

(b) Calculated $X^2 = 16.8$; table value of $X^2$ with 5 d f at .01 level is 15.09. Hence, the difference is significant.

Further, in terms of the kind of help received by the respondents, the findings presented in Table 5.1 (B) suggest that in urban area 45 (45.33) per cent of the respondents and in rural areas about 39 (39.33) per cent of the respondents have received help in the form of food/clothing/shelter. And only 3 (3.33) per cent of the urban respondents in comparison to 22 (22.00) per cent of the rural respondents have received help in land cultivation.

Thus, with regard to the source and nature of help, the data indicates that all the respondents studied have received help from one or the other source. And further, a significant majority of them have received help from close kinsmen.

The $X^2$ value indicate that there is a significant difference between the widows of urban and rural areas in respect of the type of help received.

**Persons to Share Responsibilities and Persons Approached**

The data pertaining to the opinion of the respondents about the persons who should share any of the widow's responsibilities are presented in Tables 5.2(A) and (B) given below.

**TABLE - 5.2 (A)**
**PERSONS TO SHARE WIDOW'S RESPONSIBILITIES AND PERSONS APPROACHED**

| *Persons to Share Responsibilities* | *Urban* % | *Rural* % | *Total* % | *$X^2$ Value* |
|---|---|---|---|---|
| Husband's relation | 86.67 | 73.33 | 80.00 | |
| Widow's relation | 4.67 | 13.33 | 9.00 | 9.38** |
| The State | 8.66 | 13.34 | 11.00 | |
| Total | 100.00 | 100.00 | 100.00 | |

**TABLE - 5.2 (B)**
**PERSONS APPROACHED BY WIDOWS IN DIFFICULTIES**

| *Persons Approached* | *Urban* % | *Rural* % | *Total* % | *$X^2$ Value* |
|---|---|---|---|---|
| Parents | 8.00 | 9.33 | 8.67 | |
| In-Laws | 5.33 | 8.67 | 7.00 | |
| Brothers/Sisters | 32.00 | 20.00 | 26.00 | |
| Sons/Daughters | 44.00 | 52.00 | 48.00 | 6.74** |
| Friends | 6.67 | 5.33 | 6.00 | |
| Neighbours | 4.00 | 4.67 | 4.33 | |
| Total | 100.00 | 100.00 | 100.00 | |

(a) Calculated $X^2 = 9.38$; table value of $X^2$ with 2 d f at .01 level is 9.21. Hence, the difference is significant.

(b) Calculated $X^2 = 6.74$; table value of $X^2$ with 5 d f at .05 level is 11.09. Hence, the difference is significant.

The table shows that nearly 86 (86.67) per cent of the urban widows and about 73 (73.33) per cent of the rural widows opine that the husband's relations should share the widow's responsibilities, while only 4 (4.67) per cent of urban respondents and about 13 (13.33) per cent of the rural respondents said that widows relations should also share her responsibilities. Whereas about 8 (8.66) per cent of the urban widows and about 13 (13.44) per cent of the rural widow's expressed that the state should share the responsibilities of the widows, since they are not supported either by sons or brothers. As such the data seems to suggest that a significant majority of the respondents report that husband's relations should share widow's responsibilities. However, the difference between the urban and the rural widow's attitudes toward persons to share widow's responsibilities is found to be statistically significant.

We may next consider the persons approached by widows in times of difficulties. The data presented in Table 5.2(B) indicates that a higher proportion of respondents both in the urban and the rural areas approached their own kinsmen and relatives than friends and neighbours. About 44 (44.00) per cent of the urban respondents and 52 (52.00) per cent of the rural respondents approached sons/daughters while in difficulties. About 4 (4.00) per cent of the respondents in urban areas and 4 (4.67) per cent of the respondents in rural areas approached neighbours in difficulties. As such a majority of the respondents approach sons/daughters in difficulties. However, there is no significant difference between the urban and the rural widows in respect of persons approached by them in difficulties.

**Persons Sharing Household Works and Taking Care of Widows**

The data regarding persons who have come to live with the widows to look after household work and children during the first year of widowhood-temporarily/permanently and persons taking care of widows are presented in Tables 5.3(A) and (B).

It is obvious from the table that the proportion of widows whose brothers and their wives shared household work during widowhood is higher among the urban respondents (47.33) than the rural respondents (29.33). On the other hand, nearly 6 (6.00) per cent of the respondents in urban area against only 3 (3.34) per cent of the respondents in rural areas managed household work themselves since no one has come to share the household work. In view of the above findings we may suggest that the proportion of those who are helped by their brothers and their wives in household work is highest. However, they found that there is a significant difference between urban and rural widows in respect of persons who shared their household work during widowhood.

**TABLE - 5.3 (A)**
**PERSONS SHARING HOUSEHOLD WORKS AND TAKING CARE OF WIDOWS**

| *Persons sharing household works* | *Urban* % | *Rural* % | *Total* % | *$X^2$ Value* |
|---|---|---|---|---|
| Mother | 20.67 | 30.67 | 25.67 | |
| Sisters | 14.67 | 21.33 | 18.00 | |
| Brothers/wife/ves | 47.33 | 29.33 | 38.33 | 13.12* |
| Sons/daughters | 11.33 | 15.33 | 13.33 | |
| No one | 6.00 | 3.34 | 4.67 | |
| Total | 100.00 | 100.00 | 100.00 | |

**TABLE - 5.3 (B)**
**PERSONS TAKING CARE OF WIDOWS**

| *Persons taking care* | *Urban* % | *Rural* % | *Total* % | *$X^2$ Value* |
|---|---|---|---|---|
| Parents/relatives through parents | 22.67 | 10.00 | 16.34 | |
| In-laws/relatives through in-laws | 8.00 | 10.67 | 9.33 | |
| Sons/daughters | 64.67 | 76.00 | 70.33 | 9.6* |
| No one | 7.66 | 3.33 | 4.00 | |
| Total | 100.00 | 100.00 | 100.00 | |

(a) Calculated $X^2 = 13.12$; table value of $X^2$ with 4 d f at .05 level is 9.49. Hence, the difference is significant.

(b) Calculated $X^2 = 9.6$; table value of $X^2$ with 3 d f at .05 level is 7.81. Hence, the difference is significant.

Further, the data pertaining to the persons taking care of the widows indicate that the majority of the respondents are taken care of by their sons/daughters. About 22 (22.67) per cent of the urban respondents and 10 (10.00) per cent of the rural respondents are taken care of by the parents/relations through parents as against 8 (8.00) per cent of the urban and 10 (10.67) per cent of the rural respondents who are taken care by In-laws/relatives through in-laws. And only 4 (4.66) per cent of the urban widows and 3 (3.33) per cent of the rural widows are living alone and are not supported by any one. Thus, with regard to the persons taking care of widows we may state that a significant majority of widows are taken care of by sons. However, the $X^2$ value establishes that there is significant difference between urban and rural widows in respect of the persons taking care of widows.

## 5.1 Reactions Towards Death and Widowhood

The study of the reactions of the widows toward death and widowhood gains significance due to the fact that the attitudes help us in knowing the community attitudes towards death and widowhood. With this view in mind, a few questions aimed at eliciting responses which could be taken as indicative of the respondents's reactions toward death and widowhood were included in the interview schedule. The following analysis is based on their responses.

### Reactions Toward Death and Time taken to get over the Grief

The particulars regarding the respondents towards death and time taken to get over the grief so determined are presented in Tables 5.4(A) and (B).

**TABLE - 5.4 (A)**

**REACTION TOWARDS THE DEATH OF HUSBAND**

| *Reaction* | *Urban* % | *Rural* % | *Total* % | $X^2$ *Value* |
|---|---|---|---|---|
| Took it as natural | 12.00 | 3.33 | 7.67 | |
| Become senseless | 18.00 | 3.33 | 10.67 | |
| Felt insecured | 40.67 | 61.34 | 51.00 | 29.96** |
| Felt depressed | 23.33 | 28.00 | 25.66 | |
| Shocked to hear the news of death | 6.00 | 4.00 | 5.00 | |
| Total | 100.00 | 100.00 | 100.00 | |

It is observed from Table 5.4(A) that about 40 (40.67) per cent of the respondents in the urban areas felt insecure whereas in the rural areas 61 (61.34) per cent of the respondents felt insecure. And only 12 (12.00) per cent of the urban respondents and 3 (3.33) per cent of the rural respondents took the death of their husband as a natural process. Thus, with regard to the reaction of the respondents towards the death of husbands, it may be said that a significant majority of them felt insecure and only a few felt shocked to hear the news of death. However, it is found that there is a significant difference between the widows of urban and rural areas in respect of their reaction towards death of their husbands.

**TABLE - 5.4 (B)**
**TIME TAKEN TO GET OVER THE GRIEF**

| *Time Taken* | *Urban* % | *Rural* % | *Total* % | $X^2$ *Value* |
|---|---|---|---|---|
| 0-1 year | 56.67 | 90.00 | 73.33 | |
| 1 year-above | 43.33 | 10.00 | 26.67 | 42.6** |
| Total | 100.00 | 100.00 | 100.00 | |

(a) Calculated $X^2$ = 29.96; table value of $X^2$ with 4 d f at .01 level is 13.28. Hence, the difference is significant.

(b) Calculated $X^2$ = 42.6; table value of $X^2$ with 1 d f at .01 level is 6.63. Hence, the difference is significant.

Table 5.4(B) also reveals that over three-fourth of the respondents took one years' time to get over the grief. Nearly 43 (43.33) per cent of urban respondents and only 10 (10.00) per cent of the rural respondents took more than one year's time to get over the grief. Further, it is of significance to know that a majority of the respondents in rural areas took less than one year to get over the grief because of their lack of intimacy with their husbands and more social interaction.

It is found that the statistical results indicate the significant difference between the urban and the rural widows in respect of the time taken to get over the grief.

### Feeling of Loss and Frequency of Feeling

Particulars regarding the respondents feeling of loss of their husbands and the frequency of their feeling the same are presented in Tables 5.5(A) and (B).

**TABLE - 5.5 (A)**
**FEELING OF LOSS**

| *Feeling of Loss* | *Urban %* | *Rural %* | *Total %* | *$X^2$ Value* |
|---|---|---|---|---|
| No | 6.00 | 2.00 | 8.00 | |
| Yes | 94.00 | 98.00 | 92.00 | 3.26NS |

**TABLE - 5.5 (B)**
**FREQUENCY OF FEELING THE LOSS**

| *Frequency of Feeling* | *Urban %* | *Rural %* | *Total %* | *$X^2$ Value* |
|---|---|---|---|---|
| Never | 6.00 | 2.00 | 4.00 | |
| Sometimes | 26.00 | 54.00 | 40.00 | |
| Often | 68.00 | 44.00 | 56.00 | 12.7** |
| Total | 100.00 | 100.00 | 100.00 | |

(a) Calculated $X^2 = 3.26$; table value of $X^2$ with 1 d f at .05 level is 3.84. Hence, the difference is not significant.

(b) Calculated $X^2 = 12.7$; table value of $X^2$ with 2 d f at .01 level is 9.21. Hence, the difference is significant.

It is evident from the table that about 6 (6.00) per cent of the urban respondents and only 2 (2.00) per cent of the rural respondents did not feel the loss of their husbands, whereas a majority of the respondents both in urban and rural areas felt the loss of their husbands. As such, the findings indicate that the highest number of widows (92.00) per cent feel the loss of their husbands and the least proportion do not feel the loss at all. However, the difference between the urban and the rural widows in this respect is found to be statistically significant. Further, the data also suggests that about 26 (26.00) per cent of the urban respondents and about 54 (55.00) per cent of the rural respondents felt the loss sometimes in comparison to 68 (68.00) per cent of the urban widows and 49 (49.33) per cent of the rural widows who felt the loss of their husbands often. Thus, with regard to the frequency of feeling the loss by the widows, we may conclude that over half of them (56.00) feel the loss often. As such a majority of the widows studied seem to suggest that they feel the loss of their husbands quite often. However, statistically significant difference between the urban and the rural widows is found out in terms of feeling of the loss of their husbands.

**Persons Blamed Widows and factors Responsible for Widowhood**

Table 5.6(A) provides particulars regarding the persons who blamed widows for their condition and the factors that are considered by the respondents responsible for their widowhood.

**TABLE - 5.6 (A)**
**PERSONS BLAMED WIDOWS FOR THE DEATH OF HUSBANDS**

| *Persons Blamed Widows* | *Urban %* | *Rural %* | *Total %* | *$X^2$ Value* |
|---|---|---|---|---|
| In-laws | 14.67 | 5.33 | 10.00 | |
| Parents | 3.33 | 4.00 | 3.67 | |
| Neighbours | 4.00 | 3.33 | 3.67 | |
| Myself | 62.67 | 77.34 | 70.00 | 10.66** |
| No one | 15.33 | 10.00 | 12.66 | |
| Total | 100.00 | 100.00 | 100.00 | |

**TABLE - 5.6 (B)**
**FACTORS RESPONSIBLE FOR WIDOWHOOD**

| *Factors Responsible* | *Urban %* | *Rural %* | *Total %* | *$X^2$ Value* |
|---|---|---|---|---|
| Circumstances | 6.67 | 5.33 | 6.00 | |
| Karma | 77.33 | 68.00 | 72.67 | 5.1NS |
| God's wrath | 16.00 | 26.67 | 21.33 | |
| Total | 100.00 | 100.00 | 100.00 | |

(a) Calculated $X^2 = 10.66$; table value of $X^2$ with 4 d f at .05 level is 9.49. Hence, the difference is significant.

(b) Calculated $X^2 = 5.1$; table value of $X^2$ with 2 d f at .05 level is 5.99. Hence the difference is not significant.

It is observed from the above table that over two-third of the respondents both in urban and rural area are blamed by either others or themselves for their widowhood. And about 15 (15.33) per cent of the urban respondents are not blamed for their widowhood.

Further, in terms of the persons who blamed widows, the findings suggest that about 62.67 per cent of the urban respondents and nearly 77.33 per cent of the rural respondents blamed themselves for their widowhood. Whereas about 14 (14.67) per cent of the urban widows and about 5 (5.33) per cent of the rural widows are blamed by in-laws for the death of their husbands.

Thus, with regard to the persons who blamed widows for the death of their husbands, the data indicates that a significant majority of the widows blamed themselves for their widowhood. However, it is statistically found that there is a significant difference between the urban and the rural widows in respect of persons who blamed them for the death of their husbands. Thus, with regard to the factors responsible for widowhood, over two-third of the widows both from urban and rural areas believe that Karma/ God's wrath are responsible for the death of their husbands. And only 16 (16.00) per cent of the urban respondents and nearly 26 (26.67) per cent of the rural respondents opined that circumstances are responsible for the death of their husbands. Thus, it can be said that a significant majority of the widows considered Karma as the responsibility factor while a least number of widows considered circumstances as the responsible factor for their widowhood. However, it is found that there is no significant difference between the widows of urban and rural areas in respect of their view towards factors responsible for their widowhood.

**Status of Widows in Hindu Society**

Under this heading, the status of widows in Hindu society is focused upon. The main reason behind this is to know how widows view their status and what are the factors responsible for the inferior status of widows, what are the factors and suggestions that help the cause of widows most, and attitudes of youth towards widows. In other words, an attempt is made here to ascertain the image of widows in Hindu society, which may in turn speak of values of Hindu culture.

We may first consider the status of widows in Hindu society and factors responsible for their inferior status. The particulars regarding these are provided in Tables 5.7(A) and (B).

It can be observed from the Table that 63 (63.33) per cent of the urban respondents perceived their status as inferior in Hindu society. About 36 (36.67) per cent of the respondents in urban area considered their status as just ordinary in comparison to 58 (58.00) per cent of the rural respondents. However, none of the widows either from the urban or the rural areas perceived their status as high or equal to married women. It is found that there is significant difference between the widows of urban and rural areas in respect of their view towards status of widows in Hindu society.

**TABLE - 5.7 (A)**
**STATUS OF WIDOWS IN HINDU SOCIETY**

| *Status* | *Urban %* | *Rural %* | *Total %* | *$X^2$ Value* |
|---|---|---|---|---|
| Just ordinary | 36.67 | 58.00 | 47.33 | |
| Inferior | 63.33 | 42.00 | 52.67 | 13.68** |
| Total | 100.00 | 100.00 | 100.00 | |

**TABLE - 5.7 (B)**
**FACTORS RESPONSIBLE FOR INFERIOR STATUS**

| *Factors Responsible* | *Urban %* | *Rural %* | *Total %* | *$X^2$ Value* |
|---|---|---|---|---|
| Religious conventions | 38.00 | 12.00 | 25.00 | |
| Social & caste customs | 23.33 | 6.00 | 14.67 | |
| Lack of female education | 22.0 | 11.33 | 16.67 | |
| Lack of female employment | 8.67 | 38.00 | 23.33 | 90.84** |
| Dependency resulting out of inability to earn/lack of job opportunity | 8.00 | 32.67 | 20.33 | |
| Total | 100.00 | 100.00 | 100.00 | |

(a) Calculated $X^2$ = 13.68; table value of $X^2$ with 1 df at .01 level is 6.63. Hence the difference is significant.

(b) Calculated $X^2$ = 90.84; table value of $X^2$ with 4 df at .01 level is 13.28. Hence, the difference is significant.

The difference in the perception of factors responsible for the inferior status of the Hindu widows is evident. The data reveal that in urban area 38 (38.00) per cent of the respondents considered religious conventions for the inferior status of the Hindu widows, whereas in rural areas 12 (12.00) per cent of the respondents considered the same idea. While about 8 (8.00) per cent of the urban respondents considered dependency resulting out of inability to earn/lack of job opportunities as responsible factors, as against 32 (32.67) per cent of the rural respondents. As such the data suggest that a majority of the widows considered religious conventions as responsible factors for the inferior status of the widows in Hindu society. However, the $X^2$ value establishes a significant difference between the urban and the rural widows in respect of their attitudes toward the factors responsible for the inferior status of Hindu widows.

We may next consider the factors that help widows to improve their condition and respondents' suggestions for improving their economic status. The particulars regarding these are given in the following table.

## 5.2 Factors that Help and Suggestions for Improving Economic Status

The data presented in Tables 5.8(A) & (B) shows the perception of factors that help the cause of widow's most.

It is evident from the table that nearly 48 (48.00) per cent of the urban respondents opined female education as one of the foremost and important factors that help the widow's cause most as against 20 (20.00) per cent of the rural respondents. And about 13 (13.33) per cent of the respondents in urban areas said that social institutions, workers help to improve widow's conditions. Whereas in rural areas nearly 11 (11.33) per cent of the respondents hold the same idea. In view of above findings, we may state that a majority of the widows considered female education as one of the factors that help widow's cause the most. However, it is statistically found that there is a significant difference between the urban and the rural respondents attitudes toward the factors that help to improve widow's condition.

The suggestions of the respondents for improving the economic status of the widows are presented in Table 5.8(B).

With regard to the suggestions of the respondents the findings indicate that about 44 (44.00) per cent of the urban respondents suggested a widow's absolute authority over property as against 19 (19.33) per cent of the rural respondents. And about 9 (8.67) per cent of the respondents in urban area said that a widow's share should be equal to the son's share, whereas about 32 (32.00) per cent of the rural respondents suggested the same factor. Thus, with regard to the suggestions for improving a widow's economic status, we may state that a majority of the widows suggest that preference in employment will help in improving the widow's economic status. However, the statistical result establish that there is a difference between the urban and the rural widows in respect of their suggestions toward improving widows economic condition.

**TABLE - 5.8 (A)**
**FACTORS THAT HELP CAUSE OF WIDOW'S MOST**

| *Factors that help* | *Urban %* | *Rural %* | *Total %* | *$X^2$ Value* |
|---|---|---|---|---|
| Female education | 48.00 | 20.00 | 34.00 | |
| Female employment | 20.00 | 44.00 | 32.00 | |
| Proper inheritance and succession law | 8.67 | 14.00 | 11.33 | 34.46** |
| Social institutions/Social workers | 13.33 | 11.33 | 12.33 | |
| Widows themselves | 4.67 | 7.33 | 6.00 | |
| Awareness among women in general | 5.33 | 3.33 | 4.34 | |
| Total | 100.00 | 100.00 | 100.00 | |

**TABLE - 5.8 (B)**
**SUGGESTIONS FOR IMPROVING WIDOW'S ECONOMIC STATUS**

| *Suggestions* | *Urban %* | *Rural %* | *Total %* | *$X^2$ Value* |
|---|---|---|---|---|
| Same share as Son | 8.67 | 32.00 | 20.33 | |
| Preference in employment | 29.33 | 36.67 | 33.00 | |
| Absolute authority over property | 44.00 | 19.33 | 31.67 | 40.74** |
| Right to employment of the husband | 8.00 | 8.67 | 8.33 | |
| Social institutions/women's organisations help widows in getting property | 10.00 | 3.33 | 6.67 | |
| Total | 100.00 | 100.00 | 100.00 | |

(a) Calculated $X^2$ = 34.46; table value of $X^2$ with 5 d f at .01 level is 15.09. Hence, the difference is significant.

(b) Calculated $X^2$ = 40.74; table value of $X^2$ with 4 d f at .01 level is 3.28. Hence, the difference is significant.

**Reaction of Youths towards Widows**

The reactions of the youth towards the respondents varies from disrespect to high respect. However, 50 (50.00) per cent of the urban respondents said that youths give moderate to high respect as against 37 (37.33) per cent of the rural respondents. The following Table 5.9 represents the particulars regarding the youths reactions.

About 39 (39.33) per cent of the respondents in urban area stated that the reactions of youth toward widows was indifferent, whereas 45 (44.67) per cent of the rural respondents received the same reaction. However, nearly 10 (10.67) per cent of the respondents from urban area and 18 (18.00) per cent of the rural respondents said that the youths show no respect to the widows. As such the above findings seem to suggest that a significant majority of widows state that today's youths are indifferent towards widows. While least proportion of widows state that the youths have high respect for the widows. It is also found that there is significant difference between the urban and the rural widows in respect of their view on reaction of today's youths towards widows.

**TABLE - 5.9**

**REACTIONS OF YOUTHS TOWARDS WIDOWS**

| *Reaction* | *Urban %* | *Rural %* | *Total %* | *$X^2$ Value* |
|---|---|---|---|---|
| Disrespect | 10.67 | 18.00 | 14.33 | |
| Indifferent | 39.33 | 44.67 | 42.00 | |
| Moderate respect | 46.67 | 32.00 | 39.33 | 8.08** |
| High respect | 3.33 | 5.33 | 4.34 | |
| Total | 100.00 | 100.00 | 100.00 | |

Calculated $X^2$ = 8.08; table value of $X^2$ with 3 d f .05 level is 7.81. Hence the difference is significant.

## 5.3 Views on Widows Remarriage

One of the main objective of this study is to study the attitudes of widows towards widow remarriage. The responses obtained in respect of their knowledge about widow remarriages, marriage of other widows and opinion about who can marry and who cannot marry, opinion about their own marriage, reasons for their favourable and unfavourable attitudes, opinion about the difficulties foreseen in a widow remarriage are presented in this topic.

### Social Sanction for Marriage of Widows and Frequency of its Occurrence

The data representing the respondents knowledge about the approval of widow remarriage, frequency of its occurrence is given in Tables 5.10(A) and (B).

### TABLE - 5.10 (A)
### APPROVAL OF WIDOW'S MARRIAGE

| *Approval* | *Urban %* | *Rural %* | *Total %* | *$X^2$ Value* |
|---|---|---|---|---|
| No | 40.67 | 8.00 | 24.33 | |
| Yes | 24.67 | 45.33 | 35.00 | 44.66** |
| Not approved but occurs rarely | 34.66 | 46.67 | 40.67 | |
| Total | 100.00 | 100.00 | 100.00 | |

### TABLE - 5.10 (B)
### FREQUENCY OF ITS OCCURENCE

| *Frequency* | *Urban %* | *Rural %* | *Total %* | *$X^2$ Value* |
|---|---|---|---|---|
| No | 72.67 | 56.67 | 64.67 | |
| Yes | 27.33 | 43.33 | 35.33 | 8.38** |
| Total | 100.00 | 100.00 | 100.00 | |

(a) Calculated $X^2 = 44.66$; table value of $X^2$ with 2 d f at .01 level is 9.21. Hence, the difference is significant.

(b) Calculated $X^2 = 8.38$; table value of $X^2$ with 1 d f at .01 level is 6.63. Hence the difference is significant.

The above table indicates that nearly 24 (24.67) per cent of the respondents in urban areas and 45 (45.33) per cent of the respondents in rural areas have reported that widow remarriage is permitted in their community. And about 40 (40.67) per cent of the urban respondents and 8 (8.00) per cent of the rural respondents have mentioned that widow remarriage is not permitted in their community. However, it is significant to note that nearly 34 (34.66) per cent of the urban respondents and 46 (46.67) per cent of the rural respondents have reported that widow remarriage is not approved in their community but occurs rarely. In view of the above findings we may state that a significant majority of the widows state that widow remarriage is not approved in their communities. The $X^2$ value suggests that there is significant difference between the urban and the rural widows in respect of their view towards approval of widow remarriage in their respective communities.

Further, from Table 5.10(B) it is observed that nearly 72 (72.67) per cent of the urban respondents and about 56 (56.67) per cent of the rural respondents reported that widow remarriages did not occur frequently, whereas 27 (27.33) per cent of the urban respondents stated that in their community widow remarriages occur frequently. As such the findings seem to suggest that a significant majority of the widows report that widow remarriages do not occur frequently in their communities. The statistical results establish that there is a difference between the widows of urban and rural areas in respect of their view towards the frequency of occurence of widow marriages in their communities.

## Knowledge about Widow Remarriage

An attempt is made to assess the knowledge of the respondents in respect of widow re-marriage and reaction of the society towards such marriage. The data pertaining to this is presented in Tables 5.11(A), (B), (C) and (D).

**TABLE - 5.11 (A)**

**KNOWLEDGE ABOUT WIDOW REMARRIAGE**

| *Knowledge about Married Widows* | *Urban %* | *Rural %* | *Total %* | *$X^2$ Value* |
|---|---|---|---|---|
| No | 14.00 | 6.00 | 10.00 | |
| Yes | 39.33 | 69.33 | 54.33 | |
| I heard about widow remarriage | 46.67 | 24.67 | 35.67 | 27.38** |
| Total | 100.00 | 100.00 | 100.00 | |

**(B) OBSERVED WIDOW'S REMARRIAGE**

| *Observed Widow's remarriage* | *Urban %* | *Rural %* | *Total %* | *$X^2$ Value* |
|---|---|---|---|---|
| No | 57.33 | 24.00 | 40.67 | |
| Yes | 42.67 | 76.00 | 59.33 | |
| Total | 100.00 | 100.00 | 100.00 | |

**(C) ARE THEY HAPPY**

| *Are they Happy* | *Urban %* | *Rural %* | *Total %* | *$X^2$ Value* |
|---|---|---|---|---|
| No | 10.67 | 3.33 | 7.00 | |
| Yes | 37.33 | 74.00 | 55.67 | |
| Don't know | 52.00 | 22.67 | 37.33 | |
| Total | 100.00 | 100.00 | 100.00 | |

(D) REACTIONS OF SOCIETY

| *Reactions* | *Urban %* | *Rural %* | *Total %* | $X^2$ *Value* |
|---|---|---|---|---|
| Condemned | 7.33 | 3.33 | 5.33 | |
| Intellectuals welcomed but others condemned | 80.00 | 42.00 | 61.00 | |
| Welcomed warmly | 12.67 | 54.67 | 33.67 | |
| Total | 100.00 | 100.00 | 100.00 | |

(a) Calculated $X^2 = 27.38$; table value of $X^2$ with 2 d f at .01 level is 9.21. Hence, the difference is significant.

The data given in Table 5.11(A) reveals that nearly 39 (39.33) per cent of the urban respondents as against 69 (69.33) per cent of the rural respondents have reported that they knew widows who got married. And about 14 (14.00) per cent of the urban respondents and only about 6 (6.00) per cent of the rural respondents have mentioned that they have not known widows who married. But about 46 (46.67) per cent of the urban respondents as against 24 (24.67) per cent of the rural respondents have heard about widow remarriage. However, there is a significant difference between the urban and the rural widows in respect of their knowledge toward widow re-marriages.

The Table 5.11(B) also shows that nearly 42 (42.67) per cent of the urban respondents have observed widow remarriage, while the proportion of such respondents who have observed widow re-marriage in rural areas is about 76 (76.00) per cent. And about 57 (57.33) per cent of the urban respondents and 24 (24.00) per cent of the rural respondents have not observed widow remarriage.

Further, an attempt is made to assess the knowledge of the respondents in respect of successful or unsuccessful widow re-marriage. The findings presented in Table 5.11(C) suggest that about 52 (52.00) per cent of the urban respondents as against 22 (22.67) per cent, of the rural respondents are not aware of the re-married widow's life. While, 37 (37.33) per cent of the urban respondents and 74 (74.00) per cent of the rural respondents are aware of the instances of successful widow marriages. About 10 (10.67) per cent of urban respondents and only 3 (3.33) per cent of the rural respondents are aware of instances of unsuccessful widow remarriages.

Furthermore, it may be observed from the data presented in Table 5.11(D) that a majority of the respondents 80.00 per cent from urban and 42.00 per cent from rural areas report that intellectuals welcomed but others condemned widow remarriage. And about 12 (12.67) per cent of the urban respondents and 54 (54.67) per cent of the rural respondents mention that people warmly welcomed widow remarriage. Nearly 7 (7.33) per cent of the respondents in urban area and only 3 (3.33) per cent of the rural respondents state that people condemn this practice.

Thus, with regard to the knowledge of respondents about widow remarriage, the data indicates that a majority of the urban respondents have heard about widow remarriages, but have not observed widow re-marriages, and are not aware of such successful marriages. But they are aware of the reaction of society and a majority of them state that while intellectuals welcome widow marriage others condemn it.

### Attitudes toward Remarriage - and Ideal Gap between Widowhood and Remarriage

We may next consider the attitudes of the respondents toward widow remarriage and ideal gap between widowhood and re-marriage. The particulars regarding this are presented in Tables 5.12(A) and (B).

**TABLE - 5.12 (A)**

**ATTITUDES TOWARD REMARRIAGE**

| *Can a Widow Remarry* | *Urban %* | *Rural %* | *Total %* |
|---|---|---|---|
| No | 16.00 | 10.00 | 13.00 |
| Yes | 84.00 | 90.00 | 87.00 |
| Total | 100.00 | 100.00 | 100.00 |

**TABLE - 5.12 (B)**

**THE IDEAL GAP BETWEEN WIDOWHOOD AND REMARRIAGE**

| *Can a Widow Remarry* | *Urban %* | *Rural %* | *Total %* |
|---|---|---|---|
| Within a year | 11.90 | 11.77 | 11.83 |
| After one year | 30.13 | 44.12 | 39.32 |
| After two years | 41.27 | 33.08 | 37.02 |
| After three years | 12.70 | 11.03 | 11.83 |
| Total | 100.00 | 100.00 | 100.00 |

It may be observed from the above table that a majority of the urban and the rural respondents that is 84 (84.00) per cent and 90 (90.00) respectively display favourable attitudes toward widow remarriage. And only 16 (16.00) per cent of the respondents from the urban areas and 10 (10.00) per cent of respondents from the rural areas do not favour widow remarriage. As such, the findings seem to suggest that a significant majority of the widows opine that a widow can re-marry.

Further, the data presented in Table 5.12(B) indicate that 41 (41.27) per cent of the respondents in urban areas suggest that a widow can remarry after two years whereas in rural areas about 44 (44.12) per cent of the respondents suggest one year as the ideal gap between widowhood and remarriage. And only 11 (11.83) per cent of the respondents both from urban and rural areas recommend that a widow can remarry within a year of widowhood. In view of the above findings we may state that a majority of the widows suggest one year as the ideal gap between widowhood and remarriage.

### A Widow Who Can and Cannot Marry

We may next consider the attitudes of the widows toward the widows who can and cannot marry. The relevant data is given in Table 5.13.

**TABLE - 5.13**
**WIDOWS WHO CAN MARRY**

| *Who can Marry* | *Urban %* | *Rural %* | *Total %* |
|---|---|---|---|
| Child/Young widow | 32.54 | 45.19 | 39.08 |
| All those who wish to | 11.11 | 9.62 | 10.34 |
| Childless if she is under 30 | 16.66 | 14.82 | 15.70 |
| Those who cannot control themselves, have no courage to face a life of self control and those who have no one to care for/look after | 11.11 | 16.29 | 13.79 |
| If the widow's financial condition is bad, if family ill-treats her/if she is widowed soon after her marriage, she must marry | 11.90 | 5.19 | 8.43 |
| A lonely widow has to suffer a lot | 7.94 | 5.19 | 6.52 |
| One whose family and caste has allowed her to marry | 8.74 | 3.70 | 6.14 |
| Total | 100.00 | 100.00 | 100.00 |

It is obvious from the table that nearly 32 (32.54) per cent of the urban respondents as against 45 (45.19) per cent of the rural respondents opine that a child or young widow can remarry. And about 8 (8.74) per cent of the respondents from urban area and only 3 (3.70) per cent of the respondents from rural areas have favoured those widow's marriages whose family and caste have consented to their marriages. However, it is significant to note that about 11 (11.11) per cent of the urban respondents and 9 (9.62) per cent of the rural respondents favoured all those widows who wish to marry. Thus, with regard to the attitudes of widows toward a widow who can marry we may state that a majority of them say that a child/young widow can remarry.

The data pertaining to the respondents attitudes toward a widow who should not marry are presented in Table 5.14.

The table reveals that about 20 (20.83) per cent of the respondents from urban areas and 20 (20.00) per cent of the respondents from rural areas have not favoured the marriage of those widows who are above 30 years, have had a long married life/have money and protection by the family. And about 16 (16.67) per cent of the urban respondents as against 13 (13.33) per cent of the rural respondents have discouraged marriage of those widows who have children. Only 16 (16.67) per cent of the urban respondents and 6 (6.67) per cent of the rural respondents state that it is their caste customs not to marry. Thus the data indicate that a majority of the widows report that those widows who have children should not marry.

**TABLE - 5.14**

**A WIDOW WHO SHOULD NOT MARRY**

| *Who should not Marry* | *Urban %* | *Rural %* | *Total %* |
|---|---|---|---|
| Those who have children | 16.67 | 13.33 | 15.39 |
| Those who can voluntarily restrain | 16.67 | 20.00 | 17.95 |
| Those who are rich | 8.33 | 26.67 | 15.38 |
| A widow above 30, who has had a long married life, has money and is protected by the family, should not marry | 20.83 | 20.00 | 20.51 |
| It is better for a widow to lead a life of self control and celibacy | 20.83 | 13.33 | 17.95 |
| It is the caste custom not to marry | 16.67 | 6.67 | 12.82 |
| Total | 100.00 | 100.00 | 100.00 |

**Attitudes Toward Married Widow and Living Alone**

The data representing the attitudes of widows towards married widows and those living alone are given in Tables 5.15(A) and (B).

**TABLE - 5.15 (A)**
**ATTITUDES TOWARD MARRIED WIDOWS**

| *Accepting a Married Widow* | *Urban %* | *Rural %* | *Total %* |
|---|---|---|---|
| No acceptance | 16.00 | 10.00 | 13.00 |
| Only those widows should be accepted whose caste permit remarriage | 7.33 | 3.33 | 5.33 |
| Unconditional acceptance | 76.67 | 86.67 | 81.67 |
| Total | 100.00 | 100.00 | 100.00 |

**TABLE 5.15 (B)**
**ATTITUDE TOWARDS WIDOWS LIVING ALONE**

| *Living Alone is Risky* | *Urban %* | *Rural %* | *Total %* |
|---|---|---|---|
| No | 6.67 | 3.33 | 5.00 |
| Yes | 93.33 | 96.67 | 95.00 |
| Total | 100.00 | 100.00 | 100.00 |

The above table indicates that a majority of the respondents both from urban and rural areas, that is, 76 (76.67) per cent and 86 (86.67) per cent respectively, showed favourable attitudes toward remarried widows. And about 16 (16.00) per cent of the urban respondents and 10 (10.00) per cent of the rural respondents are not ready to accept married widows. Remaining 7 (7.33) per cent of the respondents in urban area and 3 (3.33) per cent of the respondents in rural areas are ready to accept those widows whose caste permit remarriage. In view of the above findings it may be stated that a significant majority of the widows expressed that they accept the married widows.

Further it is observed that 93 (93.33) per cent of respondents from urban areas and 96 (96.67) per cent of the respondents from rural areas have uniformly felt that living alone is risky. Remaining 6 (6.67) per cent of the urban respondents and only 3 (3.33) per cent of the rural respondents have not felt that living alone is risky. Thus, with regard to the question whether living alone is risky, the findings indicate that a significant majority of the widows report that living alone is risky.

**Reasons for Unwillingness/Willingness to Remarry**

The following Tables 5.16(A), (B) and (C) provides particulars regarding the attitudes of the widows towards their own marriage and reasons for their favourable and disfavourable attitudes.

**TABLE - 5.16**

**(A) REASONS FOR UNWILLINGNESS/WILLINGNESS TO REMARRY**

| *Had any Thought of Marrying Again* | *Urban %* | *Rural %* | *Total %* |
|---|---|---|---|
| No | 88.67 | 85.33 | 87.00 |
| Yes | 11.33 | 14.67 | 13.00 |
| Total | 100.00 | 100.00 | 100.00 |

**(B) IF NO WHY**

| *Had any Thought of Marrying Again* | *Urban %* | *Rural %* | *Total %* |
|---|---|---|---|
| I hate this idea | 38.35 | 17.18 | 27.96 |
| Religion and society oppose it | 11.27 | 19.53 | 15.33 |
| Not of a marriageable age | 22.55 | 23.43 | 22.98 |
| Children will be left uncared for | 9.78 | 23.44 | 16.48 |
| Unable to forget first husband, cannot bear the idea of replacing him with another man | 6.77 | 4.69 | 5.75 |
| No one tried/thinks of second marriage | 6.77 | 4.69 | 5.75 |
| Second husband may not allow to keep the children | 4.51 | 7.04 | 5.75 |
| Total | 100.00 | 100.00 | 100.00 |

**(C) IF YES WHY**

| *Had any Thought of Marrying Again* | *Urban %* | *Rural %* | *Total %* |
|---|---|---|---|
| Young age | 29.41 | 27.27 | 28.20 |
| Provides socio-economic security | 29.41 | 31.82 | 30.77 |
| Our religion and society approved | 17.65 | 18.18 | 17.94 |
| Found suitable mate | 17.65 | 9.09 | 12.83 |
| Kinsmen forced me | 5.88 | 13.64 | 10.26 |
| Total | 100.00 | 100.00 | 100.00 |

The data presented in the above table reveals that nearly 88 (88.67) per cent of the urban widows and 85 (85.33) per cent of the rural respondents have not thought to remarry. And about 11

(11.33) per cent of the respondents from urban and 14 (14.67) per cent from rural have thought to remarry. As such the findings seem to suggest that a significant majority of the widows had not thought of marrying again.

When a majority of the widows had not thought about their re-marriage, we were interested in knowing, the reasons for their willingness or unwillingness to remarry.

The Table 5.16(B) shows that nearly 38 (38.35) per cent of the urban respondents as against 17 (17.18) per cent of the rural respondents hate the idea of remarriage. While 11 (11.27) per cent of the respondents from urban and 19 (19.53) per cent of the respondents from rural areas report that religion and society oppose it. And about 9 (9.78) per cent of the urban respondents as against 23 (23.44) per cent of the rural respondents mention that the children will be left uncared, while about 4 (4.51) per cent from urban area and only 7 (7.04) per cent from rural area report that the second husband may be averse to keeping his wife's children with them.

However, the Table 5.16(C) shows that about 29 (29.41) per cent of the urban and 27 (27.27) per cent of the rural respondents have thought of remarriage because of their young age. Whereas only (17.65) per cent of the respondents from urban area and 18 (18.18) per cent of the respondents from rural areas thought of re-marriage because their religion and society approved of it.

Thus, it can be observed that the most important reason for drawing back from remarriage seems to be fidelity of widows toward their deceased husbands. The second reason appears to be lack of religious sanction for remarriage and third one seems to be the mothers anxiety to give a fair deal to their children.

**Difficulties Foreseen in Remarriage and Knowledge about the 1856 Widow Remarriage Act**

The data pertaining to the difficulties foreseen in remarriage and knowledge about widow remarriage Act of 1856 are presented in Tables 5.17(A) and (B).

It can be observed from the table that about 32 (32.67) per cent of the urban respondents as against 15 (15.33) per cent of the rural respondents report that their caste opposes it while, 15 (15.33) per cent from urban and only 7 (7.33) per cent from rural areas state that family customs oppose it. And about 43 (43.33) per cent of the urban respondents as against 49 (49.34) per cent of the rural respondents mention that it will be difficult for a woman once married to marry again. Here the other reasons, include number of children, children may not like it, peer-group may not approve of it, etc. As such the findings seem to suggest that a significant majority of the widows state that it will be difficult for a woman once married to marry again.

**TABLE - 5.17 (A)**
**DIFFICULTIES FORESEEN IN REMARRIAGE**

| *Difficulties* | *Urban %* | *Rural %* | *Total %* |
|---|---|---|---|
| Our caste opposes it | 32.67 | 15.33 | 24.00 |
| Family customs oppose it | 15.33 | 7.33 | 11.33 |
| No one will come forward to marry | 8.67 | 28.00 | 18.33 |
| Marriage involves so many compromises and adjustments on the part of the wife, it will be difficult for a woman once married to do so. | 43.33 | 49.34 | 46.34 |
| Total | 100.00 | 100.00 | 100.00 |

**TABLE - 5.17(B)**
**KNOWLEDGE ABOUT THE WIDOW REMARRIAGE ACT OF 1856**

| *Knowledge of the Act* | *Urban %* | *Rural %* | *Total %* |
|---|---|---|---|
| No | 94.00 | 100.00 | 97.00 |
| Yes | 6.00 | - | 3.00 |
| Total | 100.00 | 100.00 | 100.00 |

Further, table shows that none of the respondents in rural areas are aware of this Act, whereas in urban area only 6 (6.00) per cent of the respondents know the Act.

It appears from the above analysis that most of the respondents are uniformly unaware of the Acts enacted for their welfare.

### 5.4 Types of Family Preferred

This section pertains to the widows preference of the type of family, reasons for their preference.

**TABLE - 5.18**
**TYPE OF FAMILY PREFERRED BY WIDOWS**

| *Type of Family Preferred* | *Urban %* | *Rural %* | *Total %* | *$X^2$ Value* |
|---|---|---|---|---|
| Joint-family with in-laws | 6.00 | 4.00 | 5.00 | |
| Joint-family with Sons | 58.66 | 75.33 | 67.00 | 13.1* |
| With parents by sharing expenses equally | 22.67 | 8.67 | 15.67 | |
| Independently | 12.67 | 12.00 | 12.33 | |
| Total | 100.00 | 100.00 | 100.00 | |

Calculated $X^2 = 13.1$; table value of $X^2$ with d f at .01 level is 11.34. Hence the difference is significant.

The data given in Table 5.18 reveals that a majority of the respondents both from urban and rural areas 58 (58.66) per cent and 75 (75.33) per cent respectively preferred to live in joint family with sons, whereas, only 6 (6.00) per cent of the urban respondents and 4 (4.00) per cent of the rural respondents preferred to live with in-laws. And about 22 (22.67) per cent of the respondents in urban area and 8 (8.67) per cent of the respondents in rural areas preferred to live independently. Thus, with regard to the type of family preferred by widows we may conclude that a significant majority of them preferred to live with their sons. However, it is statistically found that there is a significant difference between the widows of urban and rural areas in respect of their preference for the type of family.

**Reasons for Liking Joint-Family and Liking to Live Independently**

We may first consider the respondents' reasons for liking joint-family. The relevant data is presented in the following table.

**TABLE - 5.19 (A)**
**REASONS FOR LIKING TO LIVE IN A JOINT FAMILY**

| *Reasons* | *Urban %* | *Rural %* | *Total %* | *$X^2$ Value* |
|---|---|---|---|---|
| Provides cooperation and help in times of need | 35.05 | 19.33 | 26.39 | |
| Teaches tolerance and love | 26.80 | 12.61 | 18.98 | |
| Risky for widows to live alone | 20.62 | 9.25 | 14.35 | 38.73** |
| Need money and protection | 10.31 | 42.01 | 27.78 | |
| Common field/ all are minor children | 7.22 | 16.80 | 12.50 | |
| Total | 100.00 | 100.00 | 100.00 | |

TABLE - 5.19 (B)

**(B) REASONS FOR LIKING TO LIVE INDEPENDENTLY**

| *Reasons* | *Urban %* | *Rural %* | *Total %* | *$X^2$ Value* |
|---|---|---|---|---|
| Like to live independently/ can have own house | 66.04 | 25.81 | 51.19 | |
| Want to avoid quarrels | 9.43 | 58.06 | 27.38 | |
| Don't want to be a burden on any one | 24.53 | 16.13 | 21.43 | 23.69* |
| Total | 100.00 | 100.00 | 100.00 | |

(a) Calculated $X^2$ = 38.73; table value of $X^2$ with 5 d f at .01 level is 15.09. Hence the difference is significant.

(b) Calculated $X^2$ = 23.69; table value of $X^2$ with 3 d f at .01 level is 7.81. Hence the difference is significant.

It is observed from Table 5.18 that a majority the respondents that is 64 (64.66) per cent and 79 (79.33) per cent of respondents belonging to urban and rural areas respectively preferred the joint family whereas the proportion of widows who preferred to live alone is least. Further with regard to the reasons, about 35 (35.05) per cent of the urban respondents and 19(19.33) per cent of the rural respondents preferred the joint family because it provides cooperation and help in times of need. And about 10 (10.31) per cent of the respondents in urban area and 42(42.01) per cent of the respondents in rural areas preferred joint family as they need money and protection . Nearly 20 (20.62) per cent of the respondents from urban area and 9 (9.25) per cent of the respondents from rural places preferred joint family because it is risky for widows to live alone. Thus, the data indicates that a majority of widows prefer to live in joint families because they need money and protection. However, the $X^2$ value indicates that there is significant difference between the urban and rural widows in respect to their reasons for liking joint family.

Further, the data seems to suggest that a small proportion of respondents belonging to urban and rural areas liked to live independently. The data pertaining to this is presented in Table 5.19(B).

The data shows that 24(24.53) per cent of the urban respondents preferred to live independently as they do not want to be a burden on anyone as against 16(16.13) per cent of the rural respondents. Whereas about 66(66.04) per cent of the urban respondents and 25 (25.81) per cent of the rural respondents state that they like to live independently as they can have their own house. As such the findings indicate that among widows who prefer to live independently the proportion who do not want to be a burden on any one is higher. The statistical results show that there is a significant difference between the widows who belonged to urban and rural areas in respect of their reasons for liking to live independently.

### 5.5 Future Plans

We may now consider the future plans of the widows for themselves and for their children. The particulars pertaining to the respondents' future plans are presented in Tables 5.20(A) and (B).

**TABLE - 5.20 (A)**
**PLANS FOR OWN FUTURE LIFE**

| *Plans for Future Life* | *Urban %* | *Rural %* | *Total %* |
|---|---|---|---|
| To get employed | 14.00 | 6.67 | 10.33 |
| To visit all the holy places | 30.67 | 23.33 | 26.67 |
| To continue employment | 28.00 | 42.00 | 35.00 |
| To die happily | 28.00 | 28.00 | 28.00 |
| Total | 100.00 | 100.00 | 100.00 |

**TABLE - 5.20 (B)**
**PLANS FOR THE WELFARE OF CHILDREN**

| *Frequency* | *Urban %* | *Rural %* | *Total %* |
|---|---|---|---|
| To provide good education | 9.33 | 8.67 | 9.00 |
| Daughter's/ Son's marriage | 24.00 | 15.33 | 19.66 |
| Son's settlement in good jobs/ business | 30.67 | 27.33 | 28.67 |
| Children are grownup/ happily settled | 36.00 | 48.67 | 42.67 |
| Total | 100.00 | 100.00 | 100.00 |

It may be observed from the Table that 3 0(30.67) per cent of the respondents in urban areas as against 23 (23.33) per cent of the rural respondents wish to visit all the holy places, while 14 (14.00) per cent of the urban respondents and only 6 (6.67) per cent of the rural respondents want to work. And about 28(28.00) per cent of the respondents both from urban and rural areas have a desire to die happily.

Further, it is of significance to know their plans for the welfare of their children. It may be observed from the above table that about 30(30.67) per cent of the urban respondents as against 27(27.33) per cent of the rural respondents are worried about their sons' settlement in good jobs/business. And about 24 (24.00) per cent of the urban respondents in comparison to 15(15.33) per cent of the rural respondents are worried about children's marriage. A majority of them are worried about their daughter's marriage. Nearly 6 (6.67) per cent respondents from urban and 8 (8.00) per cent from rural areas are worried about possessing their own house.

Thus, with regard to the plans of the widows for their own future life it is clear from the above analysis that though they are worried about their future, they do not have any specific plans for it whereas they do have some plans in case of their children.

## Wishing to be Self Supporting

The data pertaining to the respondents wish for self support and reasons for wishing to self support sand reasons for not wishing to self support are presented in Tables 5.21(A), (B) and (C).

### TABLE - 5.21

### (A) WISHING TO BE SELF SUPPORTING AND REASON FOR FAVOURABLE AND DISFAVOURABLE ATTITUDES

### (A) WISHING TO BE SELF SUPPORTING

| *Wishing to be Self Supporting* | *Urban %* | *Rural %* | *Total %* |
|---|---|---|---|
| No | 54.67 | 56.67 | 55.67 |
| Yes | 45.33 | 43.33 | 44.33 |
| Total | 100.00 | 100.00 | 100.00 |

### (B) IF NO, REASONS

| *Reasons* | *Urban %* | *Rural %* | *Total %* |
|---|---|---|---|
| Unfavourable social attitude | 6.10 | 12.94 | 9.58 |
| Opposition by family members | 12.19 | 5.88 | 8.98 |
| Fear of disapproval by relatives/in-laws | 6.10 | 14.12 | 10.18 |
| Old age | 54.87 | 36.47 | 45.51 |
| Ill-health | 6.10 | 12.94 | 9.58 |
| Financially sound, no need to work | 14.64 | 17.65 | 16.17 |
| Total | 100.00 | 100.00 | 100.00 |

**(C) IF YES, REASONS**

| *Reasons* | *Urban %* | *Rural %* | *Total %* |
|---|---|---|---|
| Facing financial problems | 45.58 | 47.69 | 46.62 |
| Want to earn sufficient money for the proper upbringing of children | 19.12 | 24.62 | 21.80 |
| To keep myself preoccupied and kill time | 11.77 | 10.76 | 11.28 |
| I am already working | 23.53 | 16.93 | 20.30 |
| Total | 100.00 | 100.00 | 100.00 |

The data indicates that 45 (45.33) per cent of the urban respondents and nearly 43(43.33) per cent of the rural respondents are willing to be self-supporting, while 54(54.67) per cent from urban and 56(56.67) per cent from rural are not willing to be so.

The data shows that about 24(24.39) per cent of the urban respondents as against 32(32.94) per cent of the rural respondents state that family members, in-laws and relatives oppose it and social attitudes are not favourable. About 60 (60.67) per cent of the respondents from urban area and 49 (49.41) per cent of the respondents from rural areas proffer old age and ill-health as reasons, while about 14 (14.64) per cent of the urban respondents as against 17 (17.65) per cent of the rural respondents say that there is no need to work as they are financially sound. Hence, the data seems to suggest that a majority of the widows who do not want to be self-supporting are aged and not healthy.

Further, the data pertaining to the reasons for willingness to be self-supporting reveals that about 46 (46.62) per cent of the respondents both from urban and rural areas say that they are facing financial problems. And nearly 19 (19.12) per cent of the respondents from urban area in comparison to 24 (24.62) per cent of the respondents from rural areas wish to earn money for the proper upbringing of their children, while 11 (11.77) per cent of the respondents from the urban area and 10 (10.76) per cent of the respondents from the rural areas want to work just to keep themselves occupied and pass the time. Thus with regard to the widow's reasons for wishing to be self supporting, the findings suggest that a majority of them are facing financial problems.

**Job-Liked**

The data pertaining to the respondents' attitudes toward kind of employment and help needed for the same are presented in Tables 5.22(A) and (B).

**TABLE - 5.22**

**(A) KIND OF EMPLOYMENT LIKED**

| *Kind of Employment Liked* | *Urban %* | *Rural %* | *Total %* |
|---|---|---|---|
| Vegetable selling | 8.83 | 20.00 | 14.28 |
| Delivering Milk | 22.06 | 35.38 | 28.58 |
| Peon | 19.12 | 7.69 | 13.53 |
| Maid Servant | 23.53 | 18.47 | 21.05 |
| Nurse/Aya | 7.35 | 9.23 | 8.28 |
| Clerical | 7.35 | - | 3.75 |
| Kirana Shop | 8.82 | 9.23 | 9.03 |
| Teaching | 2.94 | - | 1.50 |
| Total | 100.00 | 100.00 | 100.00 |

**(B) HELP NEEDED IN GETTING THE WORK/JOB**

| *Type of Help Needed* | *Urban %* | *Rural %* | *Total %* |
|---|---|---|---|
| Financial assistance | 29.41 | 27.69 | 28.57 |
| Proper training | 29.41 | 15.38 | 22.56 |
| Preference should be given for widows | 41.18 | 56.93 | 48.87 |
| Total | 100.00 | 100.00 | 100.00 |

It is observed from the table that about 22 (22.06) per cent of the urban respondents as against 35 (35.38) per cent of the rural respondents liked the task of delivering milk. While 23 (23.53) per cent of the respondents from the urban and 18 (18.47) per cent from the rural areas wish to work as maid servants. And about 7 (7.35) per cent of the urban respondents as against 9 (9.23) per cent of the rural respondents are willing to work as Nurse/Aya. Nearly 7 (7.35) per cent and only 2 (2.94) per cent of the respondents belonging to urban area would like to work as clerks and teachers, while none of the rural widows are qualified to join these jobs. Thus, with regard to the kind of job liked by the widows, the findings seem to suggest that a majority of them want to follow self-employment like that of a milk maid.

Further the data reveals that 41 (41.18) per cent of the urban respondents in comparison to 56 (56.93) per cent of the rural respondents mention that widows should be given preference in government and private recruitments whereas 29 (29.41) per cent of the respondents in urban areas and 27 (27.67) per cent of the respondents in rural areas state that widows should be given financial assistance to carry on any self-employment scheme. Hence the data indicates that a majority of the widows suggest that they be given preference in all the fields.

### 5.6 Suggestions for the Welfare of Widows

One of the objectives is to elicit suggestions for the welfare of widows from the respondents. These suggestions may be of obvious importance in policy making.

With this view in mind, the suggestions and expectations are sought. The data pertaining to this is presented in Table 5.23.

**TABLE - 5.23**
**SUGGESTIONS FOR THE WELFARE OF WIDOWS**

| *Suggestions* | *Urban %* | *Rural %* | *Total %* |
|---|---|---|---|
| Remarriage of widows should be encouraged | 8.67 | 10.00 | 9.34 |
| Poor widows should be given widow pension | 20.00 | 20.67 | 20.33 |
| Society and people should treat the widows well | 13.33 | 5.33 | 9.33 |
| Homes for widows should be established | 8.67 | 8.67 | 8.67 |
| Financial assistance should be given for the self-employment | 10.67 | 20.00 | 15.33 |
| Free vocational training should be given | 31.33 | 30.67 | 31.00 |
| Through mass media, widows should be made aware of the facilities given by the govt/semi. govt/private agencies | 7.33 | 4.66 | 6.00 |
| Total | 100.00 | 100.00 | 100.00 |

The table shows that nearly 31 (31.33) per cent of the urban and about 30 (30.67) per cent of the rural respondents suggest that free vocational training should be given to the widows since they are interested in earning on their own. While 10 (10.67) per cent of the urban respondents as against 20 (20.00) per cent of the rural respondents say that widows should be given financial assistance for self-employment. About 20 (20.00) per cent of the respondents both from urban and rural areas mention that poor widows should be given widow pension.

Nearly 8 (8.67) per cent of the urban respondents in comparison to 10 (10.00) per cent of the rural respondents state that widow remarriage should be encouraged. While 7 (7.33) per cent from the rural area and 4 (4.66) per cent of the respondents from rural area suggest that widows should be made aware of the facilities given by the government and semi government agencies through mass media. Thus, with regard to the suggestions given to the respondents for the welfare of widows, the findings suggest that a majority of them state that free vocational training should be given to the widows in order to make them self-reliant.

### Expectations of Widows from Others

However, the expectations of widows seem to be inversely associated with the suggestions. The relevant data is given in Tables 5.24(A), (B) and (C).

**TABLE - 5.24**

**(A) EXPECTATIONS OF WIDOWS FROM OTHERS**

| *Expectations from Organizations* | *Urban %* | *Rural %* | *Total %* |
|---|---|---|---|
| Should provide free vocational training | 44.00 | 44.00 | 44.00 |
| Should provide shelter for homeless | 23.33 | 22.67 | 23.00 |
| Should provide free legal advice | 17.33 | 6.00 | 11.67 |
| Should open spinning centres | 6.67 | 20.67 | 13.67 |
| Others* | 8.67 | 6.66 | 7.66 |
| Total | 100.00 | 100.00 | 100.00 |

* Should take up widow rehabilitation programme, should educate people about new values.

**(B) EXPECTATIONS OF WIDOWS FROM THE GOVERNMENT**

| *Expectations from Government* | *Urban %* | *Rural %* | *Total %* |
|---|---|---|---|
| Provide loans with low interest | 14.00 | 25.33 | 19.67 |
| Provide job reservations in government semi-govt. and private institutions | 36.00 | 16.67 | 26.33 |
| Provide adequate pension | 32.67 | 42.67 | 37.67 |
| Provide Janata Houses | 17.33 | 15.33 | 16.33 |
| Total | 100.00 | 100.00 | 100.00 |

### (C) EXPECTATIONS OF WIDOWS FROM THE 'MATHS' AND 'MATHADHIPATIS'

| *Expectations from 'Maths'* | *Urban %* | *Rural %* | *Total %* |
|---|---|---|---|
| Prejudice against widow remarriage should be reduced | 33.33 | 36.00 | 34.67 |
| Should build Ashrams for the poor widows | 46.67 | 44.67 | 45.67 |
| Should come forward to arrange such marriages | 20.00 | 19.33 | 19.66 |
| Total | 100.00 | 100.00 | 100.00 |

The data indicates that about 44 (44.00) per cent of the respondents both from urban and rural areas expect free vocational training from voluntary organizations. While about 23.33 per cent from the urban and 22.67 per cent from the rural areas expect that homeless widows should be given shelter. And about 6.67 per cent of the urban respondents say that spinning centres should be opened as against 20.67 per cent of the rural respondents. In view of the above findings we may state that a significant majority of the widows expect free vocational training from the organizations.

It may also be observed from the data presented in Table 5.24(B) that 36.00 per cent of the urban respondents in comparison to 16.67 per cent of the rural respondents expect job reservation in government/semi-government/private institutions. Nearly 32.67 per cent of the urban respondents as against 42.67 per cent of the rural respondents expect adequate widow pension. While 17 (17.33) per cent and (15.33) per cent of the respondents from urban and rural areas respectively expect that widows should be given Janata houses. Thus, with regard to the expectations of the widows from the government, the findings seem to suggest that a majority of them expected adequate pension for poor widows.

Further, the table also reveals that nearly 46.67 per cent and 44.67 per cent of the respondents from urban and rural areas respectively expect that 'Maths' should build Ashramas for the poor widows. And about 33.33 per cent of the respondents from urban area and 36.00 per cent of the respondents from rural areas expect from the Mathadhipatis that the prejudices against widow marriage should be reduced. Nearly 15.33 per cent from urban while 12.67 per cent of the respondents from the rural areas hope that the 'Maths' would come forward to arrange such marriages. Hence, the above findings seem to suggest that a majority of the widows expect Ashramas/homes for destitute widows/women from the 'Maths' and Mathadipatis to come forward to help for the cause of widows.

SIX

# Conclusion

The purpose of the present study is to look into the problems faced by widows, the ways they manage these problems and their problems of adjustment. We have tried to analyse the consequences of widowhood on widows of different age-groups. In this study, an attempt has been made to study the factors responsible for the inferior status of widows.

Throughout this research exercise, an attempt has been made to explain how widows suffer from deprivation and social stigma in India. We have also collected the opinions/attitudes of the widows towards the status of Hindu widows, factors that improve their status and their remarriage. We have also tried to understand the relationship between background factors and the problems and the differences between the urban and rural areas, and between the upper, intermediate and lower castes.

The major variables used in the present study are :

(1) Independent variable - caste, age, income and education.
(2) Infrastructure variable - property left by the husband.
(3) Dependent variable - deprivation.

**Independent Variable**

(a) Caste: depending on the caste, widows are broadly classified as (1) Hindu lower caste (2) Hindu intermediate caste and (3) Hindu upper caste.

(b) Age: Widows are classified into three broad groups such as young, middle aged and aged widows.

(c) Income: depending on the level of income, widows are classified into (1) high (2) middle and (3) low income group.

**Background Variables (Infrastructure)**

This includes husbands' occupation, their income and the property left by them. Husbands' occupation is divided into 'high' 'medium' and 'low' occupations.

**Attitudinal Variable (Deprivation)**

This variable concerns the subjective aspect of a widow's life.

**Findings**

In this research exercise, an attempt has been made to understand widowhood, with all its important ramifications from a social problem perspective rather than a historical one.

The important findings of the study are as follows.

(1) The findings pertaining to the demographic characteristics of the widows indicate that the mean age at marriage of the urban widows is higher (13.34 years) than that of the rural widows (10.34 years). It is also found that the mean age at widowhood of rural widows is 38.11 years and of urban widows is 41.50 years.

(2) The findings pertaining to the duration of married life of widows indicate that the mean duration of married life of urban widows is higher (28.39 years) than that of rural widows (27.01 Years).

The mean duration of widowed life of rural widows is higher (14.20 years) than that of the urban widows (12.65 years).

The mean age difference between the rural spouses is higher (11.25 years) than that of urban spouses (9.87 years).

(3) With regard to the widows who started working after widowhood due to sheer economic necessity it is found that a little over half of them (25.67%) started working. It is also significant to note that a greater number of urban widows (16.00%) as compared to the rural widows (12.00%) started working after becoming widows. In both urban and rural areas a majority of widows (46.67%) are helped by their parents/brothers in getting employment, and about 40.74% of the urban widows, as against 66.67% of their rural counterparts faced problems in getting Job/work due to the

lack of proper education. It is also interesting to note that among working widows a significant majority of those based in rural areas (87.33%) are not satisfied with their present employment. The figure is much higher than that for urban widows. About 44.87 per cent of the total working widows have mentioned low emoluments, as a reason for their dissatisfaction. In support of the above-mentioned fact, it may also be stated that in urban area 42.67 per cent of the widows and in rural areas 81.33 per cent of the widows fall in the low income group.

(4) As high as 77.34 per cent of the urban widows, in comparison to 84.67 per cent of the rural widows, have stated that they are living with their children. In support of this , it may be stated that 81 (81.00) per cent of the total respondents expressed their wish to live with their children.

(5) Coming to the type of accommodation of the widows, the data indicates that about three fourths of the respondents both in the urban and rural areas are living in their own houses.

(6) A larger number of the urban widows (82.67%) expressed happiness with their earlier life than rural widows (78.67%).

(7) With regard to the age at death of the deceased husbands, the study reveals that there is no significant difference between urban and rural area. But there is a significant difference between the urban and the rural husbands as to the causes of their death. In support of this, it may be stated that about 21.33 per cent of the urban husbands died of heart attack, whereas the same number of rural husbands died of prolonged illness. This seems to have been so because a large number of rural husbands did not receive treatment as, according to the respondents, no time was left to take effective treatment. This may be mainly due to the low level of literacy among rural people, coupled with inadequate conveyance (transport services) and delay in getting the required treatment from the doctors.

(8) With regard to the educational level of the deceased husbands, the findings reveal that a significant majority of the rural deceased husbands (76.67%) were illiterate compared to

urban deceased husbands. They differed from their urban counterparts in terms of the occupation followed, income earned, savings garnered and property left behind. In support of this, it may be stated that about 47.33 per cent of the rural husbands were land labourers while about 48.66 per cent of the urban husbands were government/private employees. The urban husband's income (Rs. 20,000-above) was better than the rural husband's income (Rs.1001-2000). Further, it can be stated that urban deceased husbands left behind more savings and property than the rural husbands.

(9) A greater number of the rural widows are saddled with dependent children than the urban widows. The level of illiteracy is higher among the rural children than the urban children. Among those studying, as many as 49.33 per cent of the urban children and 20.00 per cent of the rural children did not discontinue their education.

Those who discontinued their education, started working in order to support the family. Widows received fuller financial support from the unmarried children rather than the married children. The hypothesis that 'absence of father influences the children's behaviour is not rejected'.

(10) With regard to the persons taking care of the children, a greater number of urban widows (66.67%) take care of their children than rural widows (56.00%). And it may also be said that about 71.33 per cent of the rural, and 66.33 per cent of the urban, widows have said that their children seek advice from the widows' kinsmen. And with regard to the children seeking advice from their widowed mothers, the findings indicate that majority of the total widows (71.00%) stated that their children seek advice from them sometimes, if not often.

(11) The study also reveals that a majority of the widows (43.00%) faced difficulties in controlling their children. And about 26.00 per cent of the urban widows and 57.33 per cent of rural widows have reported that they have noticed changes in their children's activities. This may be due to the absence of the male member at home. A majority of the widows (42.33%) stated that they consult close relatives while taking decisions about their children.

(12) With regard to the economic deprivation faced by the widows, the findings suggest that both urban and rural widows, irrespective of their castes, have faced economic problems. Among widows belonging to different age groups, young and middle-aged widows have faced more economic problems than the aged widows. Both working and non-working widows have faced economic problems. About 16.00 per cent of the urban widows and 12.00 per cent of the rural widows started working in order to overcome the economic deprivation. About 38.67 per cent of the total widows have found the expenses of food, clothing and shelter most difficult to meet. Economic insecurity is felt by 38.67 per cent of the widows. The first hypothesis that 'the income of the husbands has influenced on the widows level of economic deprivation' is not rejected and the second hypothesis examined in the study that 'husband's age at death has influence on the economic deprivation of widow is rejected'.

(13) With regard to social deprivation faced by the widows, the findings reveal that both urban and rural widows have faced greater social deprivation after widowhood than before . The hypothesis that 'there is a significant difference in the social deprivation level of rural and urban widows is not rejected'. Upper caste widows have faced more social deprivation than the other caste groups. Widows belonging to different age groups faced social deprivation after widowhood. Both working and non-working widows have faced social deprivation. There is a decrease in the frequency of kinsmen's visits to widows and vice-versa after widowhood irrespective of their locality, caste, age and occupational status. The frequency of visits between widows and friends was also greater before widowhood than after.

(14) With regard to the emotional deprivation, the study reveals that both urban and rural widows, irrespective of their caste, age, occupational status, have faced emotional deprivation because of their feeling of insecurity. The hypothesis that 'there is no significant difference in the emotional deprivation of rural and urban widows is not rejected'. After widowhood, over half the number of widows had indifferent health. They

suffered from headache, loss of weight, depression and falling of hair, etc. Almost all the widows are not treated warmly by the members of their family after widowhood. About 42.33 per cent of widows have said that their daughters-in-law quarrel with them. About 68.33 per cent of them have expressed the conviction that widows should not live because they find it difficult to manage the family without the bread winner. About 32.00 per cent of the widows talk to their siblings when they are unhappy. A significant majority of them (32.33%) remember their husbands on family celebrations.

(15) With regard to the cultural deprivation faced by the widows the findings indicate that both urban and rural widows have faced more cultural deprivation after widowhood. It is also found that the higher the caste, the greater the cultural deprivation (62.8%). The hypothesis that the caste has influence on the level of cultural deprivation of widows is not rejected. Aged widows faced more cultural deprivation than the young and middle aged ones. Both working and non-working widows faced cultural deprivation. A significant majority of them started eating simple food and wearing simple clothes due to economic problems. Among the upper castes this change was due to the taboos imposed on them. Over 90 per cent of the widows do not use "saubhagya" signs. Over half of them have not attended socio-religious functions because they do not feel like doing so, but send their children instead. Almost all the widows observe the practice prescribed for them in their own communities.

(16) A majority of the widows (32.67%) received help from their sons/daughters, though there is a difference between the urban and rural widows in this respect. About 45.33 per cent of the urban widows and 39.33 per cent of the rural widows received help in the form of food, clothing, shelter. About 80.00 per cent of the widows opined that husband's relations should share a widow's responsibilities while, in reality, nearly half of the widows approach their sons/daughters in difficulties because they are supported by them.

(17) With regard to reaction towards death, about 40.67 per cent of the urban widows as against 61.34 per cent of the rural

widows felt insecure. A significant majority of them (73.33%) took one year's time to get over their grief. Over 90 per cent of the widows feel the loss of their husbands. About 70 per cent of them blame themselves for their widowhood and believe that Karma is responsible for their plight. Further, regarding the status of widows in Hindu society, about 63.33 per cent of the urban widows, in comparison to 42.00 per cent of the rural widows, have stated that their status is inferior. About 25.00 per cent of them held religious conventions as responsible factors for their inferior status. A large proportion of the widows (34.00%) have reported female education as one of the factors that help widow's cause most. About 29.33 per cent of the urban widows and 36.67 per cent of the rural widows have said preference in employment improve widow's economic status. And about 42.00 per cent of them have stated that today's young adults display indifference toward widows.

(18) The findings pertaining to the approval of widow remarriage indicate that about 24.67 per cent of the urban widows as against 45.33 per cent of the rural widows have reported that widow marriage is permitted in their community. Over half of the widows (54.33%) know about the practice of widow remarriage. A significant majority of them (80.00%) favoured widow remarriage and about 39.32 per cent stated one year as the ideal gap between widowhood and remarriage. About 39.08 per cent of the widows have said that in their opinion only child/young widows should remarry while about 81.67 per cent of them have stated that they would accept/welcome remarried widows. About 87.00% of the widows had not thought of marrying again because they hate this idea or were not of marriageable age or were afraid of religious and social opposition, etc. With regard to the difficulties foreseen in remarriage, about 46.34 per cent of the widows have opined that it would be difficult for a married woman to adjust to a second marriage.

About 67.00 per cent of the widows have preferred to live in the joint family with sons, because they need money and protection.

(19) With regard to the widows' plans for their own future life and for their children's life the findings indicate that about 35.00 per cent of the women wish to continue the job and about 28.67 per cent of the widows worried about their sons' ability to find and settle down in good jobs/businesses. About 45.33 per cent of the urban widows and 43.33 per cent of the rural widows wish to be self supporting. About 31.00 per cent of them have stated that widows should be given free vocational training in order to become self-reliant.

**Recommendations**

(1) Young, illiterate and poor widows should be given opportunities by voluntary organizations and government to improve their education and profession competence to enable them to take to remunerative work.

(2) Vocational training centres should be opened at district and taluk-levels either by government or voluntary organizations.

(3) Educating the people regarding how one should face death should be introduced at higher secondary level. For rural people this should be through folk songs and dramas.

(4) Like in some Government service, a man's job should be given either to his widow or children in the private sector too.

(5) Information regarding the different welfare schemes existing in different parts of the country should be made known to people through the mass media time and again.

(6) Doordarshan covers a vast part of the country, hence programmes on marriage of widows, problems of widows, and welfare schemes for widows should be broadcast.

(7) Reservation of certain percentage of jobs in the government and public institutions for widows/children is necessary.

(8) Community-based agencies should start "the widow to widow program" i.e. a group of widows who reach out to recently-widowed women and offer support in helping them adjust to their new life.

**Areas of Future Research**

(1) Similar studies in different areas may be conducted to make generalization about the impact of widowhood on the

individual and society, which may perhaps help in redesigning our welfare programmes.

(2) Various kinds of problems faced by different categories of widows like working, non-working, educated and uneducated, rich, poor, and middle-class, should be studied in detail, which might help in formulating our welfare scheme network specially in rural areas.

(3) Indepth studies should be conducted covering not only widows but also widowers, so as to know clearly their feelings about widowhood and the problems faced by them.

(4) A systematic study concerning the effect of bereavement and adjustments during the first few months of widowhood must be planned.

(5) Forms and components of loneliness as experienced by widows and the problem of adjustment should be studied in detail.

(6) Variations in widowhood from nation to nation, from state to state and between country and city should be studied in order to understand the future trend of widowhood in this country.

(7) Roles played by widows in a community; from what phases of social life are they excluded? In what activities do they play prominent parts, etc., should be studied and a similar study of widowers can also be made.

(8) A case study of students who have suffered the loss of a parent some years ago to know how has their life been affected by this loss can be studied in detail.

**Major Findings**

1. The study indicated that intermediate agencies be developed as a follow-up programme to train the widows educationally and vocationally to find a suitable employment and to ensure social security.
2. The study also pointed out that there is a need to register the names and addresses of the widows either with Municipality or Village Panchayat Councils. This would be helpful in implementing any welfare schemes meant for widows.
3. It is evident from the study that widows' disapproval of remarriage clearly points out that religious and social sanction

for remarriage is lacking. Hence, favourable atmosphere through welfare agencies, especially religious/voluntary organizations should be oriented.

4. The study also indicates need for more social participation by widows in order to reduce their general dissatisfaction in life.

APPENDICES

# Glossary

**I Nature of the Family**

1. **Family**— It is defined as a group of persons living together, taking food from the same kitchen and related by blood, marriage or adoption (Census, 1961).

   (a) *Nuclear Family*— It consists of the married couple and their children while they are still regarded as dependants (J.E. Park).

   (b) *Joint Family*— It consists of a number of married couples and their children who live together in the same household. All the men are related by blood and the women of the household are their wives, unmarried girls and widows of family kinsmen.

2. **Caste**— According to Risley, a caste is a collection of families or groups of families bearing a common descent from a mythical ancestor, human or divine. It professes to follow the same hereditary calling. It forms a homogeneous community (Karnataka State Gazetteer).

   (a) *Hindu Lower Caste*— Lower caste includes Scheduled Caste, Schedule Tribes, backward caste and backward tribes.

   (b) *Hindu Upper Caste*— Except the above groups, all other Hindus were included in this group.

   (c) *Scheduled Castes*— Mean such castes, races or tribes or parts of group within such castes, races or tribes as deemed under Article 341 of the Constitution of India.

   (d) *Scheduled Tribes*— Mean such tribes or tribal communities as are deemed so under Article 342 of the

Constitution of India. There are 100 SCs and STs as per 1971 census. The SC and ST account for 13.14 per cent and 0.79 per cent of the total population of the state, respectively whereas in India, the proportion of these two constitute 14.6 per cent and 6.94 per cent respectively.

(e) *Dominant Caste*— A caste which is the most powerful or influential than the other castes in a particular area.

(f) *Veerashavism or Puritanic Shaivism or Lingayat Caste*— is a fullblown offshoot of earlier Shaivism popularized by Basava (1131-1167) the treasurer of Kalachuri* Bijjalla of Kalayana. The Veerashaivas do not believe in difference of caste and sex and they treat all humans as equal. Wearing Ishṭalinga on the body (this has brought the name Lingayata to the sect) and its worship and also of guru and Jangama is stressed.

3. **Marital Status** (D.K. Bharadwaj Dictionary)

(a) *Married*— Joined in Marriage

(b) *Unmarried*— Not joined in Marriage

(c) *Widow*— A Woman whose husband is dead and who has not been married again.

(d) *Widower*— A man whose wife is dead and who has not been married again.

(e) *Separated*— Here both wife and husband married but they are living separately.

(f) *Divorce*— Legal dissolution of marriage between husband and wife.

4. **Literacy Status**

(a) *Illiterate*— A person who is unable to read and write (D.K. Bharadwaj Dictionary).

(b) *Literate*— A person who is able to read and write.

*Primary School*— Ist to 4th standard.
*Upper Primary School*— 5th to 7th standard.
*High School*— 8th to S.S.L.C. (10th standard).
*University*— B.A., B.Sc., B.Com. etc.
M.A., M.Sc., M.Com. etc.
*Technical*— Diploma, Industrial training, etc.
*Professional*— M.B.B.S. B.E., LLB.

5. **Type of House**
   (a) *Kuchcha*— Materials used for construction of walls and floor are permeable to water (eg. Metal wall and floor).
   (b) *Semi-Pucca*— Materials used for construction of walls and floors are partly impermeable and partly permeable to water.
   (c) *Pucca*— Materials used for construction of walls and floor are impermeable to water (eg. Cement wall and floor).
6. **Dependency Status**
   (a) *Dependent*— Depending on others for food and shelter.
   (b) *Independent*— Not depending on others for food and shelter.
   (c) *Earning dependants*— Persons who will be earning but still depend on others for food and shelter.
7. **Pension Status**
   (a) *Pensioner*— One who receives pension i.e. periodical payment made to a person in consideration of part service.
   (b) *Non-Pensioner*— Who does not receive pension.
   (c) *Old-age Pensioner*— One who receives old age pension, which is given to the persons above 60 years of age and they should be destitutes.
   (d) *Widow-Pensioner*— One who receives widow pension, which is given to the person whose husband is dead and they should be destitutes.
8. **Religious Activities**
   - Attending fairs and festivals
   - Going to temple, Mosque, Church
   - Participating in prayers and Bhajana
   - Listening to Purana, Harikata, Keeratana.
9. **Social Activities**
   - Naming ceremony
   - Attending Marriage
   - Attending Panchayat Meeting
   - Corporation Meeting
   - Health Meeting
   - Adult Education

10. **Political Activities**
   - Participating in election
   - Giving speech in parties
11. **Socio-economic Causes**
   - Social insecurity
   - Widowhood
   - Loneliness
   - Death of children
   - Indebtedness
   - Loss of employment
   - Ill-treatment by family members
12. **Medical Causes**
   - Ill-health and disability due to old age
13. **Psychological Causes**
   - Worries
   - Inferiority complex
   - Feeling of inadequate achievement
   - Feeling of failure in life
   - Unknown fear and anxiety

14. **Mangalasutra**— a string of black beeds worn by the married women, which turns the marriage contract into a sacrament. Among almost all castes, the most important part of the marriage ceremony is the tying of the Mangalasutra by the bridegroom around the neck of the bride. It is also called *'tali'* in colloquial language.

15. **Kumkum**— Saffron or a red powder applied on the forehead by Hindu and Jain women, traditionally this is not used by widows.

16. **Co-Sister**— Wife of husband's brother or brother-in-law.

17. **Math and Mathadipathis**— A building or place where a caste head (Priest) lives and a place of worship for Hindus.
   - a person who preaches values of life and popularizes that particular caste's principles.

18. **Taluk**— a sub part of a district.

19. **Hamal**— Native labourer in India.

20. **Kirana Shop**— A grocery or domestic store.

21. **Janata Houses**— Houses given to the small and marginal farmers whose income is less than Rs. 3500 who are house-less, and site-less, by the government of Karnataka.

22. **Puranas**— Purana means 'ancient' and the title Purana signifies 'Ancient Lore', indicating that these books prefer to declare ancient lore as handed down for the most part by tradition. They expound ancient Indian theogony, cosmogony, genealogies and accounts of kings and risis, religious belief, worship, observances and philosophy, personal, social and political ordinances and opinions about all kinds of miscellaneous matters — the whole illustrated and enforced by tales, legends, old songs, anecdotes and fables.

# Centres from which data was collected

(1) Karnatak University Library
Dharwad

(2) Karnatak College Library
Dharwad

(3) Karnatak University Law College
Dharwad

(4) Kannada Research Institute
Karnatak University Dharwad

(5) The Bombay University Library
Bombay

(6) Tata Institute of Social Sciences
Bombay

(7) Asiatic Library
Bombay

(8) SNDT Women's University
Bombay

(9) ICSSR Library
New Delhi

(10) JSS Institute of Economic Research
Dharwad

# Bibliography


**Books**

Agarwal, A.G. (Ed.) 1978: *Poverty, Deprivation and Intelligence.* New Delhi, Criterian Publication.

Allen, Michael and Mukherjee. S.N. (Ed) 1982: *Women in India and Nepal.* Canberra, ANU Publications.

Altekar, A.S. 1956: *The Position of Women in Hindu Civilization.* Banaras, Motilal Banarsidas.

Andre, Beteille. 1983: *Equality and Enequality-Theory and Practice.* Delhi, Oxford University Press.

Anshen, R.N. 1949: *The Family - Its Function and Destiny.* New York, Harper and Brothers Publication.

Apte, Usha. M. 1978: *The Sacrament of Marriage in Hindu Society - From Vedic Period to Dharmasastras.* Delhi, Ajanta Publications.

Athvale, Parvati. 1930: *My Story-The Autobiography of a Hindu Widow* (Marathi) translated by Rev. Justin E. Abbott. New York, G.P. Putnams Sons.

Balasubramanian, C. 1976: *The Status of Women in Tamil Nadu During the Sangam Age.* Madras, University of Madras Press.

Banerjee, Gooroodas. 1984: *Hindu Law of Marriage and Stridhana.* Delhi, Mittal Publications.

Baron, Omar. and Rolf, Ehrenfels. 1941: *Mother Right in India.* Hyderabad, Oxford University Press.

Bhattacharya, K. 1881: *Institute of Parasara Asiatic Society of Bengal,* Calcutta.

Becker, Howard, and Hill, Rueben. 1948: *Family Marriage and Parenthood.* Boston, D.C. Health Company.

Benson, Leonard. 1971: *The Family Bond-Marriage, Love and Sex in America.* New York, Random House Inc.

Bernard, Farber. (Ed). 1966: *Kinship and Family Organization.* New York, John Wiley and Sons Inc.

Bhate, G.C. 1907: *Permitting Widow-Marriages.* Poona, Widow marriage Association.

Bhatia, H.S. 1983: *Aging and Society - A Sociological Study of Retired Public Servants*. Udaipur, The Arya's Book Centre.

Bhim, Raja. 1969: *Marriage of Hindu Widows*. (2nd Ed). Bombay, Indu Prakash Press.

Bhuler, G. (Trans.) 1886: *Laws of Manu*. Delhi, Motilal Banarsidas.

Brubaker, T.H. 1985: *Later Life Families*. London, Sage Publications.

Burgess, Ernest. W. and Locke. Hurvey, J. 1945: *The Family - From Institution to Companionship*. New York, American Book Co.

Caton, A.R. (Ed.). 1930: *The Key Progress: A Survey of the Status and Condition of Woman in India*. London, Oxford University Press.

Chattopadhyaya, Sudhakar. 1965: *Social Life in Ancient India*. Calcutta, Academic Publications.

Choubey, N.P., Pandey, L.P. and Patni, Rajani. 1986: *Deprivation and Human Personality - Current Theory and Research*. Allahabad, Indian Academy of Social Sciences.

Cherry, Russell. 1981: *The Aging Experience*. Australia, George Allen and Unwin Co.

Christensen, Harold. T. 1950: *Marriage Analysis-Foundations for Successful Family Life*. New York. The Ronald Press.

Clayton, A. Hartjen. 1978: *Crime and Criminalization* (2nd Edn.) New York. Praeger Publishers.

Coleman, James. C. 1976: *Abnormal Psychology and Modern Life*. Bombay, D.B. Taraporevala and Sons. Co.

Cooper, Elizabeth. 1983: *The Harem and the Purdah*. (2nd Edn.) Delhi, Bimala Publishing House.

Cormack, Margaret. 1953: *The Hindu Woman*. New York, Bureau of Publications, Teachers College, Columbia.

Dandavate, Pramila., Ranjana, Kumari. and Verghese, Jamila. 1989: *Widows, Abandoned and Destitute Women in India*. New Delhi, Radiant Publishers.

*Dari Deepa*. 1985: Department of Information and Broadcasting Government of Karnataka, Bangalore.

Das, Mansingh. and Badris, Panos. D. (Eds) 1978: *Family in Asia*. New Delhi, Vikas Publications.

Das, R.M. 1962: *Women in Manu and His Seven Commentators*. Varanasi, Kanchana Publications.

Datta, K.K. 1972: *Socio-Cultural Background of Modern India*. Meerut, Meenakshi Prakashan.

Datta, K.K. 1975: *A Social History of Modern India*. Delhi, The Macmillan Co. of India Ltd.

Dhar, S. and Dhar, M.K. 1986: *Evolution of Hindu Family Law*. Delhi, Deputy Publications.

Derret, J. Ducan. 1963: *Introduction to Modern Hindu Law*. Bombay, Oxford University Press.

Deutsch, M., Katz, I and Jensen, A.R. (Eds). 1968: *Social Class, Race and Psychological Development*. New York, Halt Rinehart and Winston.

Dornne, Jacobson. and Susans, Wadley. 1986: *Women in India-Two Perspective*. Delhi, Manohar Publications.

D'Souza, Alfred. (Ed) 1980: *Women in Contemporary India and South Asia*. (2nd Edn). New Delhi, Manohar Publications.

Duberman, Lucile. 1977: *Marriage and other Alternatives*. (2nd Edn). New York, Praeger Publishers.

Dubois, Abbe, D.U. 1906: *Hindu Manners, Customs and Ceremonies*. (3rd Edn). Trans. by Henry K. Beauchamp. London, Oxford University Press.

Dulude, Louise. 1978: *Women and Aging - A Report on the Best of our Lives*. Ottawa, Advisory Council on the Status of Women.

Dupaquier, J. Helin. E. and Lastett, P. (Eds) 1981: *Marriage and Remarriage in Population of the Past*. New York, Academic Press.

Durkheim, Emile. 1951: *Suicide*. New York, Free Press.

Dutt, Nripendra Kumar. 1968: *Origin and Growth of Caste in India*. Calcutta, Firma Publication.

Dutt, Romesh C. 1972: *History of Civilization in Ancient India*. Vol. II. Delhi, Vishal Publishers.

Duval, Elelyn. 1971: *Family Development*. (4th Edn). New York, J.B. Lippincott Co.

Eichler, Margri. 1988: *Families in Canada Today-Recent Change and Their Policy Consequences*. Toronto, Gage Educational Publishing Co.

Eloise, C. Sgyder. (Ed) 1979: *The Study of Women-Endangering Perspectives of Social Reality*. New York, Harper and Raw Publishers.

English, Horace, B. 1961: *Dynamics of Child Development*. New York, Holt Rinehart, Winston. Inc.

Eshleman, J. Ross. 1974: *The Family - An Introduction* (2nd Edn). Boston, Allyn and Bacon Inc.

Farmer, Mary. 1979: *The Family* (2nd Edn). London, Longman Group Ltd.

Farrel, Ronald. A. and Lynnswigrert, Victoria. 1979: *Social Deviance*. (2nd Edn). Philadelphia, J.B. Lippincott. Co.

Gajendragadkar, P.B. (1951): The Hindu Code Bill. Two lectures delivered on 12th and 13th April. Dharwad. Karnatak University.

Gandhi, M.K. 1942: *Women and Social Injustice*. Ahmedabad, Navajivan Publishing House.

———. 1964: *The Role of Women*: Bombay, Bharatiya Vidya Bhavan.

Gardner, Jane. F. 1986: *Women in Roman law and Society*. London, Groom Helm.

Gardner, Lindezey and Elliot, Aronson. 1975: *The Handbook of Social Psychology*. (2nd Edn). New Delhi, Amerind Publishing Co. Pvt. Ltd.

Gerald, L.R. 1977: *Marriage in Changing World*. New York, John Wiley and Sons Co.

———. 1979: *The Family in Social Context*. New York, Oxford University Press.

Gharapure, J.R. 1932: *Yajnavalkya*. Poona, Oriental Book Agency.

———. (1936): *Yajnavakya Smruti*. Bombay, Hindu Law Texts.

Ghosh, Jogesa Chandra 1982: *Hindu Woman of India*. Delhi, Bimala Publishing House.

Ghurye, G.S. 1969: *Caste and Race in India*. Bombay, Popular Prakashan.

Gibbons, Don. C. and Jones, Joseph. F. 1975: *The Study of Deviance Perspectives and Problems*. New Jersey, Prentice-Hall Inc.

Goffman, Erving. 1964: *Stigma-Notes on the Management of Spoiled Identity*. New Jersey, Prentice-Hall Inc.

Goode, William J. 1963: *World Revolution and Family Patterns*. London, The Free Press.

———. 1965: *The Family*. New Delhi, Prentice-Hall of India (Pvt.) Ltd.

Gore, M.S. 1968: *Urbanization and Family Change*. Bombay, Popular Prakashan.

Gorwaney, Naintara. 1977: *Self-Image and Social Change*. New Delhi, Sterling Publishers Pvt. Ltd.

Gour, Horising. 1971: *The Hindu Code*. (5th Edn). Allahabad, Law Book Publishers.

Gray, Robert, F. and Gulliver P.H. 1964: *The Family in Africa Studies in the Role of Property in Family Structure*. London, Routledge and Kegan Paul Press.

Green, Ernest J. 1977: *Marriage and Family - A Basic Self Instruction Guide*. New York, McGraw Hill Book Co.

———. 1978: *Personal Relationships*. New York, McGraw Hill Book Co.

Gulati, Saroja. 1985: *Women and Society - North India in the 11th and 12th Century*. Delhi, Chanakya Publications.

Gupta, Giri Raj. 1974: *Marriage Religion and Society-Pattern of Change in an Indian Village*. Delhi, Vikas Publishing House.

Gupta, Sankar Sen. (Ed) 1962: *Indian Folklore - A Short Survey of Their Social Status and Position*. Calcutta, Indian Publication.

Hardy, Janathan. Cathorne. 1981: *Love, Sex, Marriage and Divorce*. London, Janathan. Co.

Hate, Chandrakala. A. 1948: *Hindu Women and Her Future*. Bombay, New Book Co. Ltd.

Hilary, Standing. (Ed): *Punjab Kinship and Marriage*. Delhi, Hindustan Pub. Corporation.

Holman, Robert. (Ed). 1970: *Socially Deprived Families in Britain*. London, The Bedford Square Press.

Hurlock, Elizabeth, B. 1976: *Personality Development*. New Delhi. Tata McGraw Hill Publishing Co. Ltd.

Horner, I.B. 1930: *Women Under Primitive Buddhism*. Delhi, Motilal Banarsidas.

Huber, Joan. (Ed). 1973: *Changing Women in a Changing Society*. Chicago, The University of Chicago Press.

Hyman, Herbert. H. 1983: *Of Time and Widowhood Nationwide Studies of Enduring Efforts*. Durham, Duke Press.

ICSSR 1975: *Status of Women in India-A Synopsis of the Report of the National Committee (1971-74)*. New Delhi, Allied Publishers Pvt. Ltd.

Indira, Mahindra.: 1980: *The Rebellious Home Makers*. Bombay, S.N.D.T. Women's University Press.

Jayal, Shakambari. 1966: *The Status of Women in the Epics*. Delhi, Motilal Banarsidas.

Jersild, A.T. 1963: *The Psychology of Adolescence*. (2nd Edn). New York, MacMillan. Co.

Jessie, B. and Naik, T. (Eds). 1988: *Indian Womanhood Then and Now*. Indore, Satyaprakashan Sanchar Kendra.

Jolly, J. (Ed). 1881: *Vishnu Dharma Sutra*. Calcutta, Motilal Banarsidas.

Kaegi, A. 1950: *Life in Ancient India - Studies in Rigvedic India*. Calcutta, Susil Gupta Ltd.

Kakar, Sudhir (Ed) 1982: *Identity and Adulthood*. (2nd Edn). Delhi, Oxford University Press.

Kane, P.V. 1930: *History of Dharmashastras*. Vol. II & III. Poona, Bhandarkar Oriental Research Institute.

Kanvi, C.S. (Ed). 1977: *Women Her Problems and Her Achievements*. Dharwad, Karnatak University Press.

Kapadia, K.M. 1958: *Marriage and Family in India*. (2nd Edn). London, Oxford University Press.

Kapur, Pramila. 1973: *Love, Marriage and Sex*. Delhi, Vikas Publishing House.

Karve, Irawati. 1953: *Kinship Organization in India*. Bombay, Asia Publishing House.

Katti, Venkat Rango 1889: *Vidhawa Vapana Anachara*. (Shaving of Widows Unauthorised) Poona, Oriental Book House.

Kaur, Indrajeet. 1983: *Status of Hindu Women in India*. Allahabad, Chugh Publications.

Keith, A.B. 1971: *Rigveda*. (2nd Edn). Delhi, Motilal Banarsidas.

Kelphart, William M. 1981: *The Family, Society and Individuals* (5th Edn). Boston, Houghton Mifflin Co.

Kenkel, William F. 1977: *The Family in Perspective.* (4th Edn). California, Goodyear Publishing Co.

Kimball, Young, 1952: *Personality and Problems of Adjustment.* (2nd Edn). London, Routledge and Kegan Paul Ltd.

Lakshmi, C.S. 1984: *Women in Society - The Face Behind the Mask.* New Delhi, Vikas Publishing House.

Landis, Judson. T. and Landis, Marg. G (Eds). 1953: *Readings in Marriage and The Family.* New York, Prentice-Hall Inc.

Landis, Paul. H. 1954: *Your Marriage and Family Living.* (2nd Edn). New York, McGraw-Hill Book. Co.

———. 1955: *Making the Most of Marriage* (2nd Edn). New York, Appelton Century Crofts Inc.

Leacock, E.W. (Ed). 1971: *Culture of Poverty: A Critique.* New York, Simon and Schuster.

London, Perry. and Rosenhan, David. (Ed). 1968: *Foundations of Abnormal Psychology.* New York, Holt Rinchart and Winston. Co.

Lopata, Helena. Z. 1973: *Widowhood in a American City.* Cambridge, Schenkman Publishing Co.

Madhawadas, Rugunathdas. 1890: *Story of a Widow Remarriage.* Bombay, S.K. Khambata & Co.

Maine, Henrey, 1934: *Early History of Insitutions.* London, John Murray.

Mann, R.S. 1979: *Social Structure, Social Change and Future Trends.* Jaipur, Rawat Publications.

Marris, Peter. 1958: *Widows and Their Families.* London, Routledge and Kegan Paul Ltd.

Martinson, F. 1970: *Family in Society.* New York, Doddmead.

Maurice, Freedom. (Ed). 1970: *Family and Kinship in Chinese Society.* California, Stanford University Press.

Max, Muller, F. 1968: *The Dhammapada: Sutta Nipata.* SBE, Delhi.

Merrian, Webster. 1951: *Dictionary.* pp. 606-607.

Milford, Homparey. (Ed). 1978: *The Key Progress - A Survey of The Status and Conditions of Women in India.* London, Oxford University Press.

Mitter, Dwarikanath. 1984: *The Position of Woman in Hindu Law.* Delhi, D.K. Publications.

Monks, F.J. et al., 1972: *Determinants of Behaviour Development.* New York, Academic Press.

Mukherjee, Ila. 1972: *Social Status of North Indian Women.* Agra, Editional Publishers.

Mukherjee, Prabhatil. 1978: *Hindu Women - Normative Models.* New Delhi, Orient Longman Ltd.

Mulla, Dinshah. Fardunji. 1960: *Principles of Hindu Law.* (2nd Edn). Bombay, Tripathi. Pvt. Ltd.

Mussen, P.H., Conger, J.J. and Kegan, J. 1969: *Child Development and Personality*. (3rd Edn). New York, Harper and Raw Co.

Nagesh, H.V. and Katti, A.P. (Eds). 1988: *Widowhood in India*. Dharwad, SDMET and JSS.

Nair, P.T. 1978: *Marriage and Dowry in India*. Calcutta, Minerva Associates.

Narain, V.A. 1972: *Social History of Modern India Nineteenth Century*. Meerut, Meenakshi Prakashan.

Needam, Rodney. (Ed). 1970: *Classics in Anthropology*. Chicago, The University of Chicago Press.

Nimkoff, M.F. 1934: *The Family*. Boston, Houghton Mifflin Co.

Nye, F. Ivan. and Berardo, Felix. M. 1973: *The Family - Its Structure and Interaction*. New York, MacMillan Co.

Oldenberg, H. and Max Muller. 1886: *The Grihyasutras*. (Part 1 & 2) Sacred Books of the East Oxford.

Ostor, Akos; Fruzzetti, Lina. and Barret, Steve. (Eds). 1983: *Concept of Person, Kinship, Caste and Marriage in India*. Delhi, Oxford University Press.

Pandita, Ramabai. 1984 (C-1888): *The High Caste Hindu Women*. Delhi, D.K. Publishers.

Passow, A. Harry. 1963: *Education in Depressed Areas*. New York, Teachers College Press. Columbia University.

Pathare Reform Association 1869: *Marriage of Hindu Widows*. Bombay, Indu Prakash Press.

Peter, J.S., Judith, R. and Natalie, H. 1977: *The Family - Functions, Conflicts and Symbols*. London, Addison Wesley Publishing Co.

Peterson, James. A. and Briley, Michaell. 1977: *Widows and Widowhood - A Creative Approach to Being Alone*. Chicago, Association Press.

Phelps, H.A. 1983: *Contemporary Social Problems*. New York, Printice Hall.

Philiprice, F. 1979: *Marriage and Parenthood*. Boston, Allyn and Bacon. Inc.

Polson, Joseph, Kirk. and Bassett, Marion, 1948: *The Family and Democratic Society*. London, Routledge and Kegan Paul Ltd. Ranjana Kumari. 1989: *Women Headed Households in Rural India*. New Delhi, Radiant Publishers.

Rice, E.P. 1934: *Mahabharat*. London, Oxford University Press.

Richard, Rubin. Frank, D. and Cyril, M. (Eds). 1969: *Advance in Behavioural Therapy*. New York.

Rosow, Irwing, 1967: *Social Integration of the Aged*. New York, The Free Press.

Ross, Ralph La. 1984: *Family Case Studies-A Sociological Perspective*. New York, The Free Press.

Sachchidananda and Sinha, Romesh. P. 1984: *Women's Rights: Myth and Reality*. Jaipur, Printwell Publishers.

Sainsbury, P. 1955: *Suicide in London (Moudsley Monograph No. 1)*. London. Chapman and Hall.

Sarkar, S.C. 1928: *Some Aspects of the Early History of India*. London, Humphrey Milford.

Schneider, David J. 1976: *Social Psychology*. California, Addition-Wesley Publishing Co.

Sengupta, N. 1965: *Evolution of Hindu Marriage*. Bombay, Popular Prakashan.

Significant Six Years - 1983-1989. (1989) Department of Information and Broadcasting - Government of Karnataka Publication, Dharwad.

Singh, Kulwant, 1986: *Hindu Women's Right to Property in India*. New Delhi, Deep and Deep Publications.

Sinha, Durgananda, Tirpathi, R.C. and Misra, Girishwar. (Eds). 1982: *Deprivation-its Social Roots and Psychological Consequences*. New Delhi, Concept Publishing Co.

Sinha, B.B. 1982: *Society in Tribal India*. Delhi, B.R. Publishing Corporation.

Smart, Mollie. Stevens, and Smart, Laura. S. 1976: *Families Developing Relationships*. New York, MacMillan Publishing Co.

Spencer, H. 1934: *Sociology*. London, Harrison and Sons Ltd.

Srinivas, M.N. 1942: *Marriage and Family in Mysore*. Bombay, New Book Co.

Sudhir, Chandra. 1985: *Widow Remarriage and Later Nineteenth Century Indian Literature*. (for Private Circulation only).

Sudhir, Kakar. (Ed). 1979: *Identity and Adulthood*. Delhi, Oxford University Press.

Tabbitts, Clark, (Ed.) 1960: *Handbook of Social Gerontology- Social Aspects of Aging*. Chicago, The University of Chicago Press.

Tatvabhushan, Sitanath. 1904: *Social Reform in Bengal*. Calcutta, Papyrus.

The Mahabharat 1962: Poona, Bhandarker Oriental Research Insititute.

Thomas, P. 1939: *Women and Marriage in India*. London, George Allen and Unwin Ltd.

Travernier, B.J. 1905: *Travernier Travel in India Book III*. Calcutta. Bangbasi Office.

Troll, Lilliane. and Israel Joan, and Israel, Kenneth. 1977: *Looking Ahead - A Woman's Guide to the Problems and Joys of Growing Old*. New Jersey. Prentice - Hall Inc.

Truxual, Andrew. G. and Merrill, Francis. E. 1953: *Marriage and The Family in American Culture*. New York, Prentice-Hall Inc.

Upadhyaya, B.S. 1974: *Women in Rugveda*. New Delhi. New Delhi, S. Chand and Co.

Vaidya, P.L. (Ed). 1934: *Dhammapada*. (2nd Edn). Poona, Oriental Books Agency.

Vaidya, P. L. 1962: *The Valmiki Ramayana*. Poona, Oriental Books Agency.

Vedvyasa, 1931: *The Mahabharata*. Calcutta, Oriental Publishing Co.

Vidyasagar, I.C. 1976: *Marriage of Hindu Widows*. Calcutta, K.B. Bagchi and Co.

Waller, Willard. 1956: *The Family - A Dynamic Interaction*. New York, The Dryden Press.

White, Robert, W. and Watt, Norman. F. 1973: *The Abnormal Personality*. (4th Edn). New York, The Ronald Press. Co.

Winch, Robert, F. and Spanier, Graham, (Ed.) 1974: *Selected Studies in Marriage and Family*. New York, Holt Rinchart and Winston Inc.

Womble, Dale. 1966: *Foundations for Marriage and Family Relations*. New York. MacMillan.

Zarit, Steven. H. (Ed). 1978: *Reading in Aging and Death - Contemporary Perspectives*. New York, Harper and Row Publishers.

**Periodicals**

Abrahams, Ruby. 1972: Mutual Help for the Widowed. *Social Work*, Vol. 17. No. 5, pp. 54-61.

Agarwala, A.K. 19: Intelligence Differences and Affectional Deprivation. *Indian Psychological Review*. Vol. 28. No. 3, pp. 39-44.

Agarwala, S.N. 1962: Remarriage Rates in Some Delhi Villages. *Medical Digest* Vol. 30. No. 10, pp. 548-57.

Agarwala, S.N. 1967: Widow Remarriage in Some Rural Areas of Northern India. *Demography* Vol. 4. No. 1, pp. 126-34.

Alam, Khurshid. 1988: Categorical Organization in Free Recall as a Function of Social Deprivation and Observer Presence. *Psychological Studies*. Vol. 3. No. 2, pp. 123-128.

Alam, Khurshid. 1986: Effects of Prolonged Socio-Cultural and Economic Deprivation on Retention: A Comparative Study. *Indian Psychological Review*. Vol. 30. No. 2, pp. 21-24.

Alexander, I.E. and Adlerstein, A.M. 1958. Affective Responses of the Concept of Death in Population of Children and Early Adolescents. *Journal of General Psychology*. Vol. 93. No.2, pp. 167-77.

Anderson, Trudy B. 1984: Widowhood as a Life Transition-Its Impact on Kinship Ties. *Journal of Marriage and the Family* No. 1, pp. 105-114.

Annual Meeting Scientific Proceedings. 1967: Bereavement. *British Medical Journal* Vol. 3. No.1, pp. 232-33.

Aradhya, B.M.M. 1987: What it means to be a widow. *Social Welfare* Vol. 34. No. 9, pp. 2-3.

Arling, Greg. T. 1976: The Elderly Widow and Her Family Neighbours and Friends. *Journal of Marriage and the Family*. Vol. 38. No. 4, pp. 757-68.

Baidyanath, Saraswati. 1985: The Kashivasi Widows. *Man in India* Vol. 65. No. 2, pp. 107-20.

Balasubramanyam, V. 1970: A Saviour of Widows - A Profile on R.S. Subbalakshmi Ammal. *Social Welfare*. Vol. XVII. No. 3, p. 27.

Bankoff, Elizabeth. A. 1983: Social Support and Adaptation to Widowhood. *Journal of Marriage and the Family*. Vol. 45. No. 41 pp. 827-39.

Berardo, Felix, M. 1967: Social Adaptations to Widowhood Among a Rural - Urban Aged Population. *Washington Agricultural Experimental Station Bulletin*. College of Agriculture, Washington State University, p.4.

Berardo, Felix, M. 1968: Widowhood Status in the United States Perspective on a Neglected Aspect of the Family Life Cycle. *The Family Coordinator* Vol. 17. (July) No. 3. pp. 191-203.

Berardo, Felix. M. 1970: Survivorship and Social Isolation: The Case of the Aged Widower. *The Family Coordinator*. Vol. 19. No. 1, pp. 11-25.

Bey, Hamid. 1971: Saved from the Funeral Pyre but An eyesore *Thought*. May 22. pp. 11-12.

Bharat, Shalini. 1986: Single Parent Family in India. Issues and Implications. *The Indian Journal of Social Work*. Vol. XLVII. No. 1, pp. 55-65.

Bhaktavatsalam, M. 1964: Women in Changing India. *Women on the March*. Vol.8. No. 10, pp. 76-77.

Bhattacharya, Amitabha. 1977: Moulding Man's Attitude For Woman's Progress. *Social Welfare*. Vol. XXIII No. 4, pp. 10 & 17.

Bhushan, Jamila, Brij. 1973: War Widows. *Weekly Round Table*. July 1 pp. 26-30.

Bidarakoppa, G.S. 1971: Position and Problems of Hindu Widows. *The Journal of Karnataka University Social Sciences*. Vol. VII, No. 1, pp. 76-82.

Bock, E.W. and Webber, Irving. L. 1972: Suicide Among the Elderly: Isolating Widowhood and Mitigating Alternatives. *Journal of Marriage and the Family*. Vol. 34. No. 1. pp. 24-31.

Bose, A.B. and Sen, M.L.A. 1966: Some characteristics of the Widows in Rural Society. *Man in India*. Vol. 46, No. 3, pp. 226-33.

Chatterjee, Bishwa. B. 1980: Effects of Social Deprivation. Some Contradictory Findings. *Social Change*. Vol. 10. No.1 & 2, pp. 9-14.

Chhabra, Rami. 1975-76: Where the Wind of Change Lies Low. *Social Welfare*. Vol. 22. No. 6-7, pp. 85-86, 95.

Chevan, Albert. and Korson, J. Henry. 1972: The Widowed Who Live Alone: An Examination of Social and Demographic Factors. *Social Forces*. Vol. 51. No.1, pp. 45-53.

Cosneck, Bernard. J. 1970: Family Patterns of Older Widowed Jewish People. *The Family Coordinator*. Vol. 19. No. 2, pp. 368-73.

Dange, Sindhu. S. : Yaska on Widow's Share. *Vishveshvaran and Indological Journal*. Vol. XVIII. pp. 385-387.

Das, J.P. 1973: Cultural Deprivation and Cognitive Competence. *International Review of Research in Mental Retardation*. Vol. 6 No. 2, pp. 1-53.

Datta, Jatindra. Mohan. 1956: Is Enforced Widowhood the only Cause of the Slower Growth of the Bengalee Hindus. *Man in India*. Vol. No. pp. 272-75.

Davis, R.E. 1968: Social Deprivation and Cognitive Function in low-class Children. Dessertation. *Abstracts International*. Vol. 29. pp. 1505-07.

Das, J.P. (1973): Cultural Deprivation & Cognitive Competance. *International Review of Research in Mental Retardation*. Vol.2. pp. 1-53.

Desai, A.R. 1985: Wom'ens Movement in India-An Assessment. *Economic and Political Weekly*. Vol. XX. No. 23, p. 3.

Diane, Beeson. 1975: Women in Studies: A Critique and Suggestion. *Social Problems of Aging*. Vol. 23. No. 1, pp. 52-59.

Dubey, Bhagwant Rao. 1965: Widow Remarriage in Madhya Pradesh. *Man in India*. Vol. 45. No. 1, pp. 50-55.

Dutt, Ruby. 1965: The Property Rights of Women in the Sutra Period. *The Modern Review*. Vol. CXVIII. No. 3, pp. 239-46.

Editor 1936: Mysore Widow Marriage Bill. *The Indian Social Reform*. June 20. p. 353.

Editor 1983: Legislation on Women. *Social Welfare*. Vol. XXIX. No. 11-12, p. 20.

Eliot, Thomas. D. 1930: The Adjustive Behaviour of Bereaved Families: A New Field For Research. *Social Forces*. Vol. 8. No. 4, pp. 543-49.

———. 1932-33: A Step Toward. The Social Psychology of Bereavement. *Journal of Abnormal and Social Psychology*, Vol. 27. No. 3, pp. 380-90.

———. 1943: ... of the Shadow of Death. *Annals of the American Academy of Political and Social Sciences*. Vol. 229. No. 1. pp. 94-95.

Essex, Marilyn. J. and Nam Sunghee 1987: Marital Status and Loneliness Among Older Women: The Differential Importance of Close Family and Friends. *Journal of Marriage and the Family*. Vol. 49. No. 1, pp. 93-106.

Faroqi, M.A. (Reviewed) Misra. Girishwar and Tripathi L.B. 1981: Psychological Consequences of Prolonged Deprivation. *Psychological Studies*. Vol. 26. No. 7, pp. 72-73.

Freeman, Howard. E. and Simmons, Ozzie. G. 1961: Feelings of Stigma Among Relatives of Former Mental Patients. *Social Problems*. Vol 8. No. 4, pp. 313-21.

Fritz, Mary. 1929: A Study of Widowhood *Sociology and Social Research*. Vol. XIV No. 1, pp. 553-61.

Geschwender, J.A. 1968: Status Inconsistency, Social Isoloation and Individual Unrest. *Social Force*. Vol. 46. No. 4, pp. 477-83.

Goode, W.J. 1959: The Theoretical Importance of Love. *American Sociological Review*. Vol. 24. No.1, pp. 38-47.

Gordon, E.A. 1965: Review of Compensatory Education. *American Journal of Orthopsychiatry*. Vol. 35. pp. 640-51.

Gordon, Michael., Whelan, Brendan. and Vaughan, Richard. 1981: Old Age and Loss of Household Headship: A National Irish Study. *Journal of Marriage and the Family*. Vol. 43. No.3, pp. 741-47.

Ghurye, G.S. 1936: Marriage and Widowhood in India - A Study of a Middle-class Sample of 3400 Marriages. *Marriage Hygiene*. Vol. II. No. 3, pp. 258-70.

Harichandra, C. 1982: Socio-Economic Conditions of Widows - *Yojana*. Vol. XXVI. No. 10, pp. 11-12.

Harvey, Carol, D. and Bahr, Howard M. 1974: Widowhood, Morale and Affiliation. *Journal of Marriage and the Family*. Vol. No. 36. pp. 97-106.

Hims, S. Joseph. 1964: Some Work-related Cultured Deprivations of Lower-Class Negro Youths. *Journal of Marriage and the Family*. Vol. 25. No.2, pp. 447-48.

Hunt, J.MC. 1964: The Psychological Bais for Using Pre-school Environment as an Antidote for Cultural Deprivation. *The Mirril Palmer Quarterly of Behaviour and Development*. Vol. 10. No.3, pp. 209-243.

Hurlow, H.F. 1958: The Nature of Love. *American Psychologist*. Vol. 13, No. 4, pp. 673-85.

Hutchison, Ira. W. III 1975: The Significance of Marital Status for Morale and Life Satisfaction Among Lower-Income Elderly. *Journal of Marriage and the Family*. Vol. 32. No. 2, pp. 287-93.

Hyerah, Miriam. and Mitra, Dolly. 1988: Synthetic Perception in the Sensorily Deprived. *Psychological Studies*. Vol. 33. No.2, pp. 110-15.

Internal Encyclopaedia of Psychiatry, Psychology Psychoanalysis and Neurology. Vol. 8.

Jacobs, Selby and Ostfeld, Adrian. 1977: An Epidemiological Review of the Mortality of Bereavement. *Psychosomatic Medicine*. Vol. 39, No. 5, pp. 344-57.

Kamal, Kumar, 1987: Deoral-Before and After. *Social Welfare*. Vol. 34. No.9, pp. 7.

Kamlani, Ratu. 1978: Memories of Widowhood. *Eves Weekly*. Aug. 12-18. pp. 36-37.

Kamat, A.R. 1963: The Decline in Death Rate and its Effect on the Extent of Widowhood. *Sociological Bulletin*. Vol. XII. No. 7, pp. 18-31.

Kephart, William. M. 1950: Status After Death. *American Sociological Review*. Vol. 35. No. 5, pp. 635-43.

Karve, Neera. 1956: The Lot of a Widow. *Social Welfare*. Vol. III. No.4, pp. 30-31.

Kishwar, Madhu. : Gandhi on Women. *Economic and Political Weekly*. Vol. XX. No. 40, pp. 1691-1692.

Kitchlu, T.N. 1979: A Profile of Widows in Delhi. *Social Welfare*. Vol. 25. No. 10, pp. 33-35.

Leading Articles 1961: Broken Hearts. *British Medical Journal*. Vol. 4. No.1, pp. 2-3.

Leonard, Diana. and Speakman, Mary. Anne. 1983: The Changing Experience of Women. *The Open University a Second Level Course Unit-9*. pp. 53-57; Unit 7-8. pp. 11-12.

Lindemann, Erich. 1944: Symptomatology and Management of Acute Grief. *American Journal of Psychiatry*. Vol. 101. No. 2, pp. 141-48.

Locke, Harvey. J. and Klausner, William. J, 1948: Marital Adjustment of Divorced Persons in Subsequent Marriages. *Sociology and Social Research*. Vol. 33. No.1, pp. 97-101.

Lopata, Helena. Z. 1969: Loneliness: Forms and Components *Social Problems*. Vol. 17. No.2, pp. 248-62.

———. 1970: The Social Involvement of American Widows. *American Behavioural Scientist*. Vol. 14. No.1, pp. 41-57.

———. 1978: The Absence of Community Resources in Support Systems of Urban Widows. *The Family Coordinator*. Vol. 27. No.4, pp. 383-94.

———. 1978: Contribution of Extended Families to the Support Systems of Metropolitan Area Widows: Limitations of the Modified Kin Net-Work. *Journal of Marriage and the Family*. Vol. 40. No. 2, pp. 355-64.

———. 1981: Widowhood and Husband Sanctification. *Journal of Marriage and the Family*. Vol. 43. No. 4, pp. 439-50.

Lukose, A. 1978: Facing Widowhood. *Eves Weekly*. (Aug. 12-18) pp. 35.

Madan, T.N. 1975: Structural Implications of Marriage in North India: Wife-giver and Wife-takers Among the Kashmiri Brahmins. *Contributions to Indian Sociology*. Vol. 9. No.2, pp. 217-43.

Mackey, Richard. A. 1968: Crisis Theory: Its Development and Relevance to Social Case Work Practice. *The Family Coordinator*. Vol. 17. No.3, pp. 165-73.

Meher, Pestonji, 1978: Coping with Widowhood: A Challenge. *Eves Weekly*. (Aug 12-18). pp. 38.

Mehta, Manubhai. N. 1936: Widow Remarriage. *The Indian Social Reform*. Vol. XLVI. No. 58, pp. 757.

Mehta Manubhai. N. 1961: Widow Marriage and Hindu Society. *The Indian Social Reform*. Vol. XLVI. No. 49, pp. 775.

Menon, Lakshmi. No. 1973: Indian Women Since Independence. *Indian and Foreign Review*. Vol. 10. No. 2.

Miller, Dorothy. and Dawson, William. H. 1965: Effects of Stigma on Re-employment of Ex-mental Patients. *Mental Hygiene*. Vol. 49. No. 2.

Misra, G. and Shukla A. 1979: Experimental Deprivation and Development of Social Memory. *Psychologia*. Vol, 22, No.2, pp. 115-163.

Misra, G. and Shashi, B.P. 1977: Prolonged Deprivation and Development of Status Perception. *Journal of Psychological Research*. Vol. 21. No. 2, pp. 185-91.

Misra, G. 1982: Motivational Structure and Prolonged Deprivation. *The Indian Journal of Social Work*. Vol. XLIII. No.1, pp. 19-25.

Misra, G. and Tripathi, L.B. 1978: Prolonged Deprivation and Status Perception. *The Indian Journal of Social Work*. Vol. XXXIX. No. 2, pp. 113-37.

Moghe, Vrunda Dev. 1978: Widowhood Today- A Long Term From the Dark Past. *Eves Weekly*. (Aug 12-18). pp. 33-34.

Mohanty, B. 1980: Effects of Socio-Cultural Deprivation on Some Psychological Characteristics. *Psychological Studies*. Vol. 25. No.2, pp. 113-17.

Morgan, Leslie. A. 1981: Economic Change at Mid-life Widowhood: A Longitudinal Analysis. *Journal of Marriage and The Family*. Vol. 43. No.4, pp. 899-907.

———. 1984: Changes in Family Interaction Following Widowhood. *Journal of Marriage and the Family*. Vol. 46. No.1, pp. 222-32.

Nair, Thankappan. P. 1970: The First Hindu Widow Remarriage. *Bhavans Journal*. Vol. 17. pp. 39-41.

Nurcombe, B. 1970: Deprivation: An Essay in Definition with Special Consideration of the Australian Aboriginals. *Medical Journal of Australila*. Vol.2, No.1, pp. 82-92.

O'Brayant, Shirley L. 1988: Sibling Support and Older Widow's Well Being. *Journal of Marriage and the Family*. Vol. 50. No. 1, pp. 164-84.

Ohio State University 1988: Sibling Support and Older Widow's Well-being. *Journal of Marriage and The Family*. Vol. 50. No.1, p. 173.

Parks, Marray. C. 1967: "Bereavement". *British Medical Journal* Vol. 3. No.1-6, p. 32.

Paul, Louis. 1966: Crisis Interventions. *Mental Hygiene*. Vol. 50, No. 7, pp. 141-45.

Publisher : Widow Pension. *The Economic Studies* Vol. 4. No. 7, pp. 353-54.

Punwani, Jyoti. 1978: The Corollaries of Widowhood *Eves Weekly*. (Aug 12-18). pp. 41-42.

Pushpa, M. 1980: Social Deprivation and Cognitive Development of Primary School Children. *Social Change*. Vol. No. pp. 31-35.

Rees, W. Devi. And Lutkins, Sylvia. G. 1967: Mortality of Bereavement *British Medical Journal*. Vol. 4, No.1, pp. 13-16.

Rao, Ramana. M.V. 1956: Hindu Succession Act. *Social Welfare*. Vol. III. No. 9, pp. 18-20.

Rao, Ramana. M.V. 1956: Century of Hindu Widow's Remarriage Act. *Social Welfare*. Vol III. No. 2, pp. 11-12.

Silverman, Phyllis. Rolfe. 1969: The Widow-to-widow Programme An Experiment in Preventive Intervention. *Mental Hygiene*. Vol. 53, No. 3, pp. 333-37.

———. 1979: The Widows as a Care giver in a Program of Preventive Intervention with Other Widows. *Mental Hygiene*. Vol. 54. No. 4, pp. 540-47.

Singh Gurmeet. M.P. and Gill, Sukhdeep. 1986: Problems of Widowhood. *The Indian Journal of Social Work*. Vol. XLVII No. 1, pp. 67-71.

Singh, Gurmeet. M.P. 1988: Restraints to Widow Remarriage. *Social Change*. Vol. 18. No. 3, pp. 59-62.

Singh, Sewa., Kaur, Harjinder. and Dube, Renu. 1986: Malnutrition and Cognitive Development Among Deprived and Non-Deprived Children. *Indian Journal of Clinical Psychology*. Vol. 13 No. 1, pp. 29-34.

Singh, T.R. (1969): Widow Remarriage Among Brahmans-A Sociological Study. *The Eastern Anthropologist*. Vol. 22. No.1, pp. 75-87.

Singh, Vasta Rajendra. 1976: The Remarriage and Rehabilitation of the Hindu Widows in India. 1856-1914. *Journal of Indian History*. Vol. 54. No.3, pp. 713-30.

Shrut, Samuel, D. 1958: Attitudes Toward Old Age and Death. *Mental Hygiene*. Vol. 42. No. 2, pp. 259-66.

Shukla, Aradhana. and Misra, Girishwar. 1988: Deprivation and Development of Colour Competence. *Psychological Studies*. Vol. 33. No. 1, pp. 34-48.

Smith. Ken. R. and Zick, Cathleen. D. 1986: The Incidence of Poverty Among the Recently Widowed: Mediating Factors in the Life Course. *Journal of Marriage and the Family*. Vol. 48. pp. 619-30.

Somerville, Rose. M. 1971: Death Education as Part of Family Life Education: Using Imaginative Literature for Insights into Family Crisis. *The Family Coordinator*. Vol. 20, No.3, pp. 209-224.

Spurolock, J. 1970: Social Deprivation in Childhood and Character Formation. *Journal of the American Psychoanalytic Association*. Vol. 18. No.4, pp. 621-30.

Srinivas. P. 1982: Problems of the Aged in India. *Yojana*. Vol. XXVI. No. 10, pp. 1-15.

Stroebe, Margaret. and Stroebe, Wolfgang. 1983: Who Suffers More? Sex Differences in Health Risks of the Widowed. *Psychological Bulletin*. Vol. 93. No.2, pp. 279-301.

Sweet, James. A. (1972): The Living Arrangements of Separated Widowhood and Divorced Mothers. *Demography*. Vol. 9. No.1, pp. 143-157.

Syamla, M. 1987: Here Widows are Actually Worshipped. *Eves Weekly*. (Aug 8-14).

Tannenbaum. A.J. 1969: Some Non-intellectual Concomitants of Social Deprivation. *Israil Annals of Psychiatry and Related Discipline*. Vol. 7. No.1, pp. 9-30.

Toth, Andre. and Toth, Susan. 1980: Group Work with Widows *Social Work*. Vol. 25. No.1, pp. 63-65.

Tripathi, L.B. and Misra, Girishwar. 1976: Some Cognitive Processess as Function of Prolonged Deprivation. *Indian Journal of Psychology*. Vol. 51. Part 2, pp. 129-43.

Tripathi, L.B. and Misra, Girshwar. 1975: Cognitive Activities as a Function of Prolonged Deprivation. *Psychological Studies*. Vol. 20. No.2, pp. 54-61.

Veerasalingam, K. 1970: The First Widow Marriage. *Triveni*. Vol. 39. No.3, pp. 48-54.

Vinick, B.V. 1978: Remarriage in Old Age. *The Family Co-ordinator*. Vol. 27. No. 2, pp. 359-63.

Vohra, R.N. 1972: Women in Vedic India. *Social Welfare*. Vol. XIX No. 7.

Upadhyaya, Usha. 1986: Construction and Standardisation of a Tool to Measure Sense of Deprivation. *Indian Psychological Review*. Vol. 30. No.1, pp. 29-31.

Wight, B.W., Margaret, F.G. and Philip, Keeve. 1970: Cultural Deprivation Operational Deprivation in Terms of Language Development. *American Journal of Orthopsychiatry*. Vol. 40, No. 7, pp. 77-86.

Young, Michael., Benjamin, Bernard. and Wallis, Chris. 1963: The Mortality of Widowers. *The Lancet*. Vol. II. No.1, pp. 42-44.

Zick, Cathlein, D. 1988: Recent Widowhood, Remarriage and Changes in Economic Well-being. *Journal of Marriage and the Family*. Vol. 50, No. 1, pp. 233-44.

Zilboorg, Gregory. 1943: Fear of Death. *The Psychoanalytic Quarterly*. Vol. 12 No.1, pp. 465-75.

**Thesis and Dissertations**

1. Bansal, Vimla. 1979: Widows - Murauna. Ph.D. Thesis, ICSSR Library, New Delhi.
2. Baidyanath, Saraswati. 1983: The Kashivas Widows, ICSSR Research Project Report, New Delhi.
3. Dhumatkar, M.G. 1928: Position of Hindu Women with Special Reference to Maharashtra Ph.D. Thesis, Bombay University, Bombay.

4. Hate, C.A. 1946: The Social Position of Hindu Widows, Ph.D. Thesis, Bombay University, Bombay.
5. Jambagi, Sulochana. 1964: Life and Activities of Lingayat Widows. M.A. Dissertation. Karnatak University, Dharwad.
6. Kitchlu, T.N. 1982: "A Study of Socio-economic Condition of Widows in Union Territory of Delhi", Project Report. Dept. of Social Work, Univeristy of Delhi, Delhi.
7. Kaur, Sharanjit. 1974: Social Adjustment of War Widows M.A. Dissertation. Punjab University, Chandigarh.
8. Mehta, Vatsala. 1956: The Hindu Widow - With Special Reference to Gujarat. M.A. Dissertation, Bombay University, Bombay.
9. Nagesh, H.V. and Katti. A.P. 1983: A Study of Widows - A Project Report. JSS Institute of Economic Research, Dharwad.
10. Katti, A.P. and Nagesh, H.V. 1984: A Socio-Economic Study of Widows (in Hubli City and Neighbouring Villages) - A Project Report. JSS Institute of Economic Research, Dharwad.
11. Srinivas, M.N. 1938: Marriage and Family Among the Kannada Castes of The Mysore State, M.A. Dissertation, Bombay University, Bombay.

**Census and Official Reports**

1. Census of India, 1951-1981.
2. Karnataka State Gazetteer, Part-142. Kamat, Suryanath. (Ed). 1982. Government of Karnataka, Bangalore.
3. Gazetteer of Bombay-Karnatak, Dharwad District. Venkat, Rango, Katti, (Ed). 1894. Government Central Press, Bombay.
4. Gazetteer of Dharwar District. Palande, M.R. (Ed). (Rev. Eds) 1959, Government Central Press, Bombay.

**Private Papers (Unpublished)**

Inamdar Papers

Diary of Tirmalrao

Daftar D - No. 688 Report on Enforced Widowhood.

Daftar E - No. 704 & 688 B.M. Malabari to Tirmalrao.

Daftar M - Rao Bahadur to the Secretary of Indian Law Commission.

# Index